000:001 ANIMATION

L O

Regina Dahmen-Ingenhoven

Form Follows Fun

O K

ANIMATION

002:003 ANIMATION

Edited by Kristin Feireiss

Birkhäuser – Publishers for Architecture
Basel · Boston · Berlin

Form follows fun

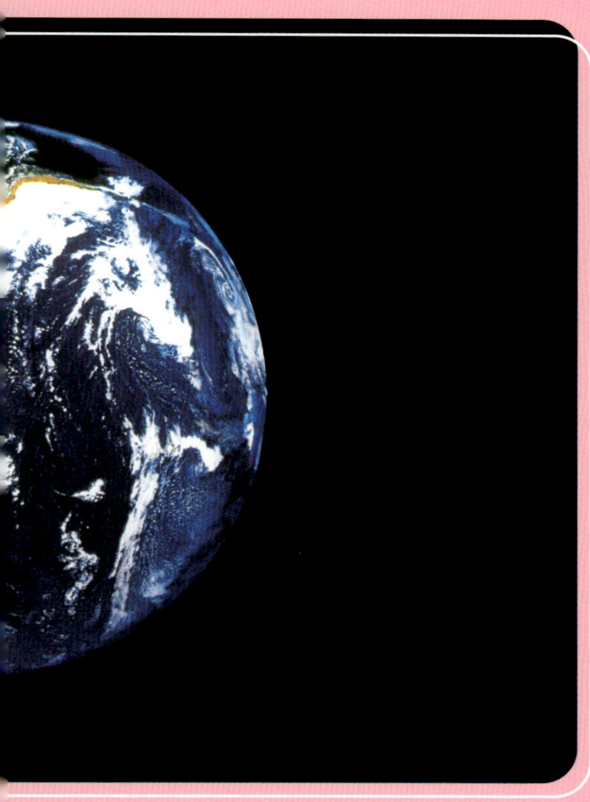

: Now is new !

CONTENT

IN TOTAL

There all is order and beauty, luxury, peace, and pleasure.

CHARLES BAUDELAIRE

Animation has infiltrated everyday life and has also left its mark on architecture in a manner that is no longer marginal. Even as recently as ten years ago, this was still a fairly exotic topic and few architects would have felt compelled to engage in this building task. Instead, actors, set builders, filmmakers and attraction designers had taken control of the field. The situation has changed since then, for even architects can longer ignore this topic! Today, everything and everyone is exposed to animation and there seems to be no escape: a bank is no longer a bank, but an experiential finance department store. The same is true for train stations and airports, which have long since ceased to be mere sites of travel. This corresponds to the adventure or experiential society, which was described as "novel" by the sociologist **Gerhard Schulze** in 1993. Today's society, Schulze declares, is subject to a kind of experiential imperative. To be deemed contemporary, you must experience something. Those who do not experience anything have only themselves to blame. Given this kind of imperative, every promise of transporting the consumer into an extraordinary experiential world beyond the everyday is a temptation. Under the influence of mass culture, a new trend has emerged in contemporary architecture: the trend of investing buildings with an experiential character employed to evoke specific emo-

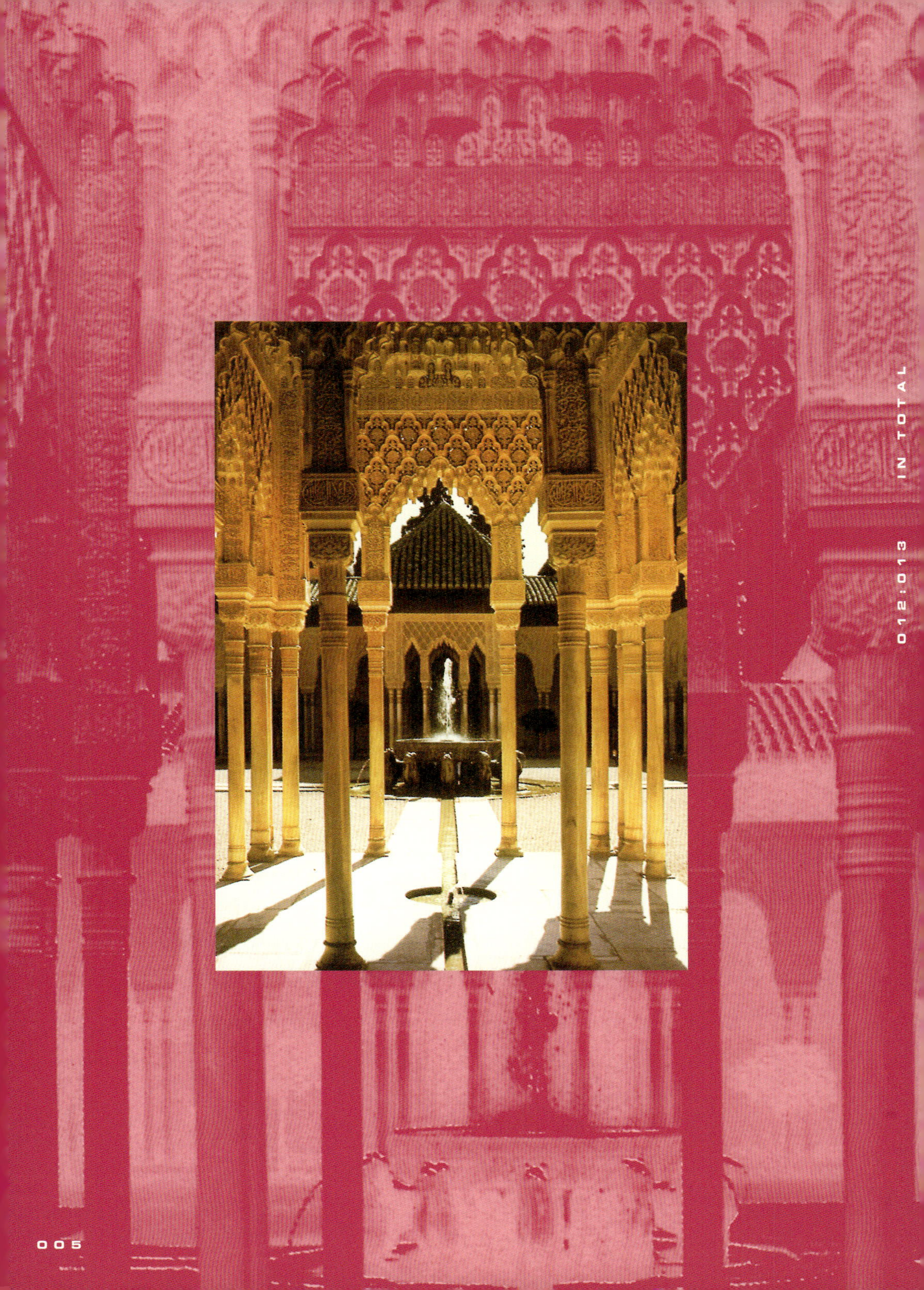

tions. This trend is most evident in, although not exclusive to, buildings that are designed for leisure activities. The primary purpose here is to animate, that is, to stimulate, to encourage, to set a mood or awaken pleasure – and to do so by a wide variety of means. 👁 Today, the gourmet has a choice that goes beyond Chinese, Italian or Indonesian cuisine, Swiss gastronomy and countless other exotic flavours. Everyone also has the choice between the Maldives or the 'Centre parc' in Belgium, which is modelled on the Maldive Islands, between Venice in Italy and Venice in Disneyworld or a stay at the Venetian Hotel in Las Vegas, between a Polynesian village in Polynesia and reconstructions in Greece or Algeria. The international industry of happiness and good taste has found a global audience. 👁 Many people increasingly spend their leisure time in synthetic 'cases' that have become wholly alienated from their original meaning and purpose – restaurants, shopping malls, fantasy parks and similar environments. Yet what is the substitute – a keyword in the context of fun parks and animation – used to generate these contradictory feelings of freedom and cosiness, of safety and adventure, of dream and déjà-vu? 👁 What is animation? What are the means of animation in each regard, in particular in terms of architecture? The exploration of this theme via seemingly outlandish topics such as the expressive quality and formal language of comic and cartoon figures also provides insight into the language and symbolism of architecture. 👁 One central effect of animation – Walt Disney describes it brilliantly as the squash and stretch of expression and proportion – lies in over-extension and exaggeration, in the exaggerated clarity of a figure conveying a clear and unambiguous meaning even to the simplest mind, regardless of how sophisticated the means of production may be. Immediate architectural parallels are evident: on the one hand, in the buildings of such leisure parks and, on the other hand, in their direct and indirect successors outside of such settings as part of the everyday urban environment. This book will make a contribution toward revealing the various animation patterns. 👁 Animation is the attempt to evoke emotions that do not necessarily correspond to the content of an object, a product, an institution or a building. Animation is, one could say, the "extra" needed to conquer the public and their emotions. 👁 In the mid-twentieth century Walt Disney dreamt of making the world a better place. He added a new dimension to leisure and amusement. Based on his expertise as a brilliant leisure entrepreneur and with the help of animation, Disney developed an entirely new concept for his amusement parks. Disneyland has been celebrated and denounced ever since it first opened in 1955: as the ultimate embodiment of a consumer society, as the harbinger of a "shopping-mall culture," as a symbol of American supremacy in the entertainment sector and as the birthplace of the idea that architecture plays an important role in the implementation. Disney's concept of the theme world has been unfailingly successful. His unique brand of fun and amusement architecture has been emulated in many areas, not only in leisure parks around the world. Catalogues of attractions and organizational models in the style of Disney have become fixed components of many shopping centres and adventure environments. Something new has been created by blending buying and experience in shopping malls, a new form of architecture, where selling and amusement are fused. 👁 This trend has also emerged in entirely different types of buildings, such as museums, tourist architecture, public pools, "car cities" or banks, all of which integrate the experiential function. There is a burgeoning evolution of architecture, which can no longer operate without animating elements. 👁 This book is about people who create mass events, design experiential worlds and conceive the corresponding architectures. Animation has become an indispensable communication tool of the early twenty-first century. We present numerous international examples that demonstrate how animation functions – with more or less success – in the domain of architecture. 👁 What are all the things we want to experience what should we experience? The contrast between the quotes that bracket this foreword – **Charles Baudelaire**'s at the beginning and **Djuna Barnes**' more sceptical statement from 1905 at the end – illustrates the contradictions inherent in the theme, oscillating between sensuality and pleasure on the one hand and doggedness and hectic determination on the other.

... some are characterized by a hurry, a doggedness, a hectic determination to amuse themselves at all costs ...

DJUNA BARNES

ZEITGEIST

Contextual Changes Today

01

The environmental planning of an age is not neutral – rather it is the expression of the prevailing attitudes ...

JEFFREY SHAW

As recently as the early twentieth century, it was by no means common for lower classes to be able to enjoy any leisure time in public recreation sites. Only the well-to-do enjoyed free time and could afford to frequent leisure settings for recreation and amusement on a regular basis. 👁 Improved living standards overall and the resulting increase in leisure time and freedom for all individuals, as well as progress in technology, have contributed to the emergence of architecture that reflects these developments. Inner cities, urban peripheries and suburbs are increasingly defined by public spaces for recreation, sports, culture and entertainment, that is, leisure sites. 👁 Access restrictions, such as were found in the eighteenth century, no longer exist. While only a few privileged individuals were able to enjoy leisure sites then, mass culture and a fundamental democratic spirit have made leisure sites universally accessible today. Mass spectacles such as sporting events or concerts unify huge crowds with a common interest. 👁 Sites and structures are created specifically for people to use in their off-work hours. There has been a fundamental shift in the ratio of work to leisure time and in living conditions. The decisive factors in this shift are the opportunities that arise from increased leisure time.

Today, work is only half of life – and leisure is the other half.
H. W. OPASCHOWSKI

MORE LEISURE TIME

More leisure time and a higher disposable income open the door to new lifestyles and also demand new ideas. Over the past several decades, there has been a considerable increase in leisure time for nearly all workers and employees. Leisure time means freedom from being governed by the demands of others or at least time during which we are at liberty to follow our own inclinations and desires. In our leisure time we can relax and be idle or seek distraction, excitement and spectacles. Amusement, pleasure, entertainment and distraction offer a variety of pastimes, which can be created, or at least encouraged, by animation. This is a fundamental prerequisite for the development of a worldwide leisure market, in which the leisure-orientated society is gaining ever more influence over the design of public space. Another prerequisite for the growing leisure industry is work itself, which provides the necessary financial means to pay for it. Whenever we speak of leisure, we must also consider work. People who are out of work are generally unable to afford leisure. **H. W. Opaschowski** describes our society as a "leisure-work society." Like **Rainer Hank**, he suggests that the two are intrinsically linked. Taking travel as an example, he explains: "The respect we have for mobility does not rule out the fact that even the increasingly travel-hungry society cannot escape what it would like to forget: the all-encompassing work society. The leisure society is not an alternative to the work society, it is its complement."

A society that is continuously engaged in hard work will have more security: and security is now being worshipped as the highest deity.

RAINER HANK

More and more, work gets all good conscience on its side; the desire for joy already calls itself a "need to recuperate" and is starting to be ashamed of itself.

FRIEDRICH NIETZSCHE

Nietzsche's observation in Book Four of *The Gay Science* (1882) seems to have been born out. Happiness is no longer identified exclusively with leisure and introspection; joy and work are no longer opposites. Many have come to regard work as part of the fulfilment of human existence. The estimation of work has changed over the course of history. Originally, it signified toil and hardship in the sense of existential survival. In the civilizations of antiquity, practical, especially physical, work was regarded as a curse and therefore delegated to the lower classes. Since the Middle Ages, in particular since the Reformation, Christian thinkers such as Benedict of Nursia or Martin Luther laid the foundations for a fundamental shift in the estimation of work. Work occupies a positive position and becomes a key factor in the self-definition of the individual. Today, work is viewed as the decisive element of self-realization, and this is not only in the professional, independent sector. 👁 Work, as **Rainer Hank** comments, became the religion of the twentieth century.

STOP

The city is always running away from itself. LARS LERUP

An important prerequisite for the emergence of mass leisure sites is the development of an infrastructure that provides universal and comfortable access. The twentieth century and the early twenty-first century have been profoundly affected by the success of the technologies that prepared the ground for mass mobility. Whereas everybody was still dreaming of owning a car in the 1950s, this dream has in the meantime materialized for most people in the Wes-tern world. Private transport and motorization experienced a massive boom through posi-tive economic developments. Automobile production became a leading sector of national economies. Mobility seems to be one of the basic human needs. In a globalized world, it is the key to a high standard of living. More and more people are reaching their destinations with ever-greater speed. Society is growing ever more mobile, be it via bus or rail, car or plane. Transportation routes are being expanded, connections are being improved and speed is being increased. As recently as the mid-twentieth century, 50 million out of a global population of 2.6 billion owned a car. While the global population has nearly tripled in the past fifty years, the number of cars has increased tenfold. This mass motorization and its consequences enable many people to enjoy a variety of leisure activities with ever greater ease and speed.

Cola
WORLD
GAMEWORKS

GRIFFEY
GRETZKY
AGASSI
ALL S
hocolates

42
ST

People as toys, enslaved by the pleasures of consumerism, addicted to the adventure of the big city, experienced in many different games. They prefer toys, lick ice cream, busy themselves with machines, dress like dolls ...
People seem to live in gambling casinos or emerge from gambling dens; they are shaped by the machines they play on, juke boxes, slot machines, pinball machines and electronic shooting alleys; the clothes they wear light up like neon signs.

WIELAND SCHMIED

As far back as 1964, the painter **Richard Lindner**, whose art was described by **Wieland Schmied** in such vivid terms, depicted a society addicted to the joys of consumerism. His favourite subjects were the amusements and amusement sites of the modern world, New York's nightlife, Hollywood's dream machine, Disneyland and Greenwich Village, Madison Avenue and Sunset Boulevard. ◉ Society has changed: superannuated patterns of cohabitation have been dissolved, new structures and orientations define community life. The term adventure society succinctly describes this variety: Live Life! – a motto that is linked to yet another appeal: Have Fun! Having fun is seen as the central criterion for evaluating experiences. ◉ So-called experience facilitators of all kinds offer their professional services to the fun market. Entertainers, animators and leisure pedagogues are creations of the twentieth and the early twenty-first century. "We are still processing how to handle this new condition, both in daily life and in the cultural sciences. We are only gradually realizing that we haven't reached the end of all problems, but new and unknown difficulties." This is how **Gerhard Schulze** describes the situation in *Die Erlebnisgesellschaft*. ◉ Some authors lament people's craving for pleasure. As Aldous Huxley remarked in *Brave New World Revisited* (1987), the civil libertarians and rationalists who are ever on the alert to oppose tyranny "failed to take into account man's almost infinite appetite for distractions." According to Huxley, people do not suffer from laughing instead of thinking, but from not knowing what they are laughing about and from having ceased to think. In his view, the spirit of culture is deteriorating into cabaret. But who doesn't like to have a lot of fun?

People must be entertained. They cannot spend all their time learning or working, they are not made for that.

CHARLES DICKENS

According to the Random House dictionary, entertainment is the act of agreeable occupation in the sense of amusement and diversion. There is a growing entertainment market, increasingly technological and run with high capital investments. Film, radio, television and computers offer new opportunities for entertainment. In the age of mass consumption, the entertainment industry is multiplied through technical developments and innovations, such as slot-machines and vending machines and through new architectures; it has become a major economic factor worldwide. One example is Germany, where more than five decades of peace accompanied by steady economic growth have created the stable conditions that support the development of this new market. 👁 **Friedrich Nietzsche** foreshadowed this trend and wrote in 1882: "Modern man no longer cares whether an experience is pleasurable or not, only that it is stimulating." 👁 **Neil Postman**'s judgment of the age of the entertainment industry is far more negative. In *Amusing Ourselves to Death*, he criticizes the gradual breakdown of cultural activity as a result of commercial illusionism – total entertainment this way: "Entertainment is the supra-ideology of all discourse on television. No matter what is depicted or from what point of view, the over-arching presumption is that it is there for our amusement and pleasure." 👁 Now and in the future, a powerful leisure production machine offers promises of happiness, dream destinations and artificial paradises, represented by an ever-increasing array of new leisure and entertainment parks, sites of pilgrimage for the twentieth and the twenty-first century. The Euro Disney Park, for example, draws twice as many visitors as the Louvre. 👁 Marketing research analyses recommend experience-oriented retail stores, because the store ambience has become the primary motivation for consumer choices. If the ambience lives up to the expectations, customers stay longer, customer numbers grow and sales increase. At the same time, a distinction is made between pure supply consumption and experiential consumption, and experience marketing has developed into a separate and expanding sector. 👁 The architects Wimberly, Allison, Tong and Goo from Sydney, for example, create sites that offer visitors a setting rich in images as respite from boredom. One of these sites is an underwater hotel.

Modern man no longer cares whether an experience is able or not, only that it is stimulating.

FRIEDRICH NIETZSCHE

015+016

Together, this ensemble of electronic techniques called into being a new world – a peek-a-boo world, where now this event, now that, pops into view for a moment, then vanishes again.

NEIL POSTMAN

The conquest of distance in the mid-nineteenth century as a result of advances in transportation went hand in hand with an expansion and acceleration of communication. In the end, **Neil Postman** suggests, the link between communication and transportation became superfluous with the invention of the telegraph. Distance no longer impedes the transfer of information. Further development of electronic, acoustic and visual transmission techniques such as photography, radio, film, television and computers generates this so-called peek-a-boo world. The eye increasingly dominates our other sensory organs. In our perception of the world it ranks higher than the olfactory sense and the more immediate tactile sense. Perception is processed more and more through a variety of filters. Images created by media are, in turn, transmitted by other media. The boundaries between reality and fiction, between image and reproduction, are becoming blurred. The eye is deliberately stimulated, as more and more emphasis is placed on the optic impulse. The Millennium festivities in London and EXPO Hanover exemplify the issue: architecture as a backdrop for multimedia images, also referred to recently as event- or media-architecture. The answer is clear for **Neil Postman**: "For the first time in history, people are getting used to seeing images of the world instead of seeing the world." 👁 To welcome the new millennium, Great Britain erected the Millennium Dome with a circumference of 1,600 m, covering an area of 90,000 m^2. At any given time 35,000 people can occupy the space . A direct competition to Expo, this vast hall is used to present contemporary themes, providing space for the new prophets: entertainers. Richard Rogers' Millennium Dome in London is a symbol of popular culture, albeit one for which a new use has yet to be found now that the millennium celebrations are over. 👁 At the same time, the gigantic Ferris wheel, the London Eye, was erected on the banks of the Thames for the millennium celebrations. Entertainment now dominates London's skyline: at 148 m, the wheel soars above downtown London.

We dream of a fantastic extraterrestrial world that is millions of light-years away ...

CLAUDE NURIDSANY

... And we haven't even begun to discover the world that is spread out at our feet: the galaxies of the small scale, a microcosm on a scale of centimetres, where tufts of grass become impenetrable forests [and] dew drops gigantic balloons ...

CLAUDE NURIDSANY

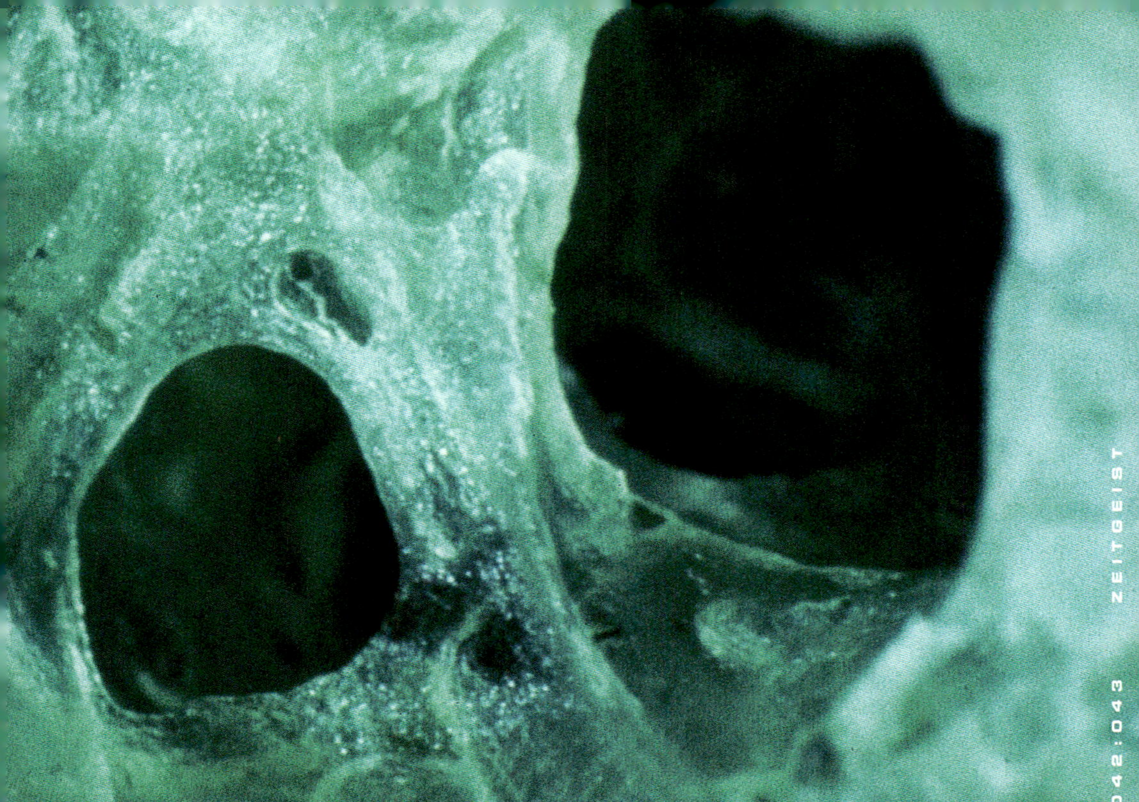

MICROCOSMS

The use of new technologies to discover microcosms also belongs to the area of animation. It is increasingly difficult to tell reality and fantasy apart. We are constantly faced with new "revelations" through ever more sophisticated technical tools such as microscopes and macro lenses. In the manifold microcosms, parallel worlds unfold before our eyes, which we can only grasp as a result of perfecting our capacity for perception through technology. Galaxies on a centimetre, millimetre or nanometre scale for example, in the animal world where 95 percent of all known species are smaller than bees. From fantastical organisms, exposed to the eye through electron microscopes, to shapes and colours in the sub-aquatic world – there are more and more things behind other things waiting to be discovered.

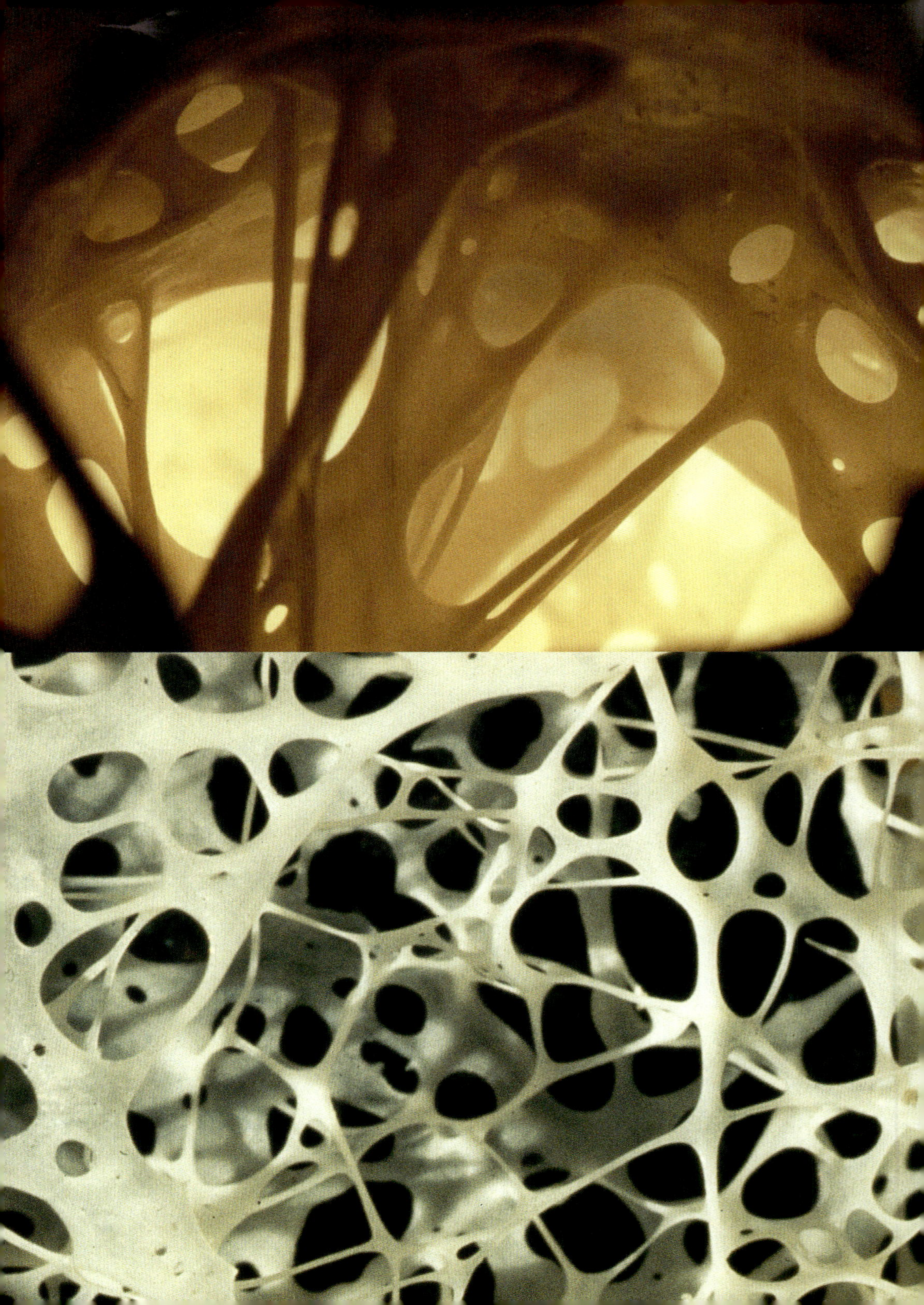

ZEITGEIST
044:045
022+023+024

The World is a Village

Globalization is making the world a smaller place, making it possible to traverse continents in no time at all with the help of modern communication tools. Globalization encompasses individualization. In the age of globalization, the life of individuals is no longer tied to a specific locale. The sociologist **Ulrich Beck** speaks of a travelling life, spent in the car, on a plane and in trains, on the phone or on the Internet – a transnational life beyond borders. According to **Bart Lootsma** and Ulrich Beck, the phenomenon of individualization, in combination with globalization, is one of the most significant changes in Western societies in the past decades. 👁 This evolution is demonstrated not only in the expansion of online connections, global changes in the economy and worldwide futuristic trends, but also in new trends in architecture. Every theme park contains multicultural potential coupled with a globalized cultural industry. The architecture of all nations is part of this animated world. The architecture of the various cultures found there is a visual proclamation of the concept of "the global village." Fascinated by the exotic and unknown, theme park designers casually combine architectural ensembles from every corner of the globe: Africa becomes Hawaii's neighbour, the Eiffel Tower stands next to Munich's Hofbräuhaus, and New Zealand shares a border with Italy. Global architecture is also the language of the International Style: be it Shanghai, Moscow or Tokyo, regional style no longer exists and the airports, shopping malls and entertainment centres with their multiplex cinemas and office towers all speak the language of a growing aesthetic and formal sameness.

ZEITGEIST 046:047

POPULAR CULTURE

One of the characteristics of popular culture is that it also delivers the emotions it aims to inspire. UMBERTO ECO

The all-encompassing motto "Have Fun" has also established roots in the cultural sector. Leisure culture paves the way for a new understanding of culture – "popular culture" in the spirit of UNESCO and the European Council. Even knowledge is to be conveyed in an entertaining manner. New word creations such as infotainment or edutainment are symptomatic of the growing integration of information and entertainment. Critics lament in vain that any and all topics are presented as entertainment today. 👁 Entertainment instead of boredom, exciting interaction instead of museological erudition. Even science is presented in a multimedia package, full of surprises and with plenty of fun. Everything is based on the popular "fun effect." 👁 One example is the science centre in Bremen designed by the architect Thomas Klumpp. The universe, a hybrid of whale and UFO, is presented as fun stage set. In Darmstadt, the Fraunhofer Institute plans to build the Cybernarium, the first theme park for virtual and expanded reality in the world. Oberhausen is currently developing a park based on the theme of human beings and life. And the meteorite designed by **André Heller**, in collaboration with the Viennese architectural firm **propeller z**, is an example of mediating knowledge through entertainment. As is the biosphere in Potsdam by Barkow/Leibinger, which is dedicated to nature and the abundance of species. In Wolfsburg, the "car city" will soon be joined by a science centre called Phaeno by Zaha Hadid. 👁 And Stuttgart has kept pace with the design for the Daimler-

Benz-museum by UN Studio. Designing experiential spaces is fashionable. ⊙ Museums, science parks and increasingly even banks and office buildings all display popular architecture. The firm of **Foster and Partners** won a competition in 2000 for a new cultural district in Hong Kong. Norman Foster demonstrates how his architecture for leisure and work, culture and sport, dominates an entire urban quarter. The mass society is beginning to leave its mark on the Western world. Its taste and preferences are taken seriously. No more "culture of deference." ⊙ As early as 1949, the visionary **Aldous Huxley** feared that we would become "a trivial culture, preoccupied with some equivalent of the feelies, the orgy porgy, and the centrifugal bumblepuppy."

11
45
45
42
41
46
44
41
07
06
02
13
28
47
28
12
49

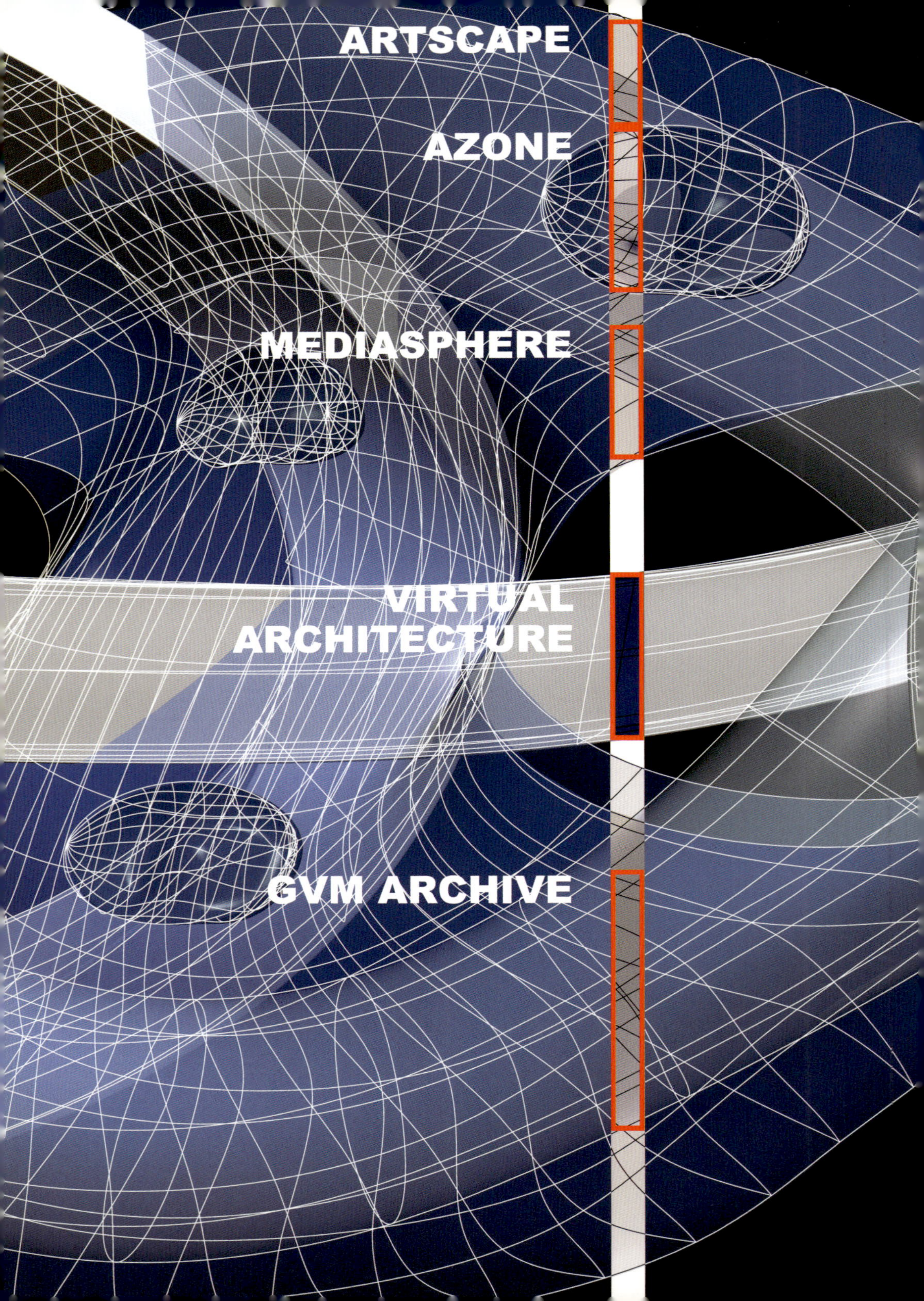
ARTSCAPE
AZONE
MEDIASPHERE
VIRTUAL
ARCHITECTURE
GVM ARCHIVE

VIRTUAL REALITY

Virtual:
... not real,
non-existent in reality
but appearing to be
real to the eye and
the sense.

RANDOM HOUSE UNABRIDGED DICTIONARY

Today, the Zeitgeist and communication are defined by entirely different and new aspects. They no longer provide only entertainment and diversion for the individual, but open up new worlds, which also influence architecture. The tradition of the panorama as a deliberate excursion into unknown worlds in painting, photography and cinematography has been expanded through the use of simulation and virtual reality. The new techniques have also enriched our vocabulary with a slew of news. In 1995, the *Year of the Media* in Germany, spelling reform was accompanied by such newly coined words as cyberspace and multimedia, virtual reality and data highway: the keywords of a new generation.

TO CONSIDER, THE PHYSICAL
AS WE HAVE ALWAYS KNOWN IT
ENCLOSURE
OF AN

HERE ENCLOSURE, FORM AND PERMANENCE WILL

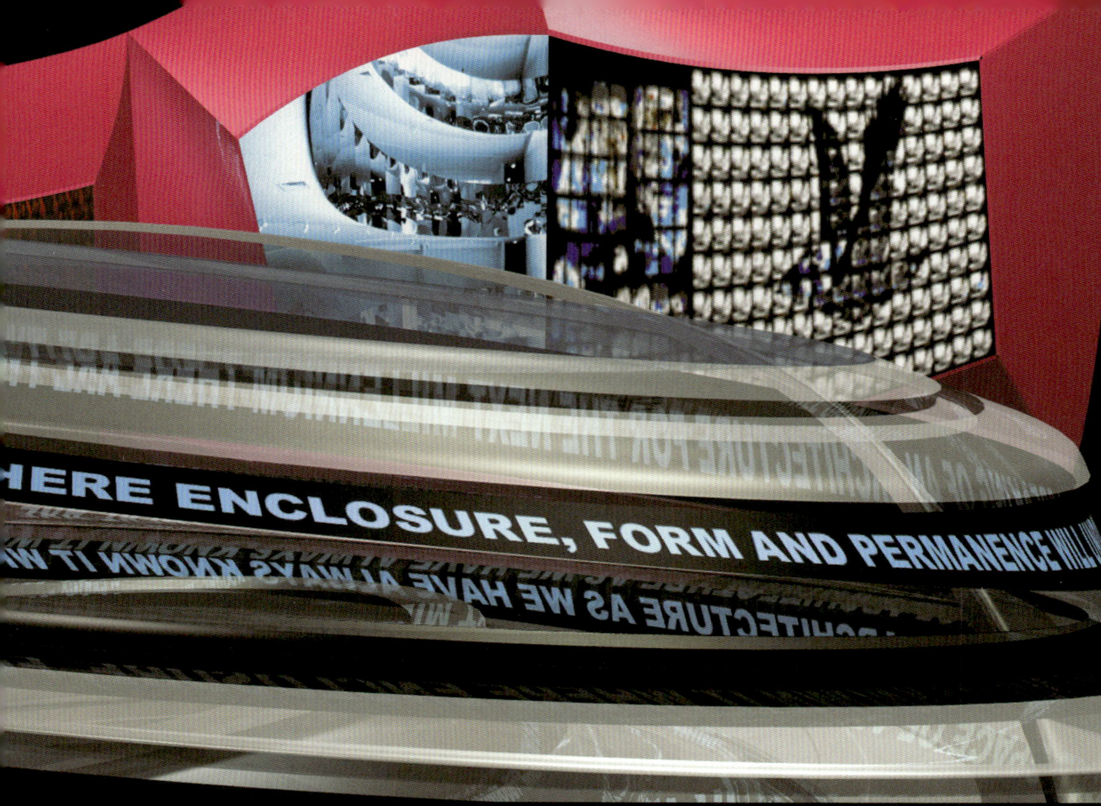

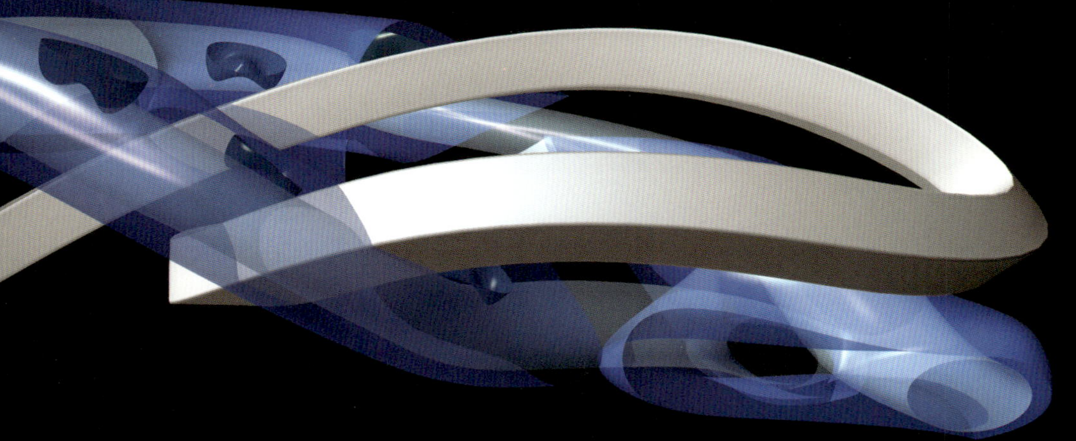

033+034

Linguists are still researching the language of computer and Internet communication with its abundance of anglicisms, and the German Brockhaus encyclopaedia, for example, has yet to record all the newly coined words linked to cyberspace. Cyberspace is a word borrowed from the science fiction novel *Neuromancer* by William Gibson (1984). It means cybernetic space. In virtual reality, cyberspace generally describes a computer-generated data or information environment that is ideally suited to visual exploration. A cyberspace is usually generated by means of computer graphics and computer animation. The user can employ a virtual reality interface such as VR-spectacles or a data glove to enter the space and interact with other users. The opportunity to run around inside such computer-generated spaces, exploring them and possibly even modifying them, is a fascinating one. It seems that virtual reality is gradually becoming a common form of communication in the twenty-first century. In an era of proliferating virtual and fictional worlds, reality is increasingly fragmented. No wonder that imaginary designs translated into tangible shape with the help of computers have also assumed concrete form in real buildings. This trend is evident in parks that are partially animated, such as Wild Blue in Japan. An artificial beach beneath a giant roof simulates a "second" nature. A network of locales offers facilities where space, time, climate and landscape are random virtual evocations. Cyber art influences architecture and vice versa. The concomitant interaction between digital design and concrete structure is also reflected in new words and phrases: expressions such as digital city, media architecture, hypersurface theory, telepolis and networked universe are used to categorize the tasks that face the architect and the urban planner in the age of data highways, cyberspace and telematic media. Samples of this new language are: multimedia, pixel, raytracing, rendering, scanning, scribble, server, shading, simulation,

state-of-the-art tools, networking, virtual vision, visualization, animation, cyberspace, digital, real time, electronic, e-mailing, extranet, photo-realism, globalization, hotline, immersion, interactive, joystick, medialization. The Guggenheim virtual museum (GVM) designed by the New York architecture firm **Asymptote** is an Internet project that carries out Web experiments with new methods of representation and new forms. This Web museum is not defined by the clumsiness of traditional wall sequences or the physical limitations of existing space. Asymptote regards virtual architecture as the most groundbreaking firm's achievement.

As human beings we are drawn to explore and comprehend the unknown using every capability available to us. Virtual reality holds immense curiosity for us, just as the oceans and the infinite expanse of universe do.

HANI RASHID, ASYMPTOTE

THE MICHELANGELOS OF THE NEW WORLD

By representing new things in new ways, we can build a new world and inhabit it, if only with our eyes. AARON BETSKY

The era we live in is characterized by a new dimension of perception. Renaissance paintings by artists like Michelangelo or Leonardo da Vinci depict stories from the Old or the New Testament. The Michelangelos of the New World dip into a bottomless pool of new sources of inspiration. Their images illustrate visions of a new way of seeing and a changed perception. 👁 The artists who design our contemporary experience are called event makers, animators, Web-designers, media artists, filmmakers, video artists, fashion designers, and slogan designers. New professions are emerging to take up the task of mediating and facilitating experience, especially in the area of new media. 👁 After all, the virtual environments of cyberspace must also be created and designed. The demand for cyberspace and animation designers – the contemporary film directors, who translate fictional ideas and experiences – will continue to grow despite the crisis of the New Economy. They develop virtual reality software in the areas of education, entertainment and architecture. Cyberspace architects design cybernetic spaces and scenarios that embody the new interpretation of their profession. In the meantime, the professional profile of a good cyberspace architect has become comparable to the talents and qualities once associated with film directors, dramaturges and video-game programmers.

PARADISE
A Perfect Plac

02

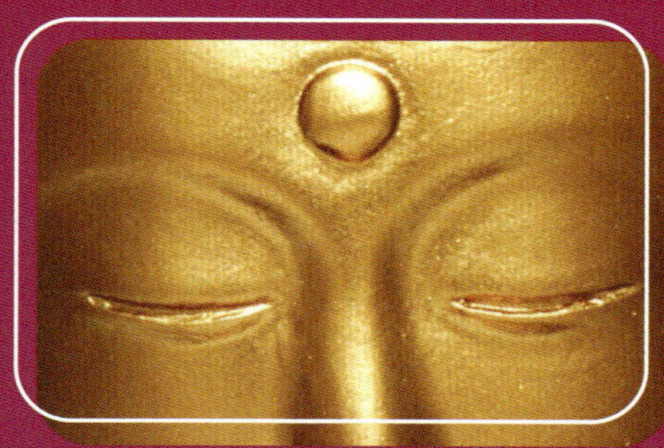

THE GARDEN OF EDEN

The idea of paradisiacal locales has existed across all centuries, right up to the present day. These sites of tranquillity, peace and happiness are gardens with an abundance of the gifts nature and a friendly animal world. All religions worldwide are based on a vision of the ancient origin of humankind before known existence. The various beliefs also share the concept of an ideal state of being and a place of eternal happiness: a perfect place. In the Old Testament, paradise is the Garden of Eden, home to the first humans. There they live in peace, unburdened by the fall from grace. They are free and happy. Their perfect lives are untroubled by threats of any kind. Genesis 2.8 tells us: "Then the Lord God planted a garden in Eden, in the East, and there he put the man he had formed." In addition to describing a site of bliss, paradise, a word originally derived from the Persian and the Hebraic, also defines the boundaries of this site: ramparts, fences and town walls. The Garden of Eden is divided by four rivers and it has a centre: the tree of the knowledge of Good and Evil.

043+044+045

PARADISE LOST

After the banishment of the first man and woman, the *Old Testament* tells us, the Garden is sealed off by cherubim. Henceforth, the paradise of Genesis is a lost site, a lost happiness. The biblical narrative predicts the return of an empire of perfect harmony – the New Jerusalem – but only at the end of time. Born out of a yearning for this lost paradise, the rediscovery of the heavenly state of paradise is a theme that recurs throughout recorded history. Even in Greek mythology, for example, the cheerful home of heroes, of the good and the just – called Elysium – is a paradisiacal configuration. Elysium is a place of eternal spring, the island abode of the blessed. This is where the blessed, to whom the Gods have granted immortality, dwell after death. The Germanic hero yearns for Valhalla, while the Egyptian aspires to reach Earu. Images of paradise are found in the myths, religions, art and literature of every epoch. In antiquity, for example, Hesiod writes of the island of the blessed, located in the Atlantic Ocean, and in his *Eclogues* Virgil describes the Golden Age of Arcadia as paradise. The Golden Age (aurea-aetas myth) is glorified in antiquity as a time when humans and nature live in perfect harmony in a paradisiacal state. Greed, war and degenerating mores, however, gradually erode the quality of life. The expression "earthly happiness" originates from the work entitled *Utopia* by the English humanist Sir Thomas More (1550). The English poet John Milton writes of paradise lost and regained. Since the Renaissance, there have been two concepts of utopia: the Christian concept of eternal happiness in a heavenly Jerusalem and the idea of the Golden Age that originated in antiquity. In the interpretation from antiquity, the concept of happiness, linked to pantheism, has a worldly orientation-imagining a bucolic life in nature. In the Christian worldview, the vision relates to the afterlife and exhorts people to productivity

Paradise regained: the New Jerusalem

and abstinence here on earth so that they may gain entry to paradise after death. Utopian visions that were independent of religions began to emerge only in the nineteenth century, when they became politically secularized and linked to inner, social, communal or even individual hedonistic desires.

THE IDEAL CITY

Jerusalem is the embodiment of the ideal city, the heavenly city on earth – all earthly cities strive to emulate it; they do not wish turn into Babylon, whose fate was destruction after it had degenerated into arrogance and excess. This image is still valid today. According to **J.-K. Schmidt** "it renders heavenly order victorious over utter chaos." 👁 The dream of the perfect society, which concludes the *Book of Revelation* in the New Testament, is a continuous theme in the history of Christendom, and also in the history of Islam. The apostle depicts the idea of a Holy or New Jerusalem as a symbol of the heavenly city: "And then I saw a new heaven and a new earth. The first heaven and the first earth had disappeared, and the sea vanished. I saw the Holy City, the New Jerusalem, coming down out of heaven from God. ... It had a great, high wall with twelve gates and with twelve angels in charge of the gates. ... The wall was made of jasper, and the city itself was made of pure gold, as clear as glass. The foundation stones of the city wall were adorned with all kinds of precious stones. The first foundation stone was jasper, the second sapphire, the third agate, ... the twelfth amethyst. ... I heard a loud voice ...: Now God's home is with people! He will live with them and they shall be his people. God himself will be with them. He will wipe away all tears from their eyes. There will be no more death, no more grief or crying or pain. The old things have disappeared." 👁 Buildings as symbols of religious ideas are erected by a wide range of civilizations and in all eras. They document ambitious political and religious endeavours. To Christian builders, New Jerusalem is an allegory for God's dwelling place. They design the divine city in accordance with the Augustinian doctrine (412–26) *De Civitate Dei*, which defines the church as the earthly manifestation of God's state. To the medieval believer, the heavenly city is thus a part of his daily

047+048

environment. The image of the ideal city in Western Europe is preserved during the Middle Ages in the monastic setting. It is expressed in two ways: on the one hand, in manuscripts in the form of illuminations of the biblical description of heavenly Jerusalem; and on the other hand, in the idealized ensembles of the monasteries themselves, which were based on the principles defined in the Carolingian ideal plan of St. Gallen (circa 820 AD). Both depictions adhere to a symmetry based on a double axis and are distinguished, by virtue of their absolute purity, from the character of those accidental real structures that are forced to adapt to the restless pace of urban life. 👁 During the Renaissance, the Carolingian ideal plan of St. Gallen nevertheless becomes the model for the restructuring of many existing cities and the design of many new cities. Where the heavenly ideal comes into contact with earthly conditions, allowances are made to deviate from the rigorous geometry, but the symbolic interpretation is maintained. In planning entirely new city ensembles, the realization of the ideal plan is supported by the might of ducal courts and strict laws, for example, in the sixteenth century when the Gonzaga dynasty commissioned the design for the city of Sabbionetta. 👁 Like the abbey of Montecassino in Italy or Cluny monastery in France, Islamic architecture also reflects the Heavenly Jerusalem. The idea of symbolically reconstructing paradise on earth by means of architecture is pursued with particular intensity in the Islamic culture. This aim, founded in the Koran, is evident in the Sah mosque of Isfahan, the Alhambra at Granada and countless other examples.

049

Ec
Para
New Je
Elys
Ut
Arc

en
dise
rusalem
ium
pia
adia

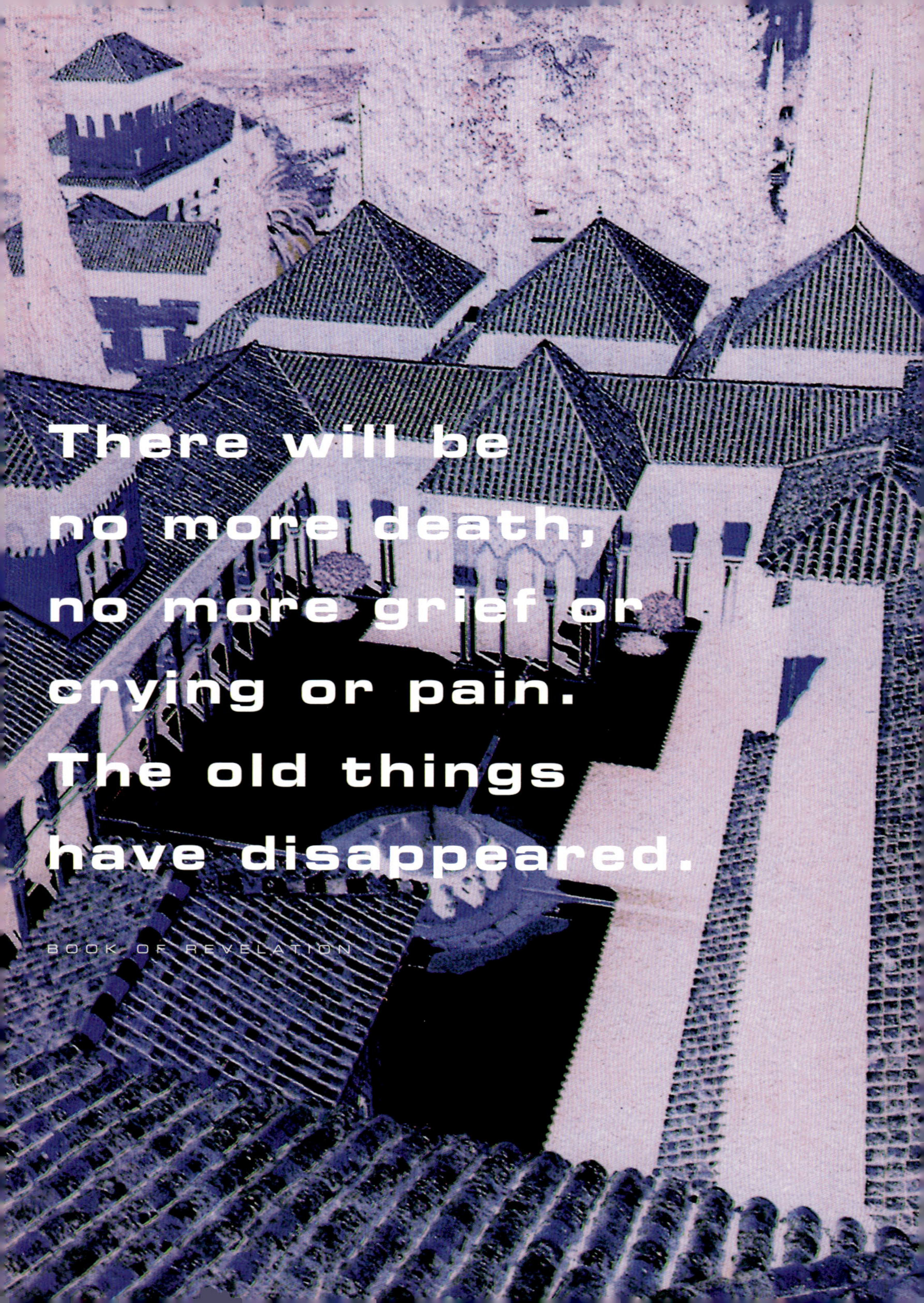
There will be
no more death,
no more grief or
crying or pain.
The old things
have disappeared.
BOOK OF REVELATION

The concept of paradise as a leitmotif is ubiquitous in the architecture of individual religious sites such as mosques, madrasas and mausoleums, as well as in palaces and in urban plans. Great architecture, especially sacred architecture, is always also an expression of emotions. It serves not only to create beautiful sites built with precious materials, but also to articulate desires and to record stories that have the power to move the life of people and the course of history. In the architecture of past centuries, this narrative quality is almost entirely based on religious content. Architecture is used to recount religious stories, which are communicated to the church visitor through the buildings themselves and their ornamentation with paintings and sculptures. The faithful are promised eternal peace upon entering into paradise at the end of life. As a symbol of this eschatological vision, the Sah mosque is transformed into an image of paradise: The ceramic tiles adorned with grapevines, garlands and flowers, whose abundance covers every surface, represents everlasting vegetation. The ideal city of Urbino exemplifies the rigorous regularity of urban design in the fifteenth century. The Carolingian ideal plan of St. Gallen exerts a profound influence not only on the architecture of churches and monasteries, it is also repeatedly employed as a model for the design of cities. The unrelieved regularity of the rationalized design and architectural order makes it impossible to add or remove anything to or from the plan. The Lion's Court in the Alhambra at Granada is also rich in religious symbols. In analogy to the biblical description of paradise, the inner courtyard symbolizes the Garden of Eden. Four streams of water flow from a central water basin in reference to the four rivers of paradise, while the solid enclosure illustrates the seclusion of the heavenly garden.

The Taj Mahal in India is widely regarded as the most famous mausoleum in the world, a symbol of paradise and of a great love. It was erected from 1630 to 1653 by Shah Jahan (reigned 1628–1657) for his second wife, Mumtaz Mahal. "Even the smallest rose, the most humble poppy on the royal tombs consists of no less than twenty or thirty carnelians, onyx, agates and chrysoberyls. Not even New Jerusalem had such a rich selection of precious stones," wrote **Aldous Huxley** in 1926. The most recent example of an ideal city is the Atlantis project by the architect Léon Krier, of which only drawings and plans exist thus far. It is the intent of the architect that Atlantis will join the long historical series of imaginary or realized ideal cities. Atlantis is to be realized on Tenerife as a small community in the south-western

mountains, far away from the tourist centres. Léon Krier's city plan combines art, music, literature and theatre into a single unit. In the hope of a better society, the architect has set himself the goal of building a perfect city.

S.J.Reynolds.
Müde bin ich, geh' zur Ruh', schließe meine Aeuglein zu:
Vater laß die Augen dein über meinem Bette sein!

REDEMPTION

The idea of paradise is found not only in numerous buildings, but also in specially designed gardens. The idealized garden landscape is a means of creating an earthly paradise. As the religious worldview was shattered in the nineteenth century, paradise began to assume earthly contours. In today's multi-faith society, characterized by a wide variety of faiths existing side by side, the exclusivity of one religion within a given cultural sphere has lost its meaning. Religious images are reinterpreted. Jesus has become part of the cultural heritage even for non-Christians. Art and architecture have explored the existential questions of the bible for two thousand years and expressed them in visual representations. Like other religious contents and depictions, the image of Jesus has changed, at least in the West. "The global religious renewal, the return of the sacred," **Roland Robertson** states in *Globalization: Social Theory and Global Culture* (1987), "is a reaction to the perception of the world as a single place." Now that the idea of divine redemption is no longer universally valid, paradise is more and more frequently transplanted onto earth. Thus the ideas of the Garden of Eden, of paradise, utopia and arcadia, no longer have any currency today. And the institutions, that communicate these ideas, have also changed beyond all recognition: whereas religion and church were in charge of promising happiness and conveying the idea of paradise in the Western world in the past, a powerful leisure industry delivers promises of happiness, dream worlds and artificial paradises today.

053+054+055

Salvation

HAPPYLAND

Walt Disney: Building a Drea

03

m

DISNEYLAND

In the twentieth century, the American Walt Disney created a modern paradise, in his own way and with his own methods. Success proved him right: when Disneyland opened its gates in July 1955 in Anaheim, USA, a mass movement was unleashed that can be compared to a constant stream of pilgrims flocking to their saviour. The extraordinary and uninterrupted acceptance suggests that Disney's concept of a good and happy place operates with elements that correspond to contemporary ideas of happiness. 👁 Disney could be compared with the French Sun King Louis XIV: both were obsessed with creating a perfect place, and both invested enormous effort, both technological and financial, into having a place constructed in accordance with their vision. The difference is that Louis XIV created the place for himself and his court. The idea behind Disneyland, conversely, was to create a happy and sunny place for all, even though a visit comes at the price of an entrance fee. Paradoxically, Disneyland is full of horror visions, artificially re-created natural catastrophes, witches and pirates. All this is overlaid with an optimism, which, as in fairy tales or Bible stories, leaves no doubt that good will win in the end.

THE PURSUIT OF HAPPINESS

"I'm building a dream," Disney commented when speaking about his Disneyland project at the beginning of the 1960s. And nothing is more real than the great American dream. But does one build a dream? How does one translate the fantasy of a good and at the same time exciting place into material form? 👁 Walt Disney's enthusiasm and imagination in solving this problem deserves our admiration. Engaged in a constant quest for a modern Happyland, he found the key to paradise: perfection was his entertainment. With the assistance of his dream engineers, he

WALT DISNEY
STUDIOS

created a world of fantasy become reality. Amusement was the cornerstone of his new genesis and also of his big business, because he catered, then and now, to the tastes of millions. 👁 He brought the same meticulous attention to detail that characterized his films to the conception of his amusement parks. Disney was a storyteller and he achieved something completely new: the combination of architecture and story. He used architecture as the medium of telling stories by translating the activities in Disneyland into a three-dimensional reality one can experience. "When we set out to plan Disneyland, we treated it as if we were making a movie." In his stories even the spooky characters and villains are presented in a cheerful, bright, shiny and merry manner. Evil, too, is put in its place and transformed, with meticulous precision, into a form that amuses. Disneyland is control and order, a place of reassurance: neither chaos nor violence threaten happiness. Nothing can go wrong here in the "happiest place on earth," for, as in the Disney cartoons, Disneyland is ruled by the classic fairy tale principle: good always triumphs over evil. There exists a quasi-religious belief that there is fun at the end of every queue. The Disney Company attracts 125,000 people day after day, and more than 20 million per year. Most people are so caught up and enchanted by the opulence and perfection of this artificial paradise that they forget all sense of time when they immerse themselves: "Here you leave today and enter the world of yesterday, tomorrow and fantasy." When Mickey and Donald control time, time is different and so is the place. The feeling of timelessness that Disney creates, gives visitors the impression of entering a different world.

Unlike any other known art form, Disney's animation has the primary goal of conveying fun, joy, even a flash of happiness. "Happiness is truth and truth is happiness." That is the simple message of Disney's magical world. And it is all that people need to know, according to his philosophy. Walt Disney figured out what the public loves and, thanks to his perfect organization, he made history – entertainment history.

WALT DISNEY

With Disneyland, Walt created the prototype for a new leisure culture. His influence is considered immeasurable and the consequences of his unconventional approach to architecture are far-reaching. In Disneyland, business and utopia form a successful union. Disney realized his personal dream in a multinational enterprise – the perfect embodiment of the American Way of Life. Disney wanted to make people happy. Throughout his long career, he often commented on the philosophy behind his animation art. He saw himself neither as an artist nor as a businessman, but as an entertainer, whose highest task it was to entertain people. "I never meant for what I do to be considered as art. It is show business, and I am a showman." His drive for perfection bordered on the fanatic. His principle was: "When we consider a new project, we really study it ... not just the surface idea, but everything about it." This was true not only for his animated films, but also for the development of his parks later on. With unbelievable effort, he studied effects, trained his animators and placed great value on one hundred percent attention to detail.

Disney, already famous as the inventor of animated films, nature films and comic strips, invented the amusement park. "I think I am an innovator. I find out what people like." He repeatedly emphasized that commercial success was not what truly mattered to him, but that he wanted to express his ideals through Disneyland. He would make enthusiastic statements, such as: "Disneyland is a work of love." Or: "All I want is that people have a smile on their face when they leave my place!" He understood his responsibility as a mass communicator. **Walt Elias Disney** said: "All of us who use the implements of mass communication have a tremendous responsibility to utilise them more fully in the interest of common humanity in the light of present world conditions." The E-Motion factor is one of the chief elements of his success. "We seem to know when to 'tap the heart.' Others have hit the intellect. We can hit them in an emotional way." And he added: "You know, the only way I've found to make these places is with animators – you can't seem to do it with accountants and bookkeepers."

The planning concept grew out of Disney's experience as a filmmaker and, in particular, the knowledge that sequences in a film can only be overlapped in exceptional cases. For this reason the paths in Disneyland follow a rigorous logic and overarching clarity: access is easy. The sequence of parking lot, ticket booth, entrance and action ensures that everything goes according to plan. The early master plan from 1950 for Disneyland in Anaheim shows the simple path layout. The central square offers easy access to the individual regions and is the basis for all subsequent Disneyland parks. Select theme park areas are the basis for this new generation of amusement parks, which revolutionized the haphazard layout of previous American and European fun fairs. Inspired by trade shows and world exhibitions, Disney developed a master plan in 1952, divided into the theme areas of Fantasyland, Tomorrowland, Adventureland and Frontierland, linked by an access road – Main Street USA. Main Street acts as a kind of entrance corridor that accommodates and disperses a large number of visitors. The individual countries radiate from this core like the spokes of a wheel. Each country, in turn, is characterized by a distinct centre and offers convenient access and exit routes, since all paths lead back to the main hub. Disney transports his public from one scene to another with gentle transitions and generates unambiguous and satisfying sequences of events. The ideas are derived not only from the theoretical principles of animation, but also from the pictorial language of Disney's films: the character of each adventure zone is unambiguously expressed.

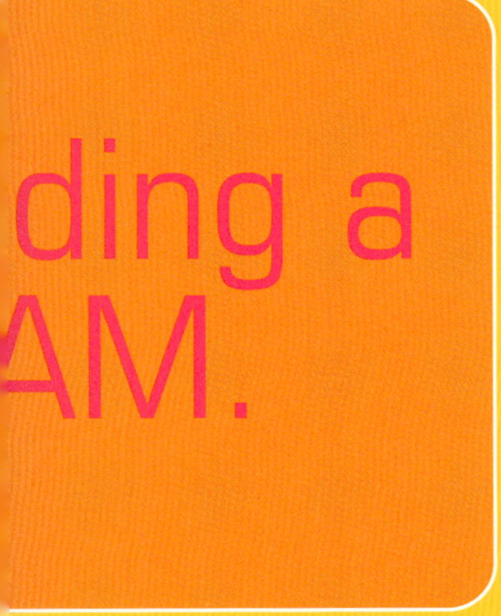

Disney's entertainment is communication without words, understood by all nations, because it is conveyed primarily by visual means. The foundation for this language, this Esperanto of fun, is perfect detail. Walt Disney surrounds his dreamland in Anaheim with a 20-foot-high earth embankment. He regrets not being able to create an encompassing green belt that would visually shield the visitors from the outside world. Emulating religious groups from the nineteenth century, Disney purchased public rights for the development of virgin land and was granted his own town ordinance. To this day, only a fraction of the land has been developed – the remainder functions as a buffer zone. For Disneyland, like paradise, is a good place – and every good place has its boundaries. "I don't want the public to see the world they live in while they're in the Park. I want them to feel they are in another world."

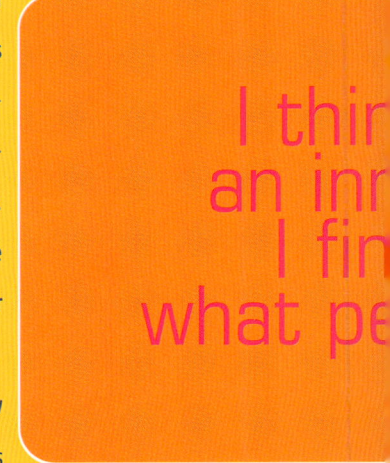

Main Street USA The prelude in Disneyland is a new version of Old New Orleans, where Main Street USA serves as an access road culminating in a central square. The varied facades that flank the street create the illusion of an individuality that has nothing to do with the rear elevation, a simple hall type. The main street depicts a New Orleans without misery: instead of poverty and violence, the scene here is dominated by countless candy shops and ice-cream parlours, a strip mall cloaked in a dazzling Victorian costume. To create a toy like ambience, Walt Disney diminishes the scale to five-eighths of the original dimension. Even the trees are adapted to this scale. Disney uses colour to generate a variety of different moods. Bright, radiant, shiny colours set a cheerful tone. Black, on the other hand, evokes a mysterious, secretive atmosphere. Life seems happy, cheerful and always beautiful on Main Street USA. There, one is surrounded by clean streets, smiling faces, cheerful colours and the assurance that everything is okay. ◉ Disney invented a series of cities. Like a king, he designed improbable pleasure gardens. First there is a fountain, then a statue and finally a castle. The staging is reminiscent of Versailles. Versailles for the masses.

I am
vator.
out
ple like.

Adventureland In Adventureland visitors travel through an artificial jungle and encounter audio-animatronic elephants, zebras, giraffes, hippos, crocodiles and snakes, which attack them. The jungle encompasses a number of different regions: the hot savannahs of Africa, the tropical islands of the Caribbean and the primeval forests of Asia. An excursion through a kaleidoscope of adventure images leads to ruins and waterfalls. The rides and conquests are based on clever technical systems that never place the adventurer in any real danger: a carefully calculated, entertaining and ultimately harmless thrill. ◉ The animator Harper Goff is the author of the jungle trip design. In many ways, the jungle trip embodies the essence of Disneyland. It is a cinematic experience, a kind of director's dream, consisting of curves and carefully placed roller coasters. In collaboration with landscape designers like Bill Evans, Walt Disney creates the perfect vegetation. With his audio animatronics, he ensures that wild, computer-controlled beasts attack the passing boats day after day, but never devour them.

Frontierland Frontierland presents the era of pioneers and conquerors circa 1840. A marshal's office and a saloon evoke the romance of cowboys and westerns. Walt Disney's idea is that Frontier Town should look like a film screen come to life. In his description of the Golden Horseshoe saloon, for example, Harper Goff copies his design for the Warner Bros. Production of *Calamity Jane* from 1953 down to the last detail. 👁 Frontierland is a perfect reflection of the cliché of the Wild West: saloon, desert, cattle farm, a lonely homestead and a prairie Indian with wigwam and reconstructed museum-quality artefacts such as costumes, tools, etc. The small town inhabited by pioneers and gold prospectors at the period of the Wild West, set in the kind of canyon and sandstone landscape that is typical of the Rocky Mountains, is the main attraction. There are rides through the maze of a mysterious gold-mine, a river trip on Mark Twain's powerful Mississippi paddle-wheel steamboat and various musical shows in the western style. 👁 In keeping with Disney's vision, his parks were never to be fully completed, but were to remain in a state of constant renewal and growth. One of the first expansions to Disneyland was New Orleans Square, a transition zone between Adventureland and Frontierland. The main attractions of New Orleans Square are the lifelike audio-animatronic figures, which were developed for the world's fair in 1964. Robots, a funhouse and pirates of the Caribbean, a haunted house and the French Quarter form a maze of small streets. Walt Disney informed the mayor of New Orleans that his West coast version was just like the real thing, only cleaner.

Fantasyland In Fantasyland, fairytale and imaginary characters live in a real place. Sleeping Beauty's castle marks the centre of the ensemble: it is the magnet for the public at the centre of Disneyland, visible from all points. ◉ Along with Main Street USA, Fantasyland is the area of Disney's park that received most attention in the planning stage. ◉ Nearly all the entertainment in Fantasyland is based on Disney's film productions. Snow White, Peter Pan, Alice in Wonderland and Mickey Mouse, the legendary figures from the early days of the studio, all are given a permanent home. This is a place for icons known throughout the world: beloved characters such as dwarfs, fairies, magicians, talking mice or baby elephants.

Tomorrowland Tomorrowland posed a challenge for Disney and his team: "The only problem with anything of tomorrow is that at the pace we are going right now tomorrow would catch up with us before we got it built." Tomorrowland speculates as to what the design of the future might be, composed from "future architectures" and equipped with innovative technologies. Modelled on the principle of a world exhibition, the pavilions are simply arranged in a row. The realization of the master plan from 1955 in Disneyland, Anaheim, California was followed by fur-ther projects: in the United States by Walt Disney World in Orlando, Florida, the Magic Kingdom (since 1971), EPCOT-Center (from 1982 onward), the Disney MGM Studios, Pleasure Island and the Typhoon Lagoon (since 1998), and since 1983 by Tokyo Disneyland in Japan and

Euro Disney in France (1992). The basic elements of the master plan are maintained throughout, creating – even before the concept of corporate identity became popular – an identity with a high recognition value, which guarantees a sense of familiarity. The iconography of the themes is adapted to regional fairy tales and national heroes, and thus varied. 👁 Disney referred to the people who realize their dreams as imagineers: a term that might be paraphrased as dream engineers. His team of studio artists included hundreds of visual artists, model builders, transport system experts, illumination and fireworks specialists, costume designers, audio-animatronic experts, event makers, show organizers and stars, interior decorators, landscape designers, graphic designers, designers, architects and writers: all of them were needed to create the entire ensemble and to cast the magic spell of the illusion of a happy life.

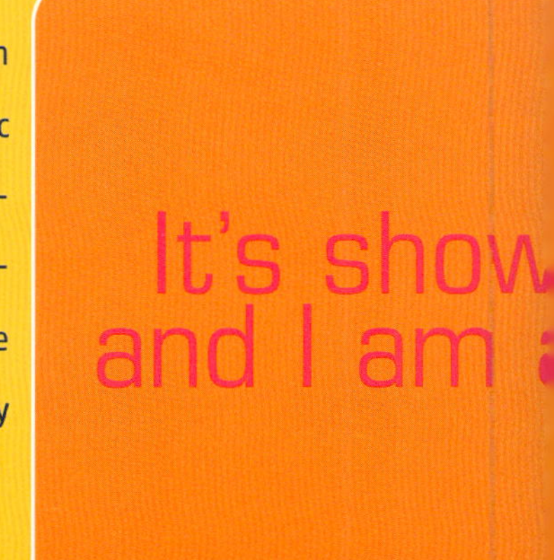

THE DISNEY COMPANY

Today, the Disney Company is an entertainment conglomerate operating on all continents. In his role as an all-encompassing leisure entrepreneur, Walt Disney revolutionized the leisure industry, from a customized code of conduct for his personnel all the way to a customized merchandising system. The economic activities of the company are comparable to a microcosm. 👁 In addition to the leisure parks, there are publishing houses, such as the Walt Disney Publishing Group, Disney Press, Hyperion Books for Children and, in Germany, the Ehapa-Comic-Verlag, Discover High Fidelity and Disney Adventures. The Disney Magic and Disney Wonder cruise ships, operated by Disney Cruise Lines, cross the high seas. The company spectrum also includes real estate, multimedia, film and video subsidiaries; the Disney Channel broadcasts into nearly one hundred percent of all American households via television and radio. As of 1995, nearly 90,000 people worldwide were employed by the Disney Company.

CROWD CONTROL

The dynamic post-war evolution toward a suburban, automobile-oriented, television society was the prerequisite for Disneyland's emergence as a mass attraction. The issue of uncomplicated arrival and uncongested movement and mass control within the parks has been solved by means of a comprehensive transportation management scheme. Buses, ferries, all kinds of boats, even steamboats and submarines, horse-drawn transportation, locomotives and a soundless monorail system are employed for crowd control and ensure a smooth flow of traffic. The Magic Kingdom also served as the testing ground for the first people movers, wide moving sidewalks that have become standard features for passenger transport in nearly every airport today. The system is computer-driven and -monitored. Disneyland serves as an experimentation environment for the latest in innovative technology, both in terms of the development of transportation systems between attractions and with regard to the mechanics of the systems themselves. The transportation solutions reflect the various epochs. From nostalgia to space travel, they represent a multitude of periods. On Main Street USA, visitors are transported in streetcars and horse-drawn carriages. Just down the road, they are moved along on the soundless monorail. Another area brings the Golden Era of the railroad back to life, and Tomorrowland features the futuristic people movers. All the transportation systems are designed not only to provide the fastest link from A to B; they are also intended to provide maximum fun. The Florida monorail, for example, offers travellers exquisite panoramic vistas across the lake and the surrounding landscape on their journey from the theme park to their hotels. 👁 The **Mark Twain steamboat** transports visitors back to a nostalgic ambience of the American South and also functions as an effective means of transportation, subject to continuous technological upgrades.

DETAIL

Part of the success of Disneyland lies in its persuasiveness as a result of the attention to detail. Disney's dedication to his projects really shows evident in those meticulous details. They demonstrate how carefully he has studied reality – in terms of the architecture, this applies to the small medieval stone house as well as to classic temples and the imaginative futuristic structures. Everything is considered with the same degree of care. From architecture to graphics, every object is invested with an identity. 👁 Total design, according to Disney, covers every conceivable aspect of design and experience: from stationery, shopping bags, furnishings and transportation to merchandising systems. The most effective impact of this attention to detail lies in achieving the goal of setting up leisure time as a positive alternative to the everyday: the fairytale and dreamlike ambience is rigorously maintained in the design. Electronic equipment and other technical requirements are hidden from the eye of the visitor. 👁 Scale and colour are carefully

People Mover

In truth, happiness can only mean: to escape.

THEODOR W. ADORNO

calibrated and manipulated to serve the illusion. There are no live animals, because their behaviour is unpredictable. Interestingly, it is precisely this artificiality, which creates the impression of reality: in the puzzle of reality versus fantasy, our sense of reality is constantly stimulated, tested and then called into question. A fantasy world that is more real than reality.

"We've been around for a long time," is the silent message of the old-fashioned lettering on windows and signage. Each locale is given the fitting idioms and the authentic materials, even the waste baskets are subject to a syncretistic design process. Leaded windows and signage, wrought iron and engraved glass in Disneyland's New Orleans Square illustrate just how true to the original each detail is reproduced.

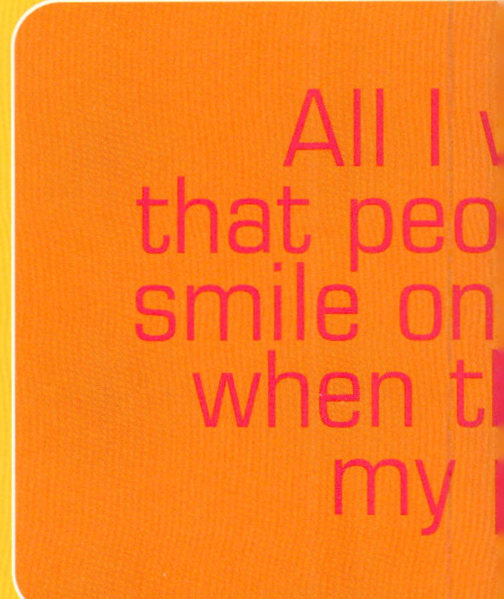

All I
that peo
smile on
when t
my

In *Travels in Hyperreality* Umberto Eco paraphrases the unreal and the real of Disneyland as follows: "The facades of Main Street USA are presented as set pieces that invite us to enter, but on the inside they are invariably disguised supermarkets, where we are shopping like mad, under the illusion that all of this is still a game. In this sense, Disneyland is hyperreal ..."

EPCOT

In 1971, a second park, Disney World, even larger and more spectacular than Disneyland, was constructed in the southern part of Florida near Orlando. After seven years of planning, the ensemble included the Magic Kingdom, a theme park comparable to Disneyland, and the EPCOT Center, a futuristic town as well as a vast vacation village, and finally, Walt Disney's World Village. In 1972, **Peter Blake** wrote: "Disney World – an absolutely staggering New Town twice the size of Manhattan, with capsulated hotels traversed by monorail trains, and a navy that ranks ninth in the world, and a submarine fleet that ranks fifth, right after the US, the USSR, Britain and France. It has cost $ 400 million so far, and that is only 10 per cent of it: When its STOL Port and its jetport and its four additional US-Steel-prefabbed hotels and its satellite EPCOT (Experimental Prototype Community of Tomorrow) are completed, Walt Disney World will run into the billions – and it will be by far the most ambitious New Town on earth." ◉ In October 1982, EPCOT provided a simulation of the utopia of ideal living conditions: in collaboration with engineers, architects and scientists, the Disney Company developed and planned the human community of tomorrow. This city for a day is based on the concept of world exhibitions and shares their optimistic view of the future. EPCOT is conceived on the basis of the motto of the World Exhibition from 1939: "Building the World of Tomorrow, for Peace and Freedom." ◉ EPCOT Center is composed of the themes transportation, communication, energy resources and agriculture. It demonstrates Disney's ideology and his unshakable

ant is
e have a
heir face
ey leave
ace.

faith in progress. Several major companies signed up as sponsors for this continuous "world exhibition." Scientists from all sectors of industry joined forces with the entertainment talents. At the time, the idea of conveying knowledge through entertainment was entirely new. EPCOT Center occupies a unique place among all Disney parks, not only in terms of content, but also with regard to form: the architecture is innovative and autonomous, consisting of Little World on one side and Future World on the other. World Showcase completes the range with a permanent exhibition that draws restaurants, landmarks and folklore from ten countries.

We see
when to 'ta
Others have
We car
in an em

Little World Little World includes famous buildings that are typical of the countries they represent. Among them are a 30-m-high miniature Eiffel Tower, the Doge's Palace and Piazza San Marco in Little Italy and a replica of Munich's Hofbräuhaus intended to communicate a piece of German *Gemütlichkeit* to the visitor.

Future World Walt Disney loved the past, but he was even more fascinated by the future. Disney's designers, the animators, collaborated with him to create countless visions of Future World. Disney met with Victor Gruen, the urban planner, to discuss the city of tomorrow. He developed the buildings and pavilions for EPCOT together with the architecture firm Welton Beckets. Spread across several pavilions, Future World features exhibitions and presentations of future technologies. The individual areas are entitled: Spaceship Earth, The Universe of Energy, The World of Motion, The Journey into Imagination and The Land. The route through this area describes a figure eight. There is no specific sequence: visitors can choose freely to avoid lengthy queues.

Spaceship Earth Spaceship Earth is the landmark of EPCOT: this massive aluminum sphere soars above the surroundings and symbolizes the Earth and is operated by United Technologies. Spaceship Earth is centrally located and looks like an oversized golf ball, as tall as an 18-storey building. Spaceship Earth is one of the first realized Buckminster Fuller geodesic domes in the world. The building consists of a steel skeleton, clad in faceted aluminum panels and raised on three pairs of steel columns. 👁 Inside, the visitor is presented with a history of communication technology narrated by means of moving pictures, beginning with prehistoric hunters communicating through calls and ending with two astronauts whose conversation is conducted via satellite. Visitors experience the show from a midway transporting them into the interior of the sphere. When they reach the top, they are exposed to a realistic simulation of weightlessness in space. 👁 The depiction is naturalistic in the extreme: the mammoth that has just been slain is still breathing a death rattle, a simulated cave fire is kept going by industrious cavemen. The press office proudly emphasises that even the hieroglyphics are authentic and that all dialects are accurately rendered. Even the costumes of the 65 figures are based on meticulous research.

to know
the heart.'
the intellect.
it them
onal way.

The Universe of Energy The Universe of Energy is sponsored by Exxon. The futuristic building designed by Disney architects distinguishes this pavilion from all the others. The pyramid structure is equipped with 80,000 solar collector cells mounted on the slanted roof facing south. Upon entering, visitors are given an introduction to the challenge of contemporary energy supply. This is provided via complex projections on one wall, consisting a hundred rotating, three-sided elements. Once the eight-minute presentation is over, doors open onto a movie theatre. An animated film illustrates the origin of fossil fuels. Suddenly the tall side walls of the theatre disappear. What was a cinema only a few seconds ago is transformed into six hovercrafts that the spectators carry into the adjacent halls, as if pulled by an invisible hand, without driver or tracks, guided by a 3-mm-thick wire in the floor. The energy supplied by the roof charges the accumulator batteries that power the vehicles.

The World of Motion General Motors presents and demonstrates the history of transportation and vehicles during a trip in a gondola. The audio animatronics simulate Neanderthals with blistered feet or farmers, building the first rafts. A sailor on the Atlantic encounters a marine monster and there are other dramatic encounters with steam-powered cars and horse-drawn carriages. Finally, the gondola glides through the modern era of cars, airplanes, space shuttles and rockets.

The Land One of the most interesting areas in EPCOT is The Land, sponsored by Kraft. The principal route through this attraction is on a boat that can ferry roughly 2,000 guests per hour. The journey leads through different landscapes: across a desert, past waterfalls and through a tropical region. The presentation begins with 150 different national crops and the corresponding methods of cultivation. The site also serves as an experimental laboratory for new cultivation methods for food production. These experiments are part of a research program conducted by the University of Arizona with the aim of increasing crop yields through vertical instead of horizontal cultivation, that is, to achieve maximum yields. In some instances, this method has achieved twenty times the standard yield. The multi-crop system is equally successful. The journey is accompanied by a soundtrack, background noise and warm breezes. The artificial chickens not only look like chickens, they smell like chickens. The experience is not only informative, but so three-dimensional as an illusion that learning is experienced as exciting entertainment. Edutainment, in short, only the word didn't exist at that time.

When
planning
we app
it as if
makin

DISNEYLAND RESORT

In the new city of Marne-la-Vallée, thirty kilometres outside of Paris, the Walt Disney Company built the largest amusement park in Europe in 1992. The area of Euro Disney equals one fifth of the expanse of the city of Paris. In addition to the Magic Kingdom, the complex contains six new hotels (15,000 beds), a 22,000 m^2 shopping centre, 30,000 m^2 of office space, 57,000 m^2 of commercial space, single-family homes and a golf course. Michael Eisner, CEO of Walt Disney, invited a wide range of famous architects, from Aldo Rossi to Rem Koolhaas, to participate in a limited competition for the six large hotels. A total of twenty European and American architects participated in the competition. The selected participants, among them international stars Aldo Rossi, Rem Koolhaas, Bernhard Tschumi, Jean Nouvel, Christian de Portzamparc, Hans Hollein,

Arata Isozaki and Frank O. Gehry, presented a broad spectrum of contemporary architecture. The proposals by the American architects Robert Stern, Michael Graves, Antoine Predock and Wimberly, Allison, Tong and the French architect Antoine Grumbach were nominated and realized. The designs by Graves, Stern, Predock and Wimberly, Allison, Tong are imitations and miniature renderings of American buildings and landscapes. The Hotel Newport Bay Club by Robert Stern recreates the scenery of the New England resort at the turn of the last century. The Hotel Santa Fe by Antoine Predock reflects the ambience of a small town in New Mexico. The Hotel Cheyenne by Michael Graves is a copy of a Wild West town. And Hotel New York features the famous skyline of the metropolis. Frank O. Gehry won the competition for Disney Village, a complex of 160,000 m^2 dedicated to retail space, restaurants and entertainment, respectively.

e were
sneyland,
oached
e were
a film.

WALT DISNEY STUDIOS PARK

On March 2002, Disneyland Resort opened the new theme park Walt Disney Studios near Paris. The park is dedicated to film, television, animation and special effects. After MGM studios in Florida, Walt Disney Studios is the second of its kind. After three years of construction and an investment of €600 million, the company hopes to attract more visitors. Located right next to Disneyland Resort, Walt Disney Studios is a new attraction with a blend of information, entertainment and interaction. Twenty-five hectares of land have been developed to this end. The four principal themes are: Front Lot, Animation Courtyard, Production Courtyard and Backlot.

Front Lot The attractions here alternate at a rapid pace. Three hundred Disney imagineers were involved in planning this mega-project. The trademark of the new theme park is the tall water tower, which also dominates the horizon at Disney studios in Burbank, California. The visitor walks through a large gate into Studio 1 and the first theme attraction, Front Lot, begins. A series of film sets are open for viewing and for a glimpse behind the scenes. Studio 1 was inspired by the Hyperion Avenue Studios in Los Angeles, where Disney produced his first major animated film, Snow White and the Seven Dwarfs.

Animation Courtyard Animation Courtyard pays homage to the father of all Disney animation characters, Walt Disney. In the attraction The Art of Disney Animation, visitors travel through the history of the art of film animation. They learn everything about Disney's animation techniques and can even try them out. Animagique is the title of a black-light presentation designed specifically for this theme park. Ultraviolet light and special effects are used to bring the heroes of Disney classics to life in a three-dimensional show.

Production Courtyard This attraction provides visitors with information about the world of film and television, how a TV-studio functions and how sets are produced. Action fans are offered a special thrill on the studio tram tour. It travels through staged catastrophes, past earthquakes and floods. Ciné Magique shows European and American film history. The TV station Television Production Tour has its studios in the park and also broadcasts from there.

Backlot The realm of action and special effects is called Backlot. Here, meteorite showers are as common as high-speed chases accompanied by rock music and stunt shows. The Russian space station Mir was reconstructed, in part to original scale and in part as a film set. Other attractions such as the Rock´n´ Roller Coaster offer loops and curves, while the Stunt Show Spectacular promises entertainment rich in action. Wild chases in cars, on motorcycles and even on jet skis can be experienced live.

You know, the only way I've found to make these places is with animators – you can't seem to do it with accountants and bookkeepers. WALT DISNEY

MOHAV
OIL CO

HISTORY
Sites of Anima

101010

001000001010111

0101000

0101010

10101001010101010

10001001001000

04

tion

BREAD AND CIRCUSES

The Roman people, who once upon a time had magisterial power and authority and legions, in short, everything at their disposal, have become modest, with a passionate desire for only two things: bread and games. JUVENAL

The historical evolution of leisure sites demonstrates that buildings and sites created specifically for use during off-work hours have existed at all times. The design of these structures was fundamentally influenced by the economic and political circumstances, the cultural trends and social customs of each epoch, the relationship between work and leisure, the importance accorded the latter and, last but not least, the financial and technological possibilities of the time. Panem et circenses or bread and games – ever since antiquity, this pairing has been synonymous with the fact that humans do not live by bread alone. The imperial strategy of government in antiquity derived its popularity even then from the ability to keep the populace happy by providing entertaining diversions in addition to the material necessities of life. This is borne out by the number and scale of buildings that served as venues for spectacles of all kinds, usually bloodthirsty and cruel, reflecting the tastes of the era. In antiquity, the spectator was treated to what is today the last remaining taboo in reality TV: a fight to the death – live. **Seneca** wrote: "I came upon a spectacle by chance and thought that I might relax in watching it – the very opposite was the case. ... In the morning they throw human beings to the lions and bears, and

118:119 HISTORY
076+077+078

in the afternoon they deliver them to the mercy of the spectators: the outcome of the fight is always death." The historicist masterpiece *Pollice verso* by **Jean-Léon Gérôme** is a dramatic depiction of a fight between gladiators with all its elements: the gigantic scale and pompous decoration of the backdrop of an antique amphitheatre, the bloodlust of the audience and the emperors' power to decide the fighters' life and death by pointing their thumbs up or down.

Colosseum The Colosseum, begun in 69 AD under **Vespasian** and inaugurated in 79 AD by his son **Titus** with a hundred-day-long celebration, served to satisfy the Roman people's thirst for spectacles even more. With a length of 185 m, a width of 156 m and a height of 48.5 m, the amphitheatre could accommodate up to 100,000 spectators. The floor construction was flexible and easily repairable because it was composed of removable board sections. It could even be submerged in water to simulate naval battles. Access was via 166 open arcades on the ground floor. There was no crush when the crowds left the theatre; the building was designed to handle the masses with ease. The public's passion for the spectacles on display led to ever more elaborate sets and additions in the subsequent decades. The 50-m-high outer facade of the amphitheatre was equipped with supports for vertical masts on which canvas sails could be raised to provide shade.

Circus Maximus One of the largest and most significant buildings was the Circus Maximus in Rome, a project on which all emperors continued to build until the reign of Constantine. After many expansions, by the fourth century AC, it had an impressive capacity of 300,000 spectators.

Be it chariot races, gladiator fights, military spectacles or the re-enactment of battles or wild game hunts – the spectacles at the circus were the centre of social life in antiquity. They marked the seasons, offered diversion, and provided topics for conversation, occasions for betting, and opportunities for rendezvous. The architectural setting was correspondingly multifunctional. This monumental entertainment venue of antiquity fulfilled many of the criteria associated with modern multi-purpose buildings. A reconstruction of the Circus Maximus clearly shows the expanse along the spine to the curved end sections. Today, large cypress trees mark the former positions of the end-posts. The flat valley forms the racecourse; the slopes of the surrounding hills provided a natural support for spectator stands, initially constructed in wood and only during Caesar's time in stone.

Baths The thermal baths created by **Emperor Caracalla** in the valley between the Caelius and the Aventine hills in 215 AD played an important role in public amusement. They were communications centres, where the sanitary purpose of personal hygiene was clearly secondary to the social benefit of hedonistic pleasures. With increasingly luxurious appointments, the bathing facilities catered to the most unusual needs, enriched with amenities for sports and games. Including the attached gymnasium – the *palaestra* – the complex covered some 109,000 m². The compact central bathhouse alone was 220 m long and 114 m wide: the complex was subsequently surpassed in scale only by the Baths of Diocletian. 👁 The individual components became standard features in subsequent public baths: the bathhouse with pool, the so-called *natatio*, the warm water pool or *caldarium*, whose domical vault projected far beyond the south facade to capture the maximum amount of sunlight and whose internal diameter measured 35 m in the Baths of Caracalla. The caldarium is flanked to the left and right by additional

122:123
081+082+083

vaulted halls for a variety of bathing rituals, such as sweat baths. From this point, patrons could walk to basilica-like halls for sports or games or follow a path across the semicircular *exedra* to the *frigidarium*, the cooling-off room, and to the changing rooms. The upper floor consisted of terraced sun patios and courtyards. The architectural ornamentation in the *thermae* created the ambience of an exclusive leisure and relaxation zone. The vaulted ceilings were magnificently decorated with coffers, the columns culminated in detailed composite capitals, and the walls were decorated with mosaics depicting sporting scenes that created a luxurious ambience.

MEDIEVAL AMUSEMENTS

Sites reserved exclusively for animation were rare in the Middle Ages. In the High Middle Ages, playgrounds for the people were usually located outside city walls. Archery grounds outside the city served as the platforms for politics, commerce and military drills, and were often reassigned to be used as sites "where persons of leisure and pleasure seekers gathered for games and entertainment," thus the description in **Dieter Hennebo**'s *Entwicklung des Stadtgrüns von der Antike bis in die Zeit des Absolutismus.* 👁 It wasn't until much later that festival and market squares as well as playhouses were no longer banished outside the city gates, but increasingly located in the cores of cities and villages at the centre of daily life. Located between church and pub, these sites played a multifunctional role. City life was vibrant. Princes making a splendid entrance, carnivals or the arrival of itinerant entertainers provided hours of amusement. When a ruler returned from battle, triumphal arches were erected, parades and spectacles were held. The celebrations of the guilds, processions and carnival festivities, all took place in the squares in front of the cathedrals, which served as a stage for comedians, artistes and dancers. 👁 The

street also acted as a stage for puppet theatres, charlatans, tightrope walkers and animal tamers. Long before the public began to pay for entertainment, the street itself was the greatest entertainment centre.

Tournaments In terms of popularity, no medieval entertainment could compete with the tournament, a staged contest in which knights set out to demonstrate courage and skill. The first tournaments were held in the eleventh century in northern France, and began to spread some fifty years later, at the beginning of the twelfth century, across the rest of Europe. Contests in front of a large audience became the favourite activity of the knights and of the public at large. A victory at a tournament meant not only fame and honour; it also promised a reward from the sovereign. 👁 Tournaments were held under the open sky. Two enormous spectator stands were raised in the contest arena. The participants set up their tents on the grounds surrounding the site. The competitions were performed in an attractive setting and accompanied by shouts of encouragement from the spectators.

THE HAPPY FEW

In contrast to the majority of the populace, sovereigns such as Louis XIV, the French "Sun King," or Ludwig II of Bavaria in a later period, enjoyed the privilege of being able to indulge freely in their desire for entertainment. They had the means to build castles to match their extravagant visions and to create formal gardens as a backdrop for their amusements. Although these projects also served to illustrate the might and wealth of the state, they were first and foremost playgrounds for feudal whims: music flowed from ornamental temples, pompous fireworks were reflected in pools and blended in with elaborate waterworks, magnificent flower borders decorated the grounds for grand balls, sumptuous sculptures facilitated flirtatious games of hide-and-seek, mazes and artfully designed labyrinths offered the thrill of disorientation. Groves and orangeries were tailor-made for a tête-à-tête. The potentates spared no effort in translating ever-new ideas for artfully designed landscape parks for diversion.

European Gardens European gardens represent the beautiful side of life. In many cultures, the design of these gardens with plants, paths, landscaping and earthworks is based on the religious motif of recreating paradise. ◉ Be it the gardens of the Renaissance or of Mannerism, the Baroque or the Rococo, English landscape gardens or French gardens, they all were designed to illustrate a better world. ◉ Arcadia, the secularized version of paradise, is a point of reference in the history of gardens. C. F. Schröer writes: "Arcadia is the land where everyday life is golden; this everyday life is completely artificial. Everything that happens is significant, exalted and essentially the exact opposite of mundane everyday life. A deep chasm separates the artificial world of Arcadia from normal, everyday life. For Arcadia is above all an aesthetic fiction and a Utopian vision of happiness." ◉ Arcadia re-emerged in the Renaissance. The court of the Medici in Florence was transformed into a work of art set into an imaginary landscape: Arcadia as a work of art, a realm between paradise and reality. Yearning for love, not its fulfillment, was the true "Arcadian sentiment." In the elaborately designed gardens of the Renaissance and later on, even more so in those of the Baroque and Mannerism, solitary or grouped statues, fountains and grottos recalled ancient mythologies. This was especially true of statues that represented the universe of Olympian gods: Pan, satyrs and nymphs are inhabitants of Arcadia. ◉ In the Renaissance, the garden ensemble was designed for the first time as a work of art and an area for relaxation and amusement, with waterworks, stairs and terraces, rock gardens and trimmed

hedges and trees – the so-called bosquet. This concept was impressively interpreted in the country estate gardens of the Medici in Florence and implemented with artful monumentality in the gardens of the Villa d'Este in Tivoli. 👁 In the sixteenth century, the Villa d'Este in Tivoli, Italy, was the seat of Cardinal **Ippolito d'Este**. The park, designed in the classic Roman spirit, was embellished with numerous waterworks, stone monuments and a penchant for the monumental. Adjacent estate buildings, stables, orchards and olive groves, fields and meadows illustrated the economic aspect of the villa garden. **Pirro Ligorio**'s garden design in Tivoli, conceived in rigorous symmetry to the principal axis, reflects the Renaissance ideal of unity between villa, park and garden. Here was horticulture in the sense of creating a world of art. Ligorio's capacity for inventiveness was overwhelming and continues to inspire awe and rapture in visitors to this day. 👁 The plan, which envisioned the garden as a complement and integral component of the house, divides it into three parts: a lower level and two additional levels, which rise in terraces toward the villa. At the very outset, the visitor is enveloped in the mood the owner wishes to create as he strolls toward the villa. 👁 Around the mid-sixteenth century, the same architect designed a sculpture park in Bomarzo. In contrast to other Renaissance gardens, this park was not ruled by the laws of order and geometry, but deliberately conceived to confuse the senses of the visitor. The monumental stone sculptures were not arranged symmetrically; instead they stand in the random order of natural boulders. A reservoir, waterworks and fountains emphasize the fairytale character. Today, the fountains have dried up and Bomarzo has become a pure rock garden. The motto of the garden, carved in stone at the entrance to the path, reads: "You who roam the world in search of sublime and fearful wonders, come hither and look upon terrible countenances, elephants, lions, bears, man-eaters and dragons." A crooked house confuses the senses of the visitors, disturbs their sense of direction as they enter and baffles them, because it disturbs the equilibrium. The sculptures evoke references to literature: giant, dragon, tortoise and elephant are reminiscent of oriental fairy tales, others of mythologies from antiquity. The monster in stone seems almost alive; one has the sense of actually hearing it roar. In the Baroque and in Mannerism, the number of structuring accessories, sculptures and small decorative buildings increased considerably, especially in the French garden. From an elevated perspective, nature was subordinated through architectonic design to a system of axes, that defined the arrangement of the borders, the ponds and the plantings. In the Baroque, the celebration at court was seen as a metaphor for life in general. **T. O. Enge** writes: "The Baroque was an epoch of fast living; the reverse side of its ever more gigantic and grandiose parties – and the

psychological reason for them – was the flight from inner emptiness." Undoubtedly the most famous example is landscape architect **Le Notre**'s park design for Versailles, realized from 1661 onward and commissioned by Louis XIV for the castle that served as the residence of the French kings until the revolution. These absolutist gardens were reserved for the exclusive use of the court. Only under the regency of Louis Philippe XIV, the so-called "Bourgeois King," were the castle and park of Versailles opened to the public, albeit with some restrictions; later still, they were used as an open-air museum and in the twentieth century they were declared a UNESCO world heritage site. ◉ A painterly style of landscape garden was developed in England circa 1720 in deliberate opposition to the geometrical and rigorously planned perspectives of the French garden. Strict geometry was rejected as unnatural; symmetrical arrangements were seen as

087+088

undesirable constraints. Curving paths and generous stretches of lawn interspersed with stands of trees were the means adopted to achieve a total work of art that creates a wide variety of images as one wanders through it. The observer was treated to a succession of new vistas and changing moods. Nature is no longer tamed, as in the French garden, but approached through the senses in an almost religious pantheistic experience. The English garden seeks to recreate the state of paradise, to awaken memories of the Garden of Eden, of Arcadia, Milton's Paradise and Elysium in the observer. Architecture was mainly represented by artificially created ruins. Structures built from natural materials, grottoes and arbours in natural stone or wood generate associations of a seemingly natural environment.

Feudal Follies In the eighteenth century the French nobility and the well-to-do bourgeoisie frolicked in their follies. These country estates were surrounded by extensive gardens with garishly designed rockeries, artificial ruins and statues. ◉ Folly, lunacy or the opposite of reason, they represent a whim.

Thus they represent the capricious design whims of noble clients, expressed most notably in the architecture of their pleasure buildings. These were a mirror of contemporary tastes, the education of the respective sovereign and his spiritual sources of inspiration. Reconstructions of antique temples or other historically relevant buildings expressed the worldliness and cultural sophistication of their builder. After a visit to England in 1772, Philippe d'Orléans commissioned the creation of the Parc Monceau near Paris in the form of a picturesque garden, a land of illusions. Mongolian and Turkish tents, gothic ruins, Roman ruins, Dutch windmills, Chinese pavilions, minarets, pyramids, and obelisks: the repertoire of atmospheric set pieces seemed endless.

Drawing on Eastern elements was another feudal whim: Philippe d'Orléans tapped into an English source of exotic inspiration, the former British colony of India. The heir to the throne, George IV (1762–1830), known for his lavish lifestyle, commissioned **John Nash** to convert the Royal Pavilion in Brighton into an elegant structure in the Indian style. With props such as Indian horseshoe and keel arches, the architect did indeed employ authentic details, but he integrated them into the whole in a completely free, individual and fantastic vision of the Orient. Nash transformed the classic summer residence of Prince George, then the Prince of Wales, into an oriental folly. The roof is a landscape of cupolas, towers and minarets, the facade is dissolved into arcades, balcony balustrades and battlements.

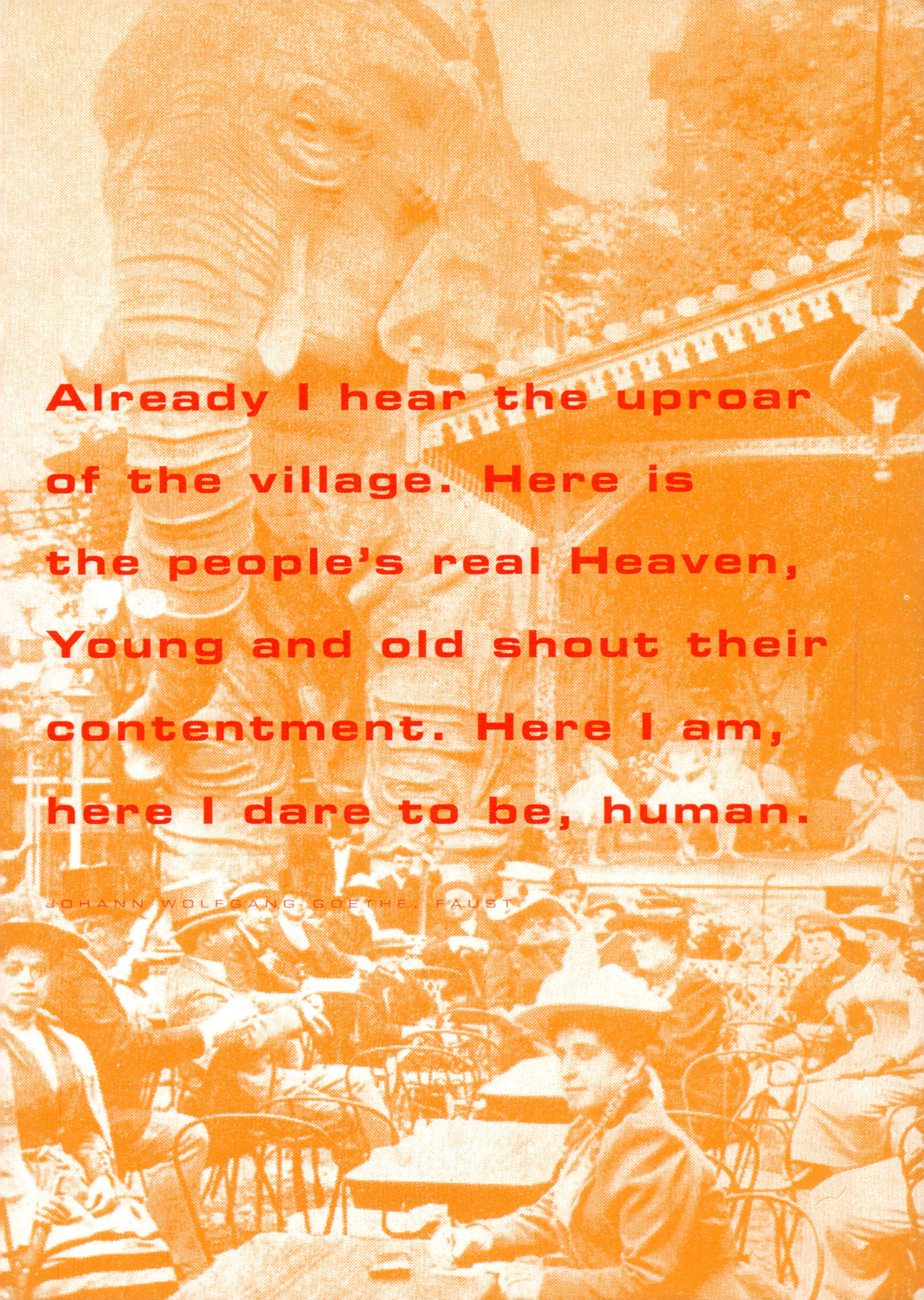
Already I hear the uproar
of the village. Here is
the people's real Heaven,
Young and old shout their
contentment. Here I am,
here I dare to be, human.
JOHANN WOLFGANG GOETHE, FAUST

PEOPLE'S PLACE

Spending time in gardens designed specifically for diversion would remain the privilege of nobility for a long time; a shift in thinking came only with the enlightened despotism of the eighteenth century. One first step towards the democratization of leisure was the opening of feudal parks to the general public: "Persons of high stature and even the noblest princes devote themselves wholly to benevolence and affability," reads the commentary in **Johann Peter Willebrand**'s *Plan for a Beautiful City* from 1775. In a humanitarian gesture – albeit one that could be revoked at will – the Baroque parks of the lesser German principalities such as Ludwigsburg, Schwetzingen, Bayreuth, Nymphenburg, Herrenhausen, Schleißheim and Kassel, which were modelled after Versailles, were opened to the lower classes. Nevertheless, strict rules as to who may or may not stroll in the parks continued to apply. The poor, beggars, the lame and domestic servants were still denied access. In the eighteenth century a sign posted at the park of Castle Herrenhausen cautioned "commoners at pain of corporal punishment" to "make use of the benches at the great fountain only when these are not required for persons of standing or elegant foreigners." Shortly before the opening of the leisure sites for the broader public, architects in France were still working predominantly for the entertainment of the court. Prior to the proclamation of the republic in 1789, the menus plaisirs contained the arrangements for the festivities at court and the design of the corresponding ephemera, set-like decorative structures. In some respects, the requirements of the menus plaisirs are comparable to the tasks of a modern animator and the flexible buildings also have much in common with the readily changeable scenery in contemporary leisure parks. When Louis Philippe, the "Bourgeois King," succeeded the Bourbons in 1830, the menus plaisirs were stripped of their function at court, and the architects shifted their attention to urban projects. Their experience was especially useful in the new design for the Champs-Elysées, which were inaugurated in May 1839 in their entirety. The nineteenth-century journal *Illustration* proclaimed: "Anything is possible in Paris now ... this city is constantly full of contrasts, here reasonable, there communist; and in the Champs-Elysées, it offers us the best display of a democratic republic." In the course of the nineteenth century, entertainment institutions were increasingly integrated with the urban image and thus taken seriously as an architectural theme in quite a different manner than before. In the years that followed a variety of buildings were erected on the Champs-Elysées, initially as decorative eye-catchers within the overall concept of different buildings whose principal purpose was entertainment. A bustling street life developed around the largest buildings, the theatre, the circus and the panorama, between coffee houses, casinos, food vendors and fairground booths. The "Café-concerts," cafés where musical entertainment was offered – a new fashion that had begun only a few years before – were popular attractions.

Pleasure Gardens From the seventeenth century onward, pleasure gardens for public access were established, beginning with the Vauxhall Gardens in London, and later in other parts of England as independent bourgeois counterparts to the courtly park and garden ensembles. Even the earliest examples of such public gardens proclaimed their purpose in their names. London's Vauxhall Gardens, for example, were a forerunner of permanent urban leisure sites. The geometrically arranged plants and flowerbeds were embellished with ornamentation in the anglo-chinois manner: grottoes, cascades, gates and light wood structures. A huge statue of an elephant was installed next to the Café Moulin Rouge. The larger-than-life replica culminated in an observation platform, which offered a panoramic view of the Belle Epoque theme park. New

attractions became popular. From the second half of the eighteenth century onward, the gardens were increasingly furnished with exotic structures and sculptures, that housed commercial establishments. The paying public replaced the aristocracy and masses flocked to the extensive outdoor restaurants. There, beer or tea gardens and cafés offered a varied menu, and animal enclosures, waterworks, musical and theatrical presentations, gambling casinos and dance halls provided an entertaining setting. The vocabulary of the design elements imitated the feudal model. The collective term for these types of grounds – Grotto Gardens – was therefore derived from the artificial grotto-like rockeries in feudal gardens.

Prater The first explicit dedication of a royal park for public use occurred in Vienna on April 7, 1766, when **Joseph II** proclaimed that "henceforth and from now on in all seasons and at all hours of the day, everyone without exception is permitted to stroll, ride or drive in the Prater and in the city's estates" and that "no person shall be excluded from seeking diversion therein with ball games, skittles and other permissible diversions to their taste." The initially temporary amusements quickly grew into permanent establishments along the western bank of the Danube. The first mechanical rides were installed in the very same year, and by 1771 the Viennese were flocking to their park for fireworks displays. The area near the entrance of the park, the so-called Wurstelprater, was crowded with carousels, swings, shooting alleys, gaming-machines, beer gardens and dance halls. Anyone wishing to escape the hectic pace could enjoy the spectacle from the lofty heights of a ride on the Ferris wheel, today protected as a heritage monument, or take refuge in the green zone. With the creation of a replica Venice in 1895, the Prater took one step further along the road towards the modern amusement park. **Adalbert Stifter** (1805–1868) tried to define the Prater in its heyday in the nineteenth century: "Is it

a park? No. A forest? No. An amusement park? No. What then? All these things combined ... an enchanting blend of meadow and forest, of park and playground, of noisy beer garden and quiet grove ... How fortunate we are to have the Prater." On the occasion of a visit to the Prater in Vienna, **Stefan Zweig** was equally enthusiastic: "The dull, muffled sound of music boomed from some unspecified place and I followed it instinctively because today everything intrigued me. I experienced this submission to chance as a sensual pleasure and to drift dully, passively amidst a softly pulsating crowd is wonderfully exciting. My blood seethed in this thick boiling stew of humanity. Everything that had previously repulsed me as ordinary, plebeian, common, all that the sophisticated gentleman in me had haughtily avoided all my life, magically enticed my new instinct as if I were sensing in me for the first time a kinship with the animalistic, the compulsive, the common ... Here ... I felt happy in a way that I could not understand."

Tivoli In France, the universal movement toward democracy after 1789 was soon evident in the typology of the leisure facilities. Over the course of the nineteenth century, the Tivoli gardens gradually replaced the pleasure gardens. The princely estates of the follies were confiscated and declared public amusement gardens. At the same time they were renamed "Tivoli," a word that became the dedicated term for similar sites in other countries. The name is a reference to the mountain village near Rome, which already served as a summer retreat for Roman emperors and which is home to the famous Renaissance gardens of the Villa d'Este. The Tivoli in Copenhagen is one of the most enduring amusement parks in the world. Opened in 1843 in the centre of the city on a former military parade ground, it was founded by the Algerian-born Dane Georg Carstensen (1802–1857), who began his career as a journalist and then organized public festivals and also worked as an architect. The concert hall in the oriental style, with cupolas, minarets

and an arcade with horseshoe arches, followed in the footsteps of the two predecessor buildings from **Harald Stilling** (1844) and **Johann Stillmann** (1865). Carstensen's building was destroyed in the Second World War. In Berlin-Kreuzberg another Tivoli was established in 1829 near the national monument. Others followed, for example in Hamburg, Hanover and Vienna. Progress in technology was increasingly evident in the design of the amusement parks. Even a full century later, Disney was inspired by Carstensen's park, fascinated, in particular, by the illumination at night. Numerous buildings were erected in the Tivoli over the course of several years: concert halls and ballrooms, cafés and restaurants, music pavilions and slides. Many are still being converted and enlarged to this day. Permanence is not the intended goal.

Bois de Boulogne The Champs-Elysées were not the only area to undergo a structural change. The grounds of the Bois de Boulogne were also transferred by the state to the city of Paris in 1852 on condition that the city would carry out similar improvements there. The attention given to such entertainment venues in city planning and their placement in the centre of the city were an expression of the social acceptance of the human need for entertainment: there was a deliberate move to no longer separate high and low culture. The Hippodrome, erected in the Bois de Boulogne in 1855, is a major attraction. This phenomenon was appreciated even at the time as an expression of a gradual process of democratization. It was also evident in the colourful design of the buildings. In the Bois de Boulogne, not only the theatres, but the circus buildings too, were rendered in a rich polychromatic palette inspired by Greek temple decor to create an atmosphere of freshness, cheerfulness and opulence. The same care was given to other

Buildings are by no means conceived for eternity. They should be renewed like flowers that fade at the end of the season.

THOMAS VON JOEST

building types, such as restaurants and cafés. But the colourful decorations were not designed to last. In his essay on the Cirque d'Été, **Thomas von Joest** explained: they should by no means be conceived for eternity and "be renewed like fresh flowers that fade at the end of the season."

Panoramas Monumental panorama paintings, which surround the viewer on all sides and create the illusion of being in the middle of a real landscape, began to proliferate after 1799. In Paris alone a number of such edifices were created. These cleverly staged pseudo-experiences corresponded with the interests of the bourgeois audience. People loved having the wool pulled over their eyes, they wanted to be amazed and, incidentally, also learn about current events and expand their knowledge. All these yearnings were satisfied by the panorama, which therefore possesses many of the characteristics of a modern mass medium – the more perfect the illusion, the better. Thus it was the declared goal of the architects of such buildings to subordinate the construction to the illusion, that is, to relegate structural details to the background as far as possible so as not to interfere with the imagination. 👁 In 1831, the rotunda was erected in the Rue des Marais-du Temple at the initiative of Colonel Jean Charles Langlois (1789–1870). The inauguration featured a painting of the naval battle at Navarino. A replica warship stern occupied the centre of the space, allowing each visitor to slip into the dramatic role of naval commander. The illusion was perfect. In the following years, there was a boom in designs for spherical projection surfaces or presentation spaces such as Phonorama, Coupolorama, Circarama, Cinetarium, Specarium, and Panrama. All were attempts to enable the viewer to forget the existence of a screen and to offer the sensation of immersing oneself completely in the projected image, accompanied by overpowering sensory experiences and "thrills." 👁 A visit to the Neorama, which was simply an architectural variation of the Georama and the Panorama, allowed the visitor to temporarily be immersed in a foreign atmosphere without having to travel to a different place. It depicted the interiors of famous buildings, for example, of St. Peter's Basilica in Rome. In the centre of Paris one could thus be transported to the core of the Vatican. However, the enthusiastic reception was soon followed by criticism. The discrepancy between the highly realistic backdrops and the static repertoire of figures was too great. Nearly a century later, Walt Disney would correct this illusion-destroying shortcoming in his amusement parks with the help of audio-animatronics. In the 1920s the Frenchman Delanglard developed the idea of the Georama, an idea that was as simple as it was inspired. He solved the problem of depicting the world on a globe, which only allowed partial views at any given time, with a simple trick. By turning the earth's surface inside out, so to speak, and placing the observer on a platform in the centre of a spherical view of the world, he was able to offer a continuous panoramic view of the globe. At the time, the primary interest in the Georama was for its informative content. But formally and psychologically it also catered to the self-image of the cosmopolitan. Like the Neorama, it was a precursor to the kind of compression that would recur at a later date in creating a close proximity of the most diverse geographic and historical zones in modern amusement parks. The panorama rotunda by **Jacob Ignaz Hittorff** on the Champs-Elysées, Grand Carré, depicted an illusion of reality. The architecture was based on the model of an antique amphitheatre. The London Coliseum in St. Regents Park, opened in 1829, was the specific model. When the boom in panorama buildings faded for some decades in the middle of the century, only to come alive again in the late 1870s, the building was expanded and integrated into the Paris World Exhibition of 1855.

Coney Island The highlight in the history of public entertainment came with the three adjacent amusement parks that were created at the beginning of the twentieth century on the Atlantic Ocean on the peninsula of Coney Island near New York: Steeplechase Park in 1898, Luna Park in 1903 and Dreamland in 1904. In 1978, **R. G. Blomeyer** and **B. Tietze** wrote about the phenomenon of Coney Island: "This was no longer a fairground, but a place of experimentation with a new kind of urban planning and with the socio-technology of the metropolis. It was in the snack bars on Coney Island that the Frankfurter metamorphosed into the hot dog and ground beef into the hamburger." 👁 To begin with, the peninsula with its wide beach was a popular summer destination for New Yorkers, until Coney Island developed a reputation as a commercial amusement site. 👁 After a trip to the Columbian World's Fair in Chicago, whose greatest sensation was a giant Ferris wheel designed by **George W. Ferris** to rival the Eiffel Tower in Paris, George C. Tilyou founded the Steeplechase amusement park in 1893. Tilyou purchased a smaller version of the Ferris wheel and installed it on Coney Island. In 1895 he was faced with competition in the immediate vicinity from the Sea Lion Park, the first amusement park to charge admission. Tilyou upgraded his park with rides such as a water slide, a miniature steam-powered railroad, and simulated horse racing, as well as a variety of precursors of the modern-day roller coaster. The speciality of Steeplechase, which was later overtaken by ever more spectacular machineries of illusion, was the interactive participation of the visitor. Even the logo on the entrance ticket gave a hint of the mood in the park: a devious and diabolically grinning face with 44 teeth, which announced the high-spirited, unchecked exuberance that awaited the visitor in the park. The Streets of Cairo opened in 1897. Minaret-flanked buildings, narrow lanes, camel rides and dancers in glittering costumes evoked the atmosphere of a miniature Egypt.

It was in the snack bars on Coney Island that the Frankfurter metamorphosed ...

... into the hot dog and ground beef into the hamburger.

R. G. BLOMEYER / B. TIETZE

Steeplechase was soon outstripped by the sensations of Luna Park and of Dreamland. Luna Park designed by **Frederick Thompson** – named after Luna Dundy, the founder's sister – was a tremendous financial hit upon opening. The program included parades with exotic animals and human beings, a Venice in New York, Cycloramas such as Darkness and Dusk and the first theme rides such as *A Trip to the Moon* or *20,000 Leagues under the Sea* after the Jules Verne novel. Dreamland was developed at the same time as Luna Park: its name reflected the common denominator in all three parks. They were fairytale sets, especially with the illuminations at night: an intoxicating array of colour, light and unfamiliar animated effects. ◉ In *New York – Stories and Reports from a Metropolis* **Djuna Barnes** writes on Coney Island: "Slides polished to a high shine beckoned to us and we donned carnival costumes and dared to ride down and down and further down, with a feeling in the pit of our stomach as if the world had suddenly foundered on a rock. A sudden immersion in a bowl, where we were tossed around with wild abandon, finally ended on rotating disks that deprived our lives of all dignity [taking us] back to our great-great-uncles ... On a rotating platform I spied Bob, who was riding around like a walnut on a wedding cake, all the while grinning idiotically. It doesn't matter, after all that's what we're here for and now we're going to go down and have a drink." ◉ Coney Island drew huge crowds, tens of thousands at first, then hundreds of thousands and finally, in the 1920s, one million visitors on a single weekend.

Luna Park As the nineteenth century drew to a close, the name Luna Park – like Tivoli before it – became synonymous with amusement parks throughout the world. Luna Parks based on the model of Coney Island were created in many European cities. In contrast to conventional parks, designed for rest and leisure, the amusement park was not intended to offer peace and relaxation, but thrills, fast consumption and bustling activity. Technical progress, experimentation with new lifestyles and utopian as well as exotic settings fascinated a broad public. The attractions and themes of Luna Park were developed in imitation of the world exhibitions. Aside from the panoramas of the nineteenth century, Luna Park was seen as a travel substitute for the people. Like contemporary amusement parks, Luna Park used every conceivable trick, special effects and stage techniques, to entertain the visitors with adventures and sensations. The real boom in the amusement business came after the First World War, which marked the beginning of a true entertainment culture. Luna Park, Berlin, was opened in 1910 on the Halensee and expanded and embellished in 1920. Among the special attractions were Europe's first wave pool and the illuminations, which transformed night into day. The symbiosis of "Sunday architecture"

and attractions translated into big business and the Berlin-based company continued to thrive until the rise of the Third Reich forced it into bankruptcy. The National Socialists converted Luna Park into a people's park, which was closed in 1933. ◉ Similar grounds, also called Luna Park, were created during the same period in Cologne, Hamburg and Paris. However, they proved to be unsustainable. The Luna Park in Cologne was in operation from 1909 to 1927, and the Luna Park in Hamburg, opened in 1913, lasted only for a few years after the First World War. Some of the parks fell into disrepute because of gambling, prostitution and alcoholism. A new aspect was the combination of Luna Park settings and the business interests of smaller and larger enterprises. The amusement park served as a testing ground for the latest technologies. Companies like AEG, Siemens and Schaub-Lorenz provided financial backing for individual park projects. ◉ In contrast to today's leisure parks, the Tivolis and Luna Parks were concentrated in and on the edge of large cities. As a result of expanded traffic and transportation systems, leisure parks have been almost exclusively developed in the surroundings of cities or in rural settings since the 1960s. Today, new leisure areas are created on the periphery, where building lots are inexpensive.

Piers The development of seaside resorts on Britain's coast in the nineteenth century gave rise to a new and original form of leisure architecture. The role of the piers as landing stages for boats and ships became increasingly less important in comparison to their function as promenades. Without getting their feet wet, spa patrons strolled back and forth on the solidly anchored piers high above the water and enjoyed the view of the sea and boats dancing on the waves. Pavilions on the promenade offered food, refreshments and shopping, even theatre visits. In 1823, the Chain Pier in Brighton was deliberately designed as the first amusement pier in England. It was demolished in 1896 and replaced with the extravagant orientalized Palace Pier. 👁 Erected from 1891–1899, the Palace Pier in Brighton is one of the most beautifully appointed piers in Great Britain. Twenty-eight cast-iron columns rise from the sea bottom at intervals of 19 m. The pier projects 521 m into the sea, with a minimum width of 15 m. The deck is 16 m above the sea floor, 12 m above the water surface during low tide, and 6 m above water during high tide. A weather screen – the dominant and unifying element of the structure – provides wind protection and, thanks to its transparency, a view of the sea through numerous windows and openings.

POPCORN

109+110+111

WORLD'S FAIRS

The world's fair has a 150-year history. Since the first great exhibition of 1851 in London's Crystal Palace, which was erected especially for the occasion, twenty-three world's fairs have been held around the world. These events illustrate the social changes of an era, especially in the fields of architecture, technology and design. To begin with, the world's fairs served as showcases of economic performance for the participating countries. With increasing economic growth over the course of the nineteenth century and the easing of trade through amended import laws, the fairs took on greater international significance. The function of promoting understanding between nations became increasingly important. To this day, world's fairs are based on the idea that world trade is intrinsically linked to world peace. 👁 Time and time again, the organizers were faced with the challenge of dazzling the world with the very latest thing in each field. The innovative products were to be showcased in a fitting setting: exhibition architecture became an experimental stage for sensational designs. 👁 The exhibition buildings of the first world's fair were above all extraordinary feats of engineering. New building materials such as glass and iron were tested, while larger spans made rapid and inexpensive construction possible. The Crystal Palace, erected for the occasion of the Great Exhibition of the Works of Industry of all Nations in London, 1851, was a symbol of a new era. The purpose of the Crystal Palace as an exhibition hall for "a comparative overview of the industrial products of all educated nations of the earth," (EXPO 2000 *World Exhibition* brochure, Norbert Bargman, Hubertus von Bothmer), was as new as its construction was innovative. 👁 **Gustave Eiffel**'s tower, a symbol of progress in technology, was the highlight of the Exposition Universelle in Paris in 1889. This architectural attraction, a spectacular feat of engineering, made the exhibition an unforgettable experience. 👁 The proto-

112 + 113 + 114

type of an exhibition pavilion similar to the Crystal Palace, a basilica with several aisles, was gradually replaced by hyper-individualistic architecture. Unique structures such as the Eiffel Tower in Paris contrasted with the plaster facades of conventional, classicistic buildings. The latter have long since disappeared, while the Eiffel Tower of 1889 or the Atomium in Brussels (1958) survive to this day and have become symbols of their cities. ◉ The Columbian World's Fair of 1893 in Chicago had a fairytale quality that seemed to fore shadow modern amusement parks: a city rendered in dazzling white, with imitation marble porticoes overlooking the large pond, as well as Venetian gondolas and magnificent illumination at night, to the delight of all visitors. To all this was added the Ferris wheel, named after its inventor **George W. Ferris.** ◉ By the end of the nineteenth century, the universal exhibitions were accompanied by special fairs. Fairgrounds and picturesque historic villages, which had been fashionable since the last quarter of the nineteenth century, were not only standard features of these fairs but their key attractions. This change in the exhibition went hand in hand with a new strategy. The world's fair was to become a public place for amusement, accessible for the price of an entrance fee. This functional shift marked the beginning of a new era. Amusement became an important business factor. The organizers quickly realized that world's fairs should be combined with entertainment. ◉ The world's fair in Antwerp in 1930 even had space for a Luna Park and a historic Belgian village. The plan for the New York World's Fair in 1969 showed parallels with the concepts for other leisure parks being developed around the same time. At EXPO 1967 in Montréal, the German Pavilion by Frei Otto and Rudolf Gutsbrod accommodated hundreds of people thanks to its expansive roof covering. The free formal language was cheerful, open and bright, and was employed as a symbol of the democratic spirit some years later for the design of the Olympic Stadium in Munich.

FORD
GENERAL MOTORS
DU PONT
GREECE
VATICAN
TEXAS
WESTINGHOUSE
PEPSI-COLA
HALL OF EDUCATION
CENTRAL
PARKWAY
EXPRESSWAY
LOUISIANA
MEXICO
DENMARK
UNITED STATES SPACE PARK

Around the mid-twentieth century, this led to the creation of cosmopolitan windows onto art, history, natural sciences and technology, all presented in an entertaining manner and shaping the expectations of entire generations. The evolution of world's fairs is remarkably similar to the development of leisure parks. In both cases, architects are charged with designing architecture that does not resist serving the popular taste, either in form or in content. They also wield considerable influence on the social functions of public space. EXPO 2000 in Hanover was a blend of multiplex cinema and Documenta, fairground and adult education centre. One of the goals of EXPO 2000 was to thematicize the motto "Man, Nature, Technology." From the outset, the intent was also to develop world exhibition grounds with a view to sustainability.

HISTORY 164:165

World's fairs become a public place for amusement for the price of an entrance fee. Amusement became an important business factor.

Fair organizers promise the discovery of a new world. Adventure pavilions such as Cyclebowl, PLANET M and Scape attempt to merge real and virtual worlds. The exhibition makers offer multi-sensory experiences. Ambience, light, colours and sounds reflect the lifestyle of the @ generation. ◉ In PLANET M, for example, designed by **Triad Architekten Karl Karau** in collaboration with **Axel Büther** and **Becker, Gewers, Kühn & Kühn Architekten**, visitors can step onto another planet without leaving Earth. The take-off alone is an adventure, as the Space Lift transports the visitors without gravity to the planet floating 9 m above ground level. The pavilion of the media conglomerate Bertelsmann thematicizes the history, variety and importance of media

in multi-vision shows, images and projections. • A visit to the theme parks at EXPO 2000 was intended not only to provide new insights, but above all to be fun as a multimedia adventure trip into the future. In addition to this, a 100,000 m² theme park, designed as an adventure landscape by Kamel Louafi, along with numerous music, dance and art events, fireworks and Disco Fun, as well as an open-air cinema, offered a cultural program with an emphasis on entertainment. • Many of the temporary structures on the pavilion grounds have a future. Some will be fully recycled, others can be reassembled in other cities or even other countries, thereby bearing out the claim of sustainability.

ANIMATION
The Illusion of I

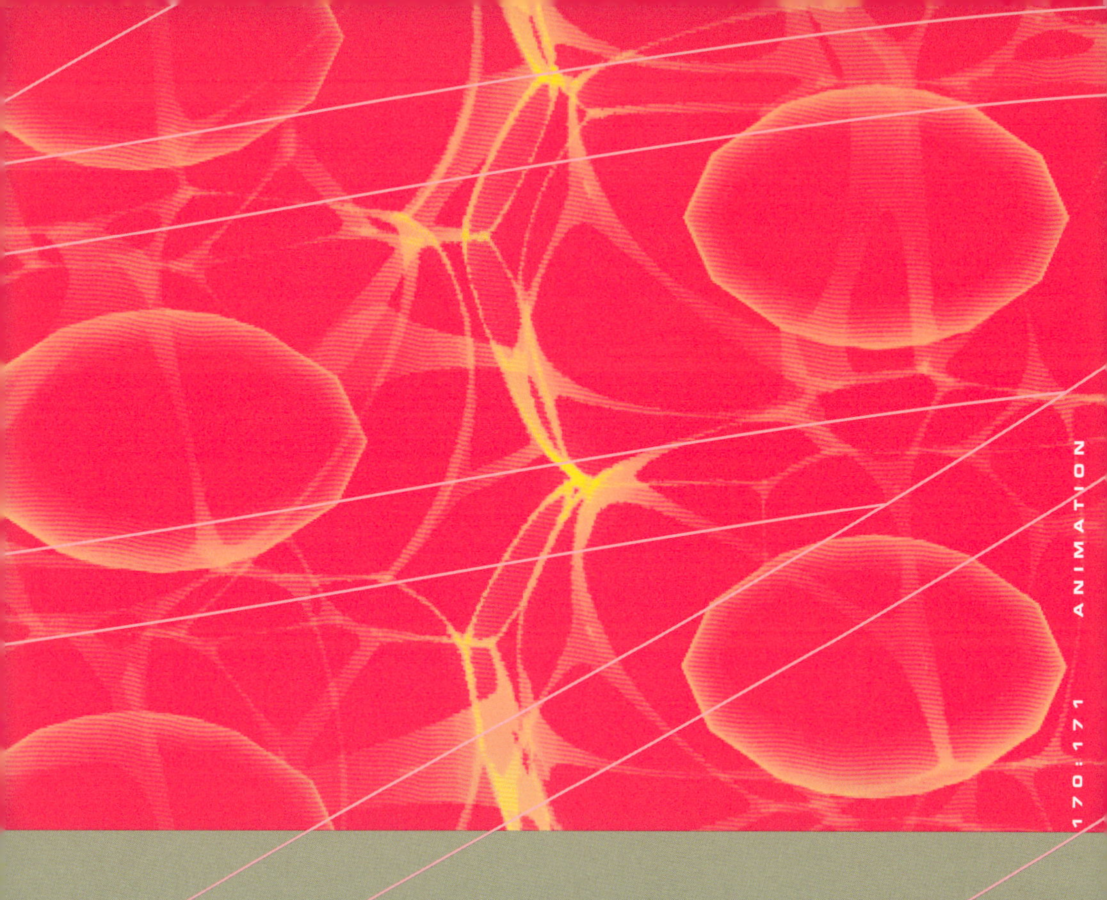

05

.ife

ANIMATION

When we explore the theme of animation, our first realization is that there is no final definition at this point and, consequently, that there is unlikely to be one in the future. The natural recourse is to look at a dictionary. The number of interpretations and derivations for the word indicate that the definition of this term is still in progress and can differ widely depending on the context.

Animation, n.

1) *general:* the process of making inanimate objects appear to move.

The representation of animate and multi-dimensional images is increasingly computer generated (computer animation).

2) *film:* in animated films, the act of bringing inanimate objects to life, e.g. drawings, puppets; today, most animated images in film and video are created with the help of digital animation techniques; these are complemented by other methods in which animated scenes are combined with real film sequences.

3) *tourism:* the act of providing activities and entertainment for tourists at tourist destinations.

Animate, v.

1) *general:* enliven, make lively, encourage, create a mood.

2) *film:* the act of filming the individual sequences of movement in animated cartoons.

Anima (*Latin* breath of air, breath). 1. soul (*philos.*)

Pinocchio can be brought to life through special effects; even a wooden doll can be animated – if only as an illusion. The word "animation" means just that.

172:173 ANIMATION

120+121

ANIMISM IN ARCHITECTURE

A brief excursion into the past reveals that the term animation also has a historical background. The literal rendering of animated architecture is architecture with a soul, that is, endowing an inanimate building with life. The spiritual-ethnological term animism suggests that both animate and inanimate natural phenomena possess a personal soul. According to this view, devices and objects for daily use are also inhabited by individual spirits or souls. The idea that buildings are autonomous individuals is common among some primitive peoples. "The Dasun in Borneo," writes **Edward O. Wilson** in *Consilience* (Berlin, 1998), "humanize each house as a body with arms, head, belly, legs and other body parts. They believe that this body can only 'stand' properly if it faces in a specific direction. Houses built into a slope, for example, are thought of as upside down. In other contexts, the house is categorized as thin or fat, as young or old or even as exhausted. The interiors are designed with careful consideration for meaning. Every room and each piece of furnishing is linked to seasonal rituals, superstitions and social

mores." ◉ The longhouse of the Dasun in the Dyak in Borneo symbolizes the original social structure of the tribes: each extended family lives independently under a common roof in a separate structure equipped with all domestic facilities. Life is regulated by a strict code of behaviour. Infringements of this code threaten the spiritual unity of the society. A longhouse that has been ritually damaged becomes "hot" or "feverish" and can only "heal" through rituals of atonement or the payment of a fine. ◉ The external structure of a longhouse has symbolic and cosmological meaning. Thus, certain ritual ceremonies include a procession of warriors and women along the gallery. The procession represents the act of traversing the universe and re-enacts the journey of the gods to join in the celebrations of humans. ◉ The construction of a longhouse is always dependent on specific omens: if there is a bad omen, a longhouse must be abandoned for a time or even permanently. The entire housing complex is raised on 3-to 6-metre-high posts and accessed via a notched tree trunk.

122+123+124

DISNEY'S PRINCIPLES OF ANIMATION

Disney established twelve principles of animation:

1 – Squash and Stretch

The most important invention is undoubtedly that of squashing and stretching: the overstretching and exaggeration of each character in expression and proportion. For example, not only the mouth but the entire body must be involved in giving a figure expression. Disney uses the example of a squashed sack as a vivid illustration of how expression can be created by very simple means, even without details such as eye or lip movements. The famous example of the half-filled sack of flour demonstrates the distribution of volume within a graphic contour and helps us identify the change in mood, which even the tiniest variation in the outline is capable of expressing: squashed means sad and stretched means happy. Squash and stretch.

2 – Anticipation

Anticipation is an important principle for establishing contact with the viewer. Planned sequences of actions are meant to guide the public from one activity to another. Even in real life, few movements occur without prior notice of some kind. Viewers must be prepared for the next movement and anticipate it before it actually happens. The movements in early animated films are too abrupt and unexpected.

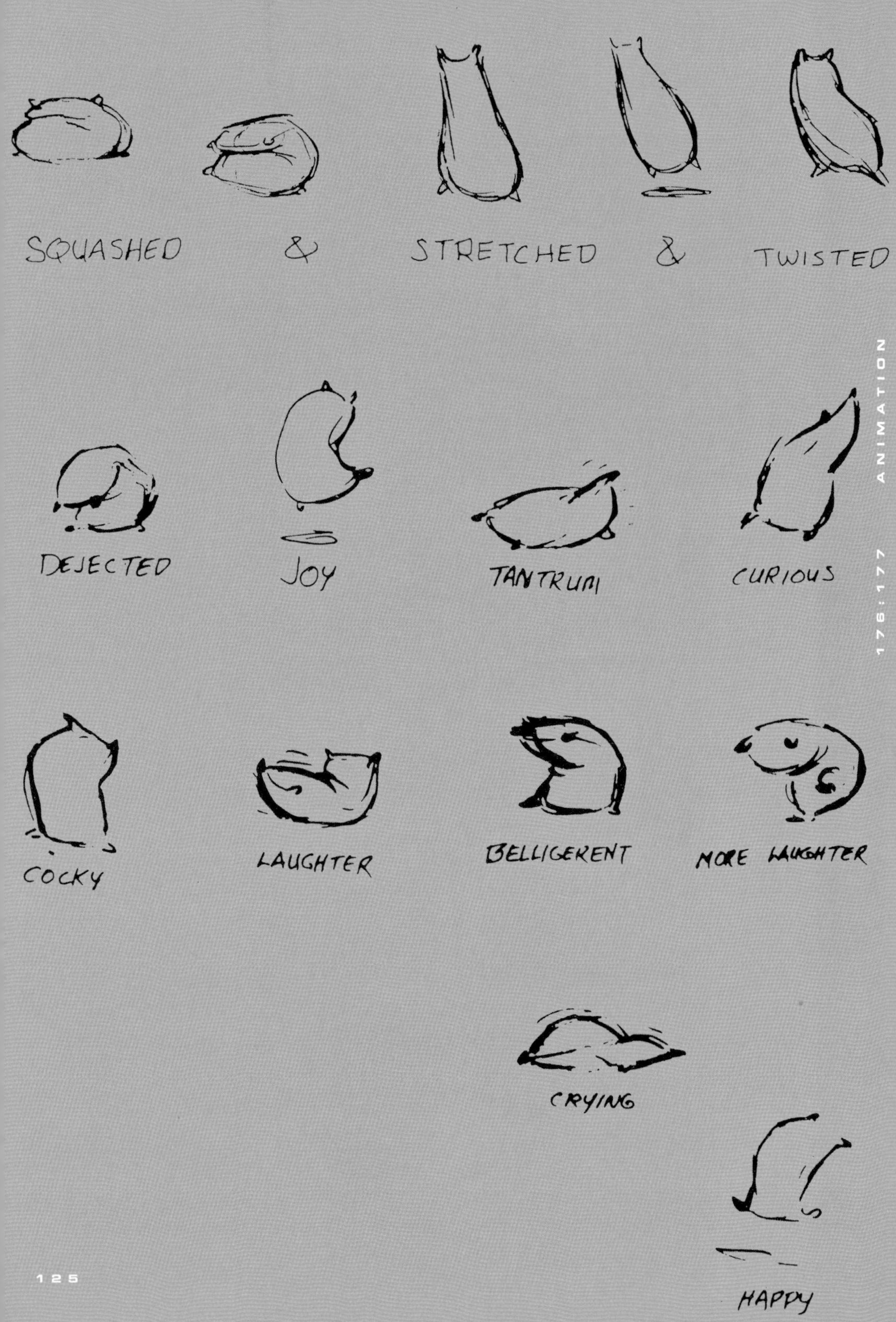
SQUASHED & STRETCHED & TWISTED
DEJECTED
JOY
TANTRUM
CURIOUS
COCKY
LAUGHTER
BELLIGERENT
MORE LAUGHTER
CRYING
HAPPY

The public is therefore often unprepared for what comes next and misses the gag. This was one of the first aspects that Disney began to correct early on.

3 – Staging

Staging is a key principle because it affects so many areas and has a long-standing tradition in the world of the theatre. Staging is the presentation of any idea in a manner that is so convincing as to render the idea completely and unmistakably comprehensible. If an eerie mood is desired, then the scene is crowded with symbols that represent a creepy situation: an old house, howling wind, rustling leaves or paper in a courtyard, clouds obscuring the moon, a threatening sky, perhaps the sound of bare branches tapping against a window pane or a flittering shadow – all these images clearly communicate one and the same thing: an eerie atmosphere.

4 – Straight-ahead Action and Pose to Pose

There are two main approaches to animation. The first is known as "straight-ahead action," because the animator creates the scene directly from his first drawing. In minute steps, he creates one drawing after another, gathering new ideas until he reaches the end of a scene. The second approach is called "pose to pose." In this instance, the animator plans the action in advance and decides which drawings are required to animate the entire sequence. He then creates separate drawings, establishing a context between each drawing, as well as scale and action sequences.

JOY

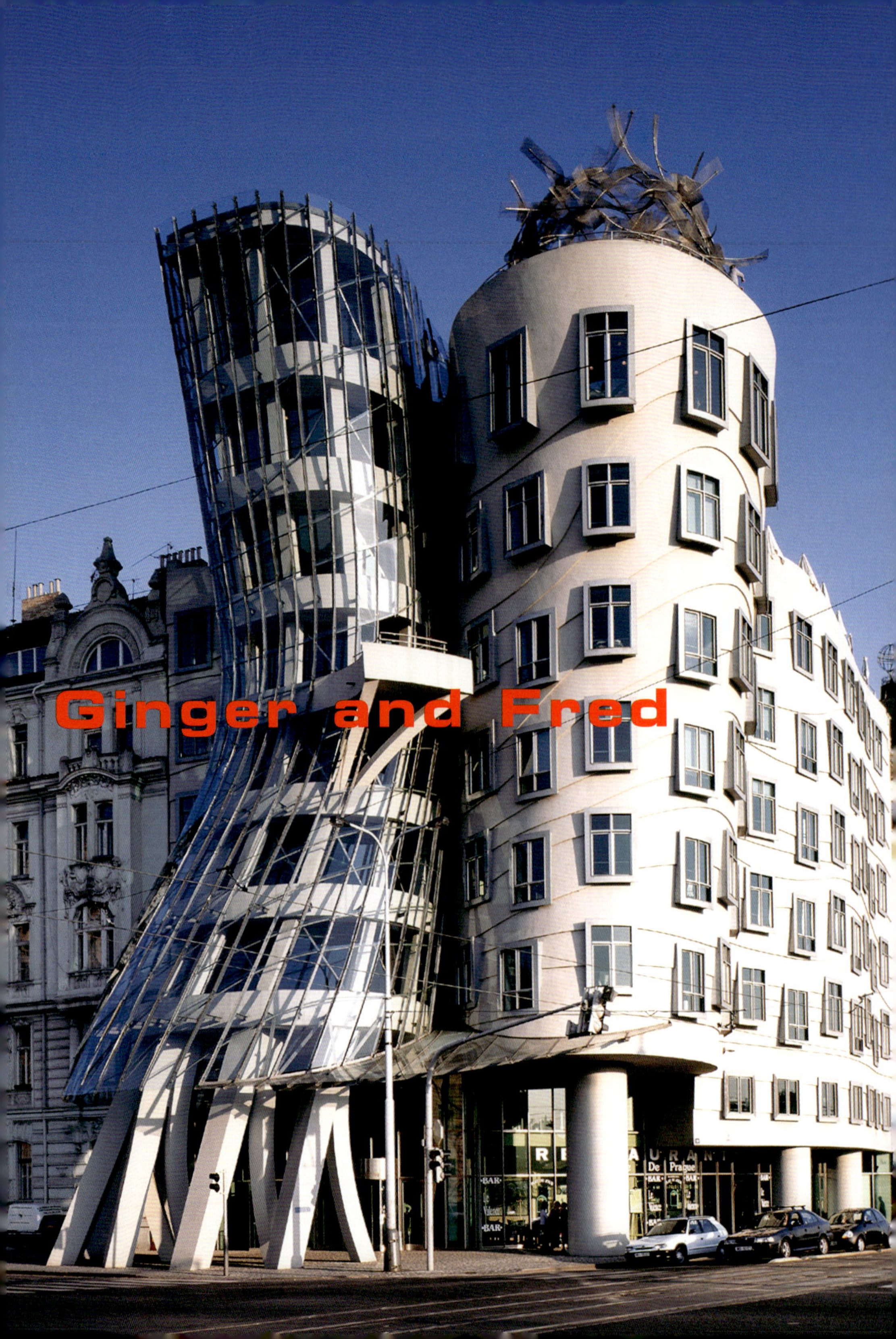

Ginger and Fred

Mickey's Toontown in Disneyland, Anaheim, seems to be in motion. Everything is topsy-turvy in the hometown of the cartoon characters: the buildings bristle, chirp and squeak, overflow, and shake themselves. But Mickey's loony city isn't the only one where everything dances to a tune. The office building for the "National-Niederlanden" in Prague by **Frank O. Gehry** is another example. The two glass-and-stone towers seem to sway back and forth like a dancing couple. The building – nicknamed **Fred and Ginger** by the locals – exemplifies the strong pictorial effect of Gehry's architecture. 👁 The Team Disney Building in Orlando, Florida, USA, designed by Arata Isozaki, is a wild mix of shapes, patterns, and colours. **Robert Stern**'s preview centre for Euro-disney, Paris and **Frank O. Gehry**'s festival Disney are further examples of architectures reminiscent of stage design. The witch as an embodiment of evil reveals her character at the first glance: long, bony fingers, large, bulging eyes, humpback and ugly chin – this is treachery personified. The design of Dumbo, the baby elephant from the film of the same name, exaggerates the emotive child pattern. Oversized ears, which enable him to fly, grace a head that is too large for its body; the trusting eyes and humble posture complete the image, which is appealing enough to melt the viewer's heart.

Finally, he hands the scene to his assistant who will draw the "in-betweens."

5 – Follow-through and Overlapping Action

The principal action can be followed by one or several secondary actions, either consecutively or simultaneously.

6 – Slow In and Slow Out

Most movements are more effectively rendered when the so-called softening approach is used. Each movement is slowed down at the beginning and at the end. Disney works on the mechanics of movement, stating that movement lies at the very heart of his work.

7 – Arcs

Few living organisms are capable of executing mechanical movements. Most movements describe a kind of arc. A movement is all the more beautiful and clear when it follows the line of an arc. Therefore, the animator must mark the phase position with a curved line.

8 – Secondary Action

The idea of a scene can often be strengthened through secondary actions performed by a character. A sad figure wipes away a tear as it turns. Someone caught by surprise or astonished, shakes his head as he rises. When these incidental details are employed to serve the principal action, they are called secondary action, which is always subordinate to the principal action.

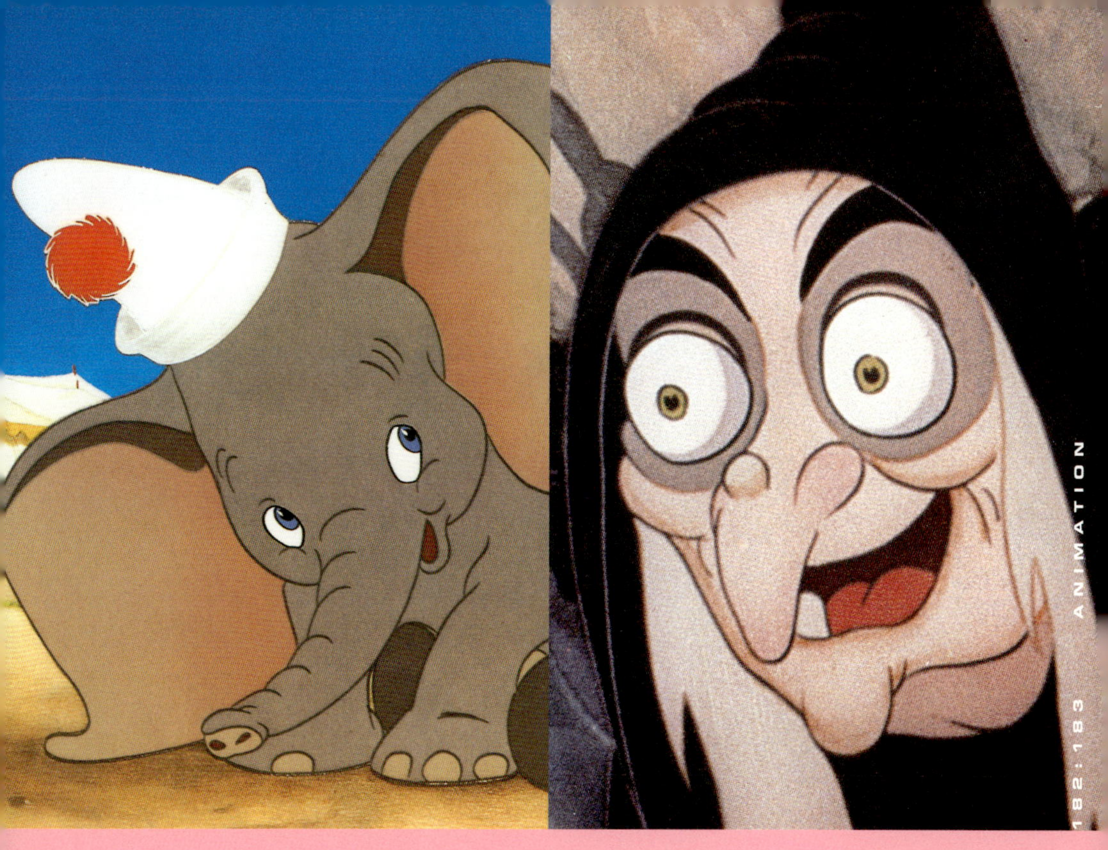

The villain must be just as appealing as the hero. WALT DISNEY

129+130+131

9 – Timing

In animation, timing means how the passage of time is managed. One second may contain some 24 frames. The secret of good animation lies in what can be drawn within this length of time.

10 – Exaggeration

Finally, exaggeration is an especially effective means of enhancing the impact. Disney wants to make the dead come alive. To this end, he instructs his animators: "Whenever a character is sad, make him even sadder, when he's happy, make him happier, if he's wild, make him wilder ... Take it to such extremes that it'll drive me crazy."

11 – Solid Drawing

The basis for animation is a sound knowledge of three-dimensional drawing: "You should be quite a skilful draughtsman before beginning with animation." (Gwin Patwick, animator)

So-called twins, that is, drawings that are too similar, should be avoided. To create a dynamic image, animators experiment with countless variations on possible movements.

12 – Appeal

Appeal is an important factor from the very outset. The term encompasses everything from beautiful design to charm, attractive form, movement, simplicity, and expression. The villain must be just as appealing in his own way as the hero. On stage, the actors must have charisma; in animation the characters must have appeal.

Philippe Starck's Super Dry Hall in Tokyo, Japan, possesses a Disneyesque popular appeal. The golden object is an eye-catching symbol of the function of the black granite building: it crowns the tapering form of the building like a head of beer in a glass. 👁 Perhaps the Dutch architectural firm MVRDV was familiar with Disney's principles of animation when they staged an imaginative gag for EXPO 2000 in Hanover. The Big Mac by MVRDV stacks natural elements one on top of another like so many hamburger ingredients. The roof is transformed into an egg yolk and is integrated in an entertaining fashion.

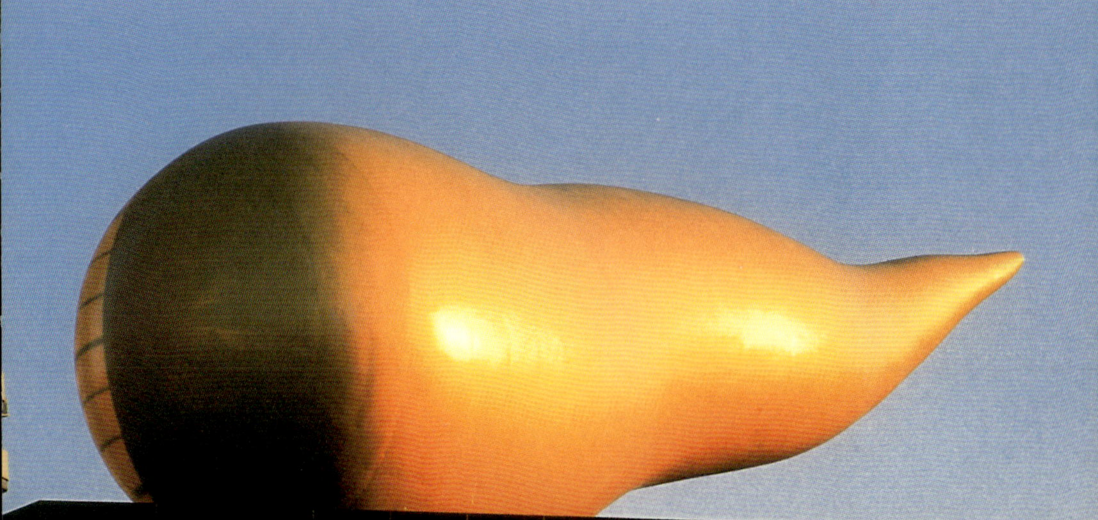

MOVIE JARGON

In addition to the principles, there are other characteristic components of cartoon animation expressed in a specialized movie jargon.

Audience *The basic goal of all animation is to reach the audience. The following rules apply: "Always look at a project through the eyes of the audience." "The public has paid good money and expects to be entertained. They're not there to help you do your job." "Don't expect any energy to flow from the audience to you ... The energy should come from the actor, you have to reach out [to the audience] and touch them."*

Emotion *Emotion, involving the public by engaging their feelings, is the very soul of entertainment. To begin with, the cartoon medium was no more than a novelty. It only began to really connect with the public when Disney's crew had more to offer than mere tricks by creating personalities. Disney's movies are successful above all because of the characters and emotions they portray. From the very start, the emotive quality of Disney characters creates the illusion that they are alive, inviting the loyalty of the laughing audience. Disney comments: "We seem to know when to 'tap the heart.' Others have hit the intellect. We can hit them in an emotional way."*

The dwarfs from Snow White are examples of how Disney's artists evoke emotion in the viewer. Walt Disney gives each figure its own personality, a distinct character: Happy, Bashful, Sleepy, Clumsy,

and so on, allowing each audience member to identify with one of the figures. Every detail in the body outline and facial features is important.

Storyboard *In the early days of animation, Walt Disney developed the idea of the storyboard, a visual concept of the story by means of a sequence of sketches. A storyboard is a tool for developing the story, the characters and their relationships; it illustrates how the story unfolds and it facilitates work on the sequences. The visual communication of the content takes precedence over the verbal unfolding of the plot.*

Story Sketchman / Stylist *A story sketchman is usually an artist with a special sense of how illustration, design, and appearance work in unison to create a whole and a unique talent for combining sequences. A stylist, on the other hand, is only called upon to create individual images that are outstanding in quality and filled with dynamic energy. This means that he must be able, first and foremost, to infuse the animation with a unique appeal.*

Gagman *Gagmen create gags and moments of surprise to move the story forward in an entertaining fashion.*

Animator *The animator has the most difficult job. Story sketchman, stylist, painter, and gagman are all creative artists, who are usually focussed on finding the solution to a specific problem. But animation is magic. It is a matter of creating appeal. The main question is: Is it alive? You can copy techniques, reproduce mechanics, or trace drawings. But it is*

the animator who adds the real spark. His taste, judgement, and ideas are the components that make his work unique, for animation is a highly individual matter. Years of experience in the area of film animation have taught Disney artists how to handle movement. Thus the impression of reality can often be more convincingly rendered by avoiding large movements. For example, a character's surprise is better expressed by raising an eyebrow than by throwing up his hands. An animated cartoon is an act of communication. It consists of ideas, shown as clearly and simply as possible, to allow the audience to understand them. The animation is the most controlled aspect, since the imaginative power of the entire film depends to a large degree upon its quality.

Make it believable!

The task of animation is: make it believable! Regardless of whether the scene is suspenseful, sad, dramatic or peaceful, what matters is the public's identification with it. Disney achieves this goal by including familiar elements: for example, the obvious character of a figure is emphasized by a matching assemblage of background noises: loud and heavy breathing, echoes, the familiar sound of footsteps – and the audience is captivated. This process of identification springs from the emotions of the audience, not of the actor. This is the main basis on which animation operates. It takes imagination to reach into the minds and the hearts of the audience.

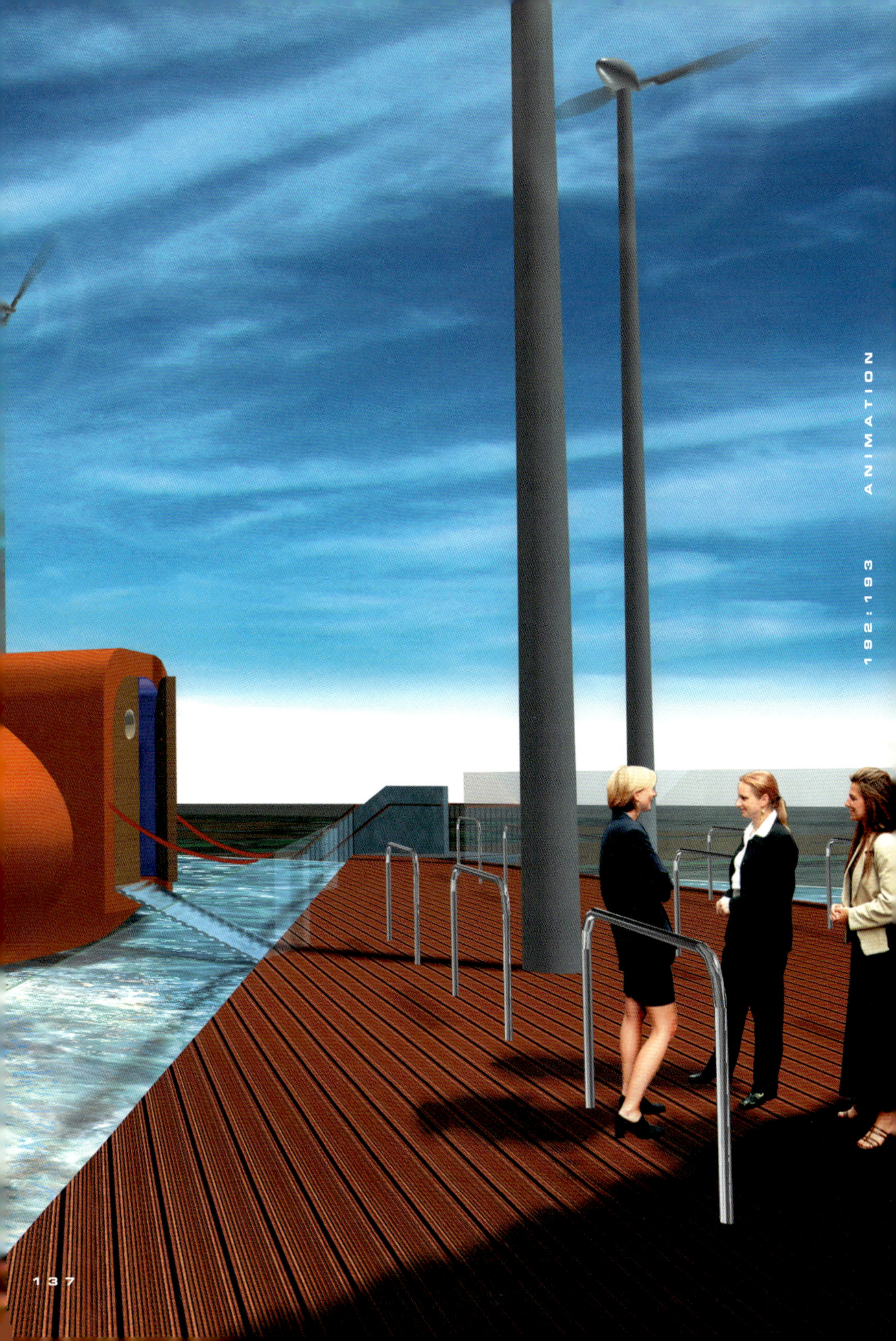

ANIMATED ARCHITECTURE

Classic animation refers to animated cartoons; computer animation, too, is based on the rules of cartoon animation pioneered by Walt Disney. His treatise *Animation, the Illusion of Life* describes the sequences and tools employed to animate the inanimate, the combined use of which is called animation. Disney's technique and methods were outlined for the first time in that document. 👁 Disney's ideas on animation have thus far received little attention outside the domain of animated film, although they offer information pertinent for other areas. His principles of animation can also be applied to architecture, where they are sometimes employed deliberately and sometimes unconsciously. Like an animator, the architect animates inanimate objects, especially in the area of entertainment. The production schedule of the Walt Disney imagineers frequently includes projects that are realized in collaboration with architects. With Euro-Disney, for example, the corporation sought to develop a new, worldwide image that was to be increasingly expressed in the architecture. Michael Eisner, who spearheaded this development, commissioned star architects from the 1980s and 1990s to design so-called "entertainment architecture," clearly identified as such for the first time and in accordance with Disney's motto of "Building a Dream." The precepts of film animation are predominantly translated into architecture by proponents of postmodernism. As early as 1991, **Paul Goldberger** wrote in the *New York Times*: "Disney deserves credit for inspiring a rapprochement between architecture and entertainment and for launching a potent overlapping of these aspects." 👁 Animation breathes life into things – animated architecture activates buildings, thus increasing their popular effect. Buildings of this kind are intended, for example, to create a sense of disorientation by turning standard dimensions upside down and by using unusual colours and ornamentation. Be it

Roman columns, dancing fish, flying swans or dwarfs transformed into giants, these designs dip into the annals of historic architecture, playfully remixing art historical contexts. This type of fantasy architecture aims to disrupt everyday perception and transport the observer into a different time and another world. But its principal goal is to provide fun. ◉ Arquitectonia designs using gigantic cowboy boots, a banjo, and musical notes are the unmistakable symbols that decorate the country music sector of the motel complex All-Star Resorts. This complex with its different theme areas is conceived as a three-dimensional comic book: the idea is that this will be to architecture what Pop Art is to art. In 1992, Robert Stern designed a preview centre for Eurodisney. Mickey Mouse as the sorcerer's apprentice in the animated film *Fantasia* inspired the architect's design of the expressive facade for the preview building. Mickey's sorcerer's hat crowns the tempietto above the entrance and the unmistakable silhouettes of his group of friends grace the facade and the entrance structure. The preview centre at Eurodisney in Paris transports visitors into the film *Fantasia*.

DECORATED SHED

In 1972, Robert Venturi and Denise Scott Brown analyzed a specific new building type by taking Las Vegas as an example. The work is a polemical rejection of the doctrines of classic modernism. The billboards and neon signs of a message town, consisting entirely of signs and symbols, are a welcome source of inspiration to Venturi, whose ambition is to call for a renewal of symbolism in architecture. He looks upon the elements of "low" culture, for example, the Las Vegas strip, as a challenge for architects and pushes the envelope even further: the city becomes a learning object for the significance of symbolic and communicative architecture. According to their study, the buildings are divided into, on the one hand, a front with oversized symbols and, on the other hand, the structure itself as a modest necessity. The billboards, neon signs and colourful facades are more important to Venturi than the actual structures. Venturi refers to this type as the decorated shed. Form and content are separate and independent. At times the building itself is a sign, for example, the store selling ducks, which is constructed in the shape of a duck. ◉ At first, Venturi's critical stance inspired a lively debate, but soon many American architects began to share his antipathy toward rigid, rationalistic principles. By the 1980s at the latest, his motto "The less form follows function, the better," began to take hold around the world. Postmodernism gave expression to Venturi's call for a renewal of architecture. Symbols, historical quotes and fictitious worlds have been integrated into architecture since the 1980s. ◉ **James Stirling**'s museum building in Stuttgart demonstrates how an abundance of form and gestures can create synthesis between contradictory styles and vocabularies. The legendary Piazza d'Italia in New Orleans by **Charles Moore** also uses a stylistic vocabulary rich in quotations. Postmodernism, like Disney, creates an invented world where the most divergent forms of representation and contents can be freely chosen. In this example, the choice is to cite classic Italian motifs.

FONS SANCTI JOSEPHI

AVANT-GARDE – BUBBLES AND CLOUDS

In addition to postmodernism, devoted to the "decorated shed" and the celebration of ornamentation and staging, other positions began to emerge at the same time. Artist-architects like Haus-Rucker-Co and Coop Himmelb(l)au were ahead of their time. Archigram and their heyday in the 1960s have regained currency in the debate. Archi-Week, Truth Commandos, Zoneworks, Kamakazi, Space Cowboys, Superstudio, Onyx, Crash City, The Grocery Store, Mind House, Instengible, and Art Farm joined the avant-garde movement. In the decade of the Beatles, the landing on the moon, of cybernetics and mega-cities, new forms and structures were being created, which turned the established values upside down. Tapping into the trends of the time, technology and art, political protest, comics and science fiction or the fantasy worlds of amusement parks, the result is a cheerful flower-power architecture. Archigram, in particular, experimented with new forms and explored new models for living. To this end, the group imagined autonomous environments constructed from tubes, capsules and scaffolds, pop-up envelopes and disposable buildings. A series of projects followed, for example, the Seaside Bubble, Plug-in City, Walking City, and Blow-out Village, which look like computers and robots, comparable to the film sets for *2001: A Space Odyssey* or *Star Wars*. Writing on Archigram, Herbert Lachmayer

comments: "Archigram tuned into the broad innovative impulses of the 1960s – advanced technology and space travel, science fiction and comics, pop culture, (...) and fused them into an architectural vision that swept aside the vocabulary of Classic Modernism." Instead of style, the conceptual work of Archigram deals with social themes, with the complexity of work, consumption, pleasure and realizing happiness. Another avant-garde element of Archigram is the prioritization of individualism, along with the individual's pursuit of liberty and personal right to happiness. Coop Himmelb(l)au from Vienna is another group that cannot be tied to a single style. Since 1968, this group of architects has made feelings run high with provocative exhibitions, projects, happenings, appeals and buildings. **Wolf Prix** described the group with the following words: "Coop Himmelb(l)au is not a colour but an idea – the idea of having architecture with fantasy, as buoyant and variable as clouds." Slightly less than a decade later, Wolf Prix stated: "We are tired of seeing Palladio and other historical masks. Because we don't want architecture to exclude everything that is disquieting. We want architecture to have more. Architecture that bleeds, that exhausts, that whirls and even breaks." Like Archigram, this group attempts to dematerialize form and visualize individual dreams. "Our architecture is based on a psychological rather than a physical plan."

AMAZING ARCHIGRAM 4
ZOOM
ISSUE

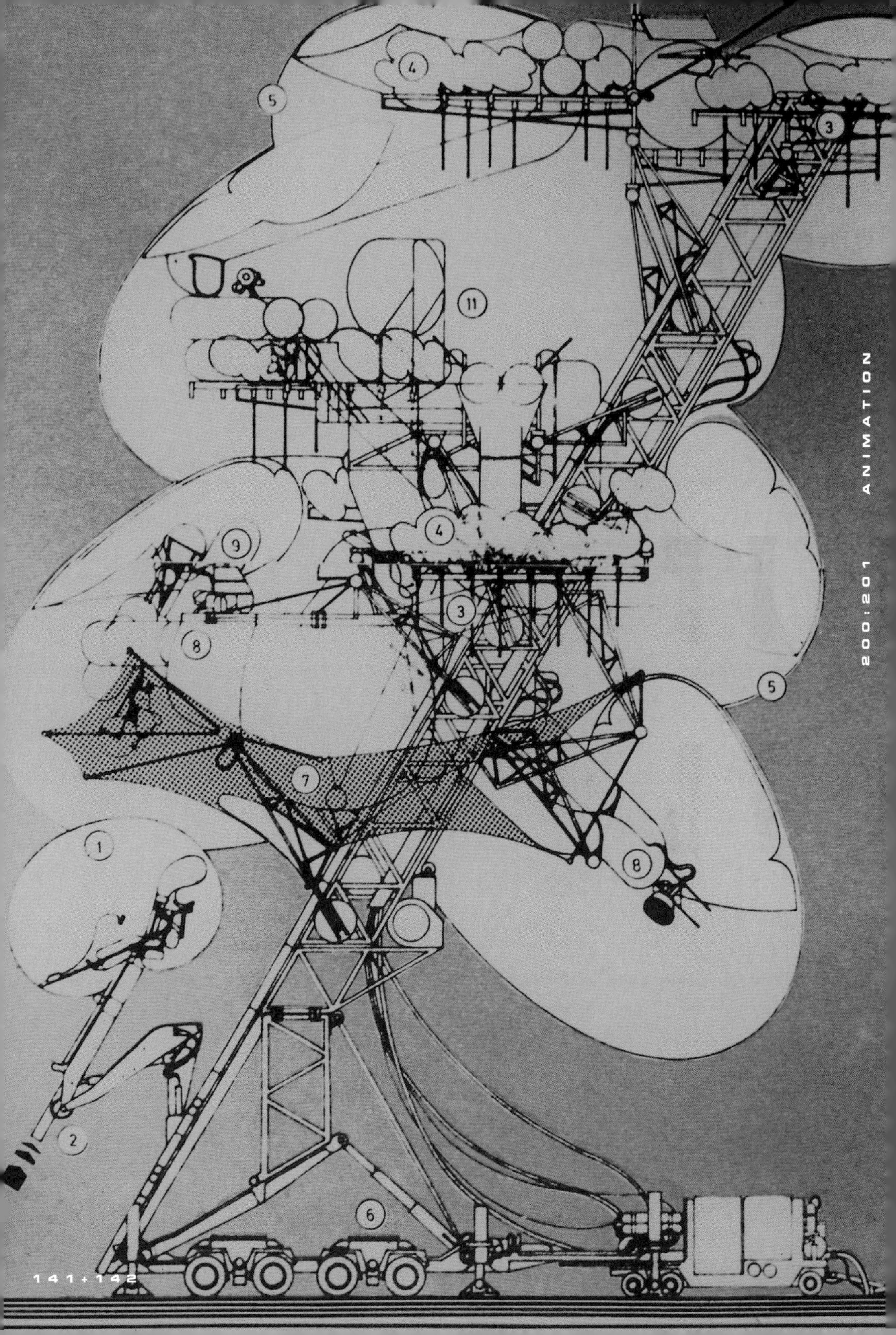
4
5
3
11
4
9
3
8
5
7
1
8
2
6

BIONICS – BIOLOGY AND BUILDING

A new science, bionics, tries to establish itself with the goal of learning from living nature.

FREI OTTO

According to the dictionary definition, bionics is the science of applying biological principles to the study and design of engineering systems, especially electronic systems. Bionics also describes a movement in architecture that takes natures as its model. Architecture that is animated in this manner generates natural structures. It is the result of an attempt to interpret nature from the perspective of studying its structural principles. Scientific discoveries are the basis for form-finding methods when designing tents, inflatables, tensile structures, shells, arches, cupolas or vaults. 👁 Buckminster Fuller and Frei Otto, the pioneers and spiritual fathers of this idea, translate the complicated and complex laws of nature into structure and form on the basis of mathematical principles. The exploration of nature is far from complete in this field. 👁 Frei Otto, who prefers to use the terms biology and building in combination instead of bionics, states: "In addition to the pure adaptation of the forms of nature in painting, sculpture and architecture as motifs without reference to their structures, there is a growing trend of applying biological constructional principles to technology. This is called bionics. The proponents of bionics take the evolutionary state of biological objects, which technology could do little to improve, as their point of departure. They believe that this transfer to technology will benefit the latter. Architects hope that the approximation and integration of biological aspects will bring their buildings into greater harmony with nature and achieve an elevated aesthetic component. Some biologists recommend the structure of animals and plants for technical products. The opposite route, counter to that of bionics, is to continue the development of technical structures independent of the models in living nature; the new results of this approach can also offer new perspectives on biological objects. Buckminster Fuller's tensegrity structures, for example, led to the understanding of the construction of diatoms and Radiolaria and, after Fuller's death, even to the discovery of new carbon molecules, the fullerenes. The development of the lightest and largest-span pneumatic halls led to the realization that all biological objects, without exception, are constructed on the basis of a single principle, namely a water-filled flexible skin (pneumatic structure). This seems to be particularly significant for the still open explanation of the creation of life and development in the field of the biological evolution of species."

Buildings should therefore not imitate nature but be created in the spirit of nature.

ARTHUR SCHOPENHAUER

Fuller does not see himself as a copyist of natural forms. He writes: "What really interests me therefore in all these recent geodesic tensegrity findings in nature is that that they apparently confirm that I have found the coordinate mathematical system employed in nature's structuring." ◉ In addition to classic bionics, the structural or aesthetic adaptation of biological models, new directions, such as "genetic architecture" and biological architecture have emerged, especially in recent years. ◉ The origins of genetic architecture lie in computer simulation employed, for example, to simulate static systems and to modify them independent of context. The proponents of this movement not only adhere to the aesthetics and formative laws of nature, they also strive to achieve a fusion of biology, technology and architecture. For the time being, attempts to create architecture that resembles a living organism are virtual. ◉ In his introduction to the work of Nox Architects in *Hybrid Space*, Peter Zellner writes: "Through a kind of digital genetic engineering, NOX crossbreeds the body's motorized biology with electronic life, generating liquid forms in which human action and architecture are synthesized." Studies of human tissue reveal structures that correspond to wickerwork. The combined action of muscle and bone can also be understood as a tensegrity structure, as can the filaments and needle-like cytoskeletons of cells.

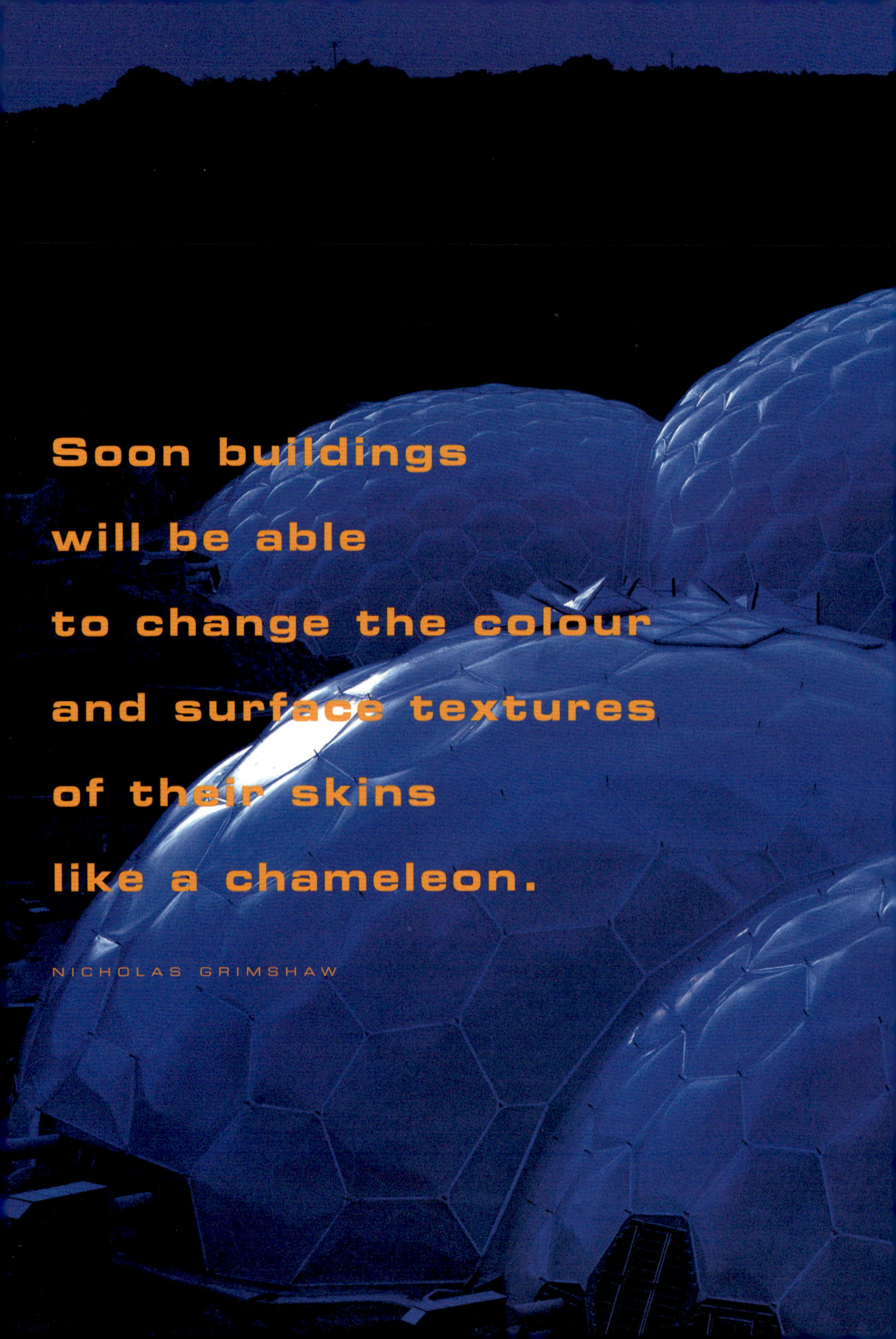

Soon buildings will be able to change the colour and surface textures of their skins like a chameleon.

NICHOLAS GRIMSHAW

The Eden project designed by **Nicholas Grimshaw and Partner** in Great Britain is reminiscent of such a living organism. The gigantic greenhouse is conceived to intensify our awareness of the environment. Since glass alone would have been too heavy a material to fill the steel hexagons with a diameter of roughly 9 m each, the architect stretched a paper-thin Teflon film across the honeycomb structure. The load-bearing structure reminds one of foam. 👁 The architecture firm **3deluxe**, which presented the Bionic Pavilion Case Study at EXPO 2000 in Hanover, writes: "We can discover sensuality in the computer, nature in genetic engineering and philosophy in bionics. Or biology in technology ... ." Their bionic pavilion is intended to symbolize the fusion of biology and technology. The goal is to create a genetic architecture, originating from computer simulation, which is as close an approximation of a living organism with an autonomous metabolism as possible. 👁 The youth pavilion, scape, by the same group creates an architectural spatial landscape that can be physically experienced – a multi-sensory and visionary journey through the world of the media of the future. The pavilion, covering an area of 4,000 m² and with a height of 8 m and a capacity of 500 visitors, features an inner zone at the core divided by gauze veils, where interactive games and installations invite visitors to explore themes in five lounges: leisure lounge, living tunnel, fashion studio, omnium and cyclone lounge. Scape becomes a living organism – "genetic architecture." An elastic floor even creates a sense of weightlessness.

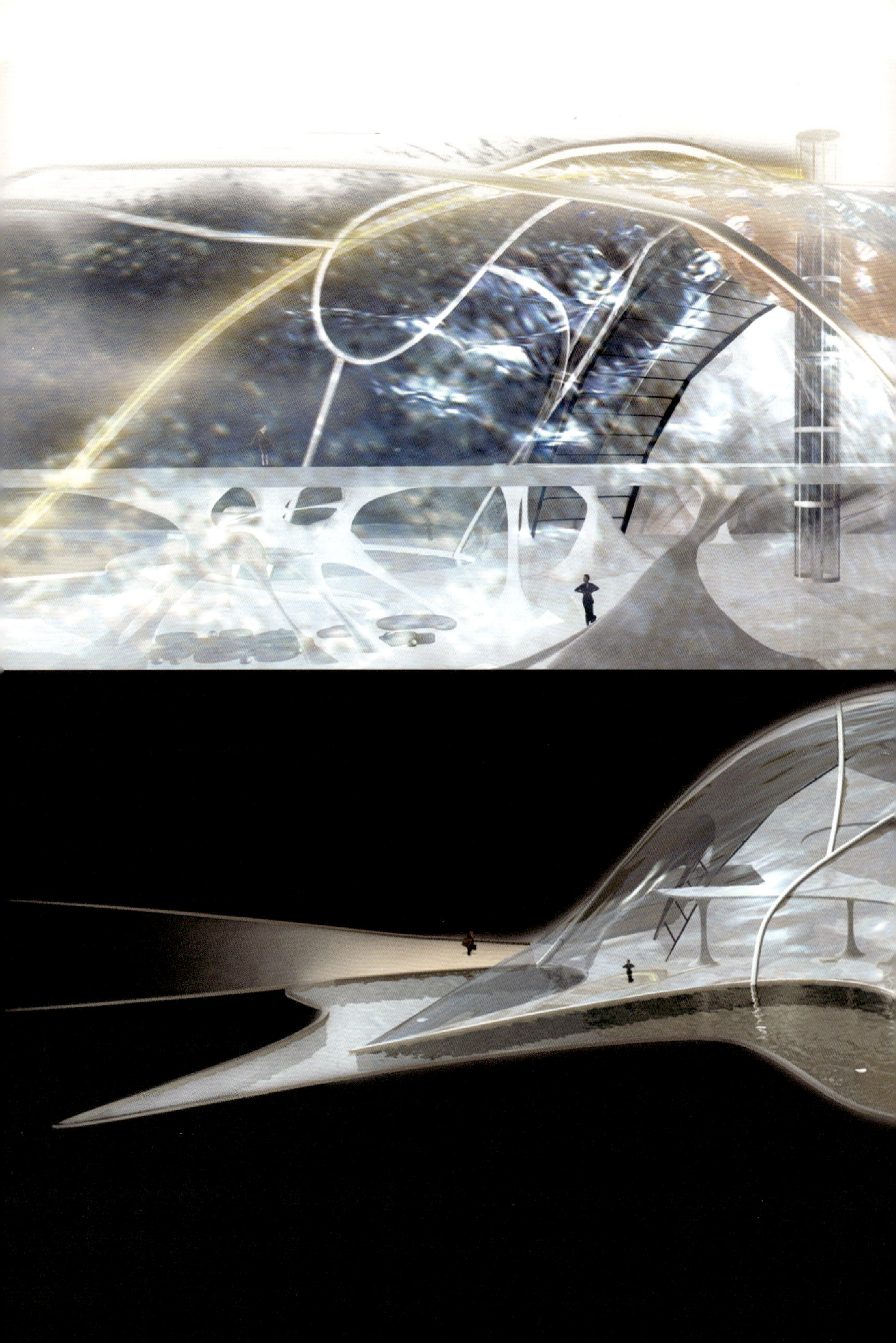

We can discover sensuality in the computer, nature in genetic engineering and philosophy in bionics. Or biology in technology ...

3DELUXE

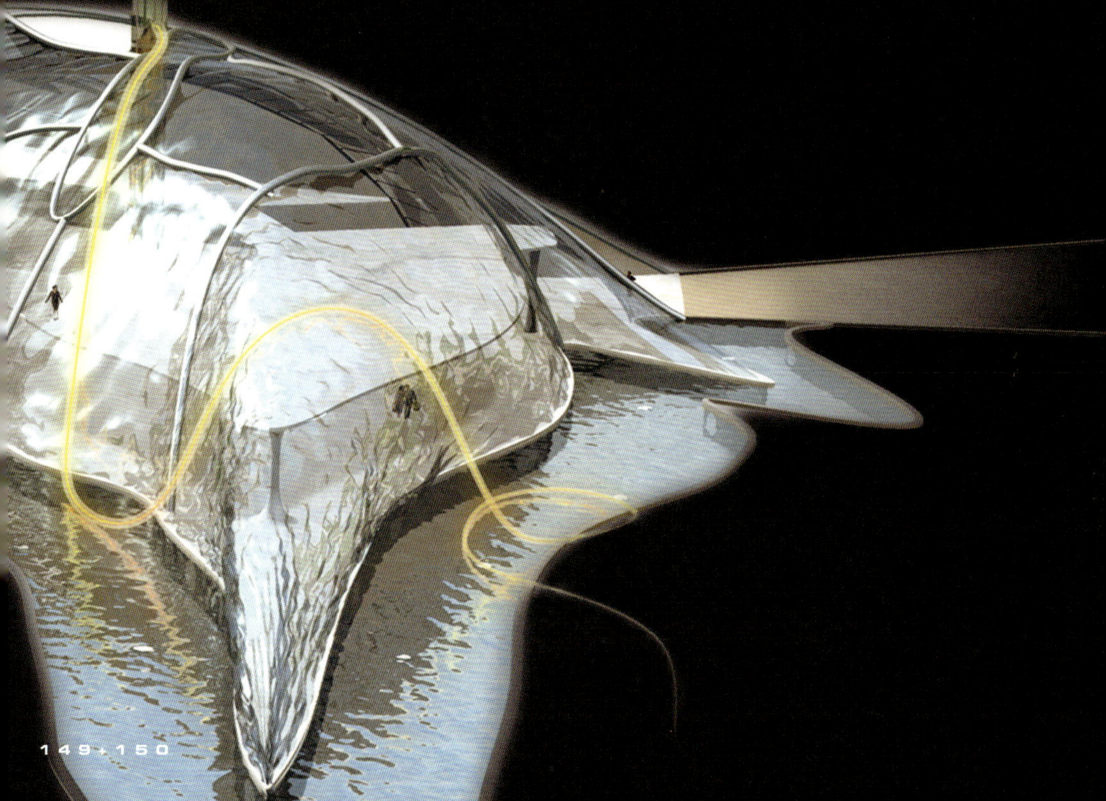

149+150

DIGITAL REAL

Many other innovative aspects are also expressed in animated architecture: Movement, speed, virtual realities, new media, and digital techniques combine into new architectural forms. The world of data opens up endless possibilities. Digital technologies, in particular, are not only means to an end, but a challenge to discover a new formal language. They have imbued architecture with a new sense of departure, similar to that at the beginning of the last century. ◉ In recent times, new media are inspiring architects to develop innovative design methods and concepts. Computers are used both in the design and in the building process. In the meantime, the means of the various computer-assisted animation patterns are further differentiated. For the design of the future, computer technology opens up new creative possibilities for architecture. Virtual city, shape grammar, rapid promoting genetic algorithms, process data visualization and neutral networks are some examples. ◉ While some architects see little promise in the new design methods, a steadily growing number of colleagues regard computer technology not only as a working method, but as a basis for research. The interior of three-dimensional objects can be studied and explored on the computer, taken apart as needed and reassembled. This changes

... animation implies the evolution of a form and its shaping forces.

GREG LYNN

both the requirements and the results of the architectural work. The architecture practice of the future is a virtual studio, the architect of the future an animation designer – this is the motto of the proponents. 👁 Whether computer technology will truly bring about a dramatic change in architecture remains to be seen. It is possible, however, that this technical development will provide suitable means for supporting the implementation of current requirements in the area of animated architecture. Cyberspace, for example, is a medium that gives people the sensation of having been bodily transported away from their everyday physical world into a world of pure fantasy. This fantasy world is influenced by the new everyday experiences, on the one hand, and changes the perception of the everyday world, on the other. In combination with other factors, such as universal social activation or the simultaneous coexistence of local differences and a growing global homogeneity, the fantasy world thus contributes to a kind of dilution of the experiential event. The translation of these categories into built architecture, into concrete and not only virtual spaces, can be promoted and supported by the new digital technologies. 👁 Some architecture firms have already seized the opportunity to explore new spaces with the help of animation software. Free-form areas are designed that are no longer based in conventional geometries, but are developed with specialized high-end software. The first built examples illustrate that cyber artists are anything but unrealistic dreamers. The exhibition entitled *digital real. blobmeister – first built projects* at the German Museum of Architecture in Frankfurt on Main featuring realized objects. 👁 Architecture firms such as Marcos Novak, California, Ocean North, London, Oosterhuis Associates, Rotterdam, Nox, Rotterdam, Stephen Perella, New York and Greg Lynn, Los Angeles, develop new spatial structures and explore new ideas on the nature of architecture. Thus Greg Lynn elaborated on his meta-blob model studies in 1999:

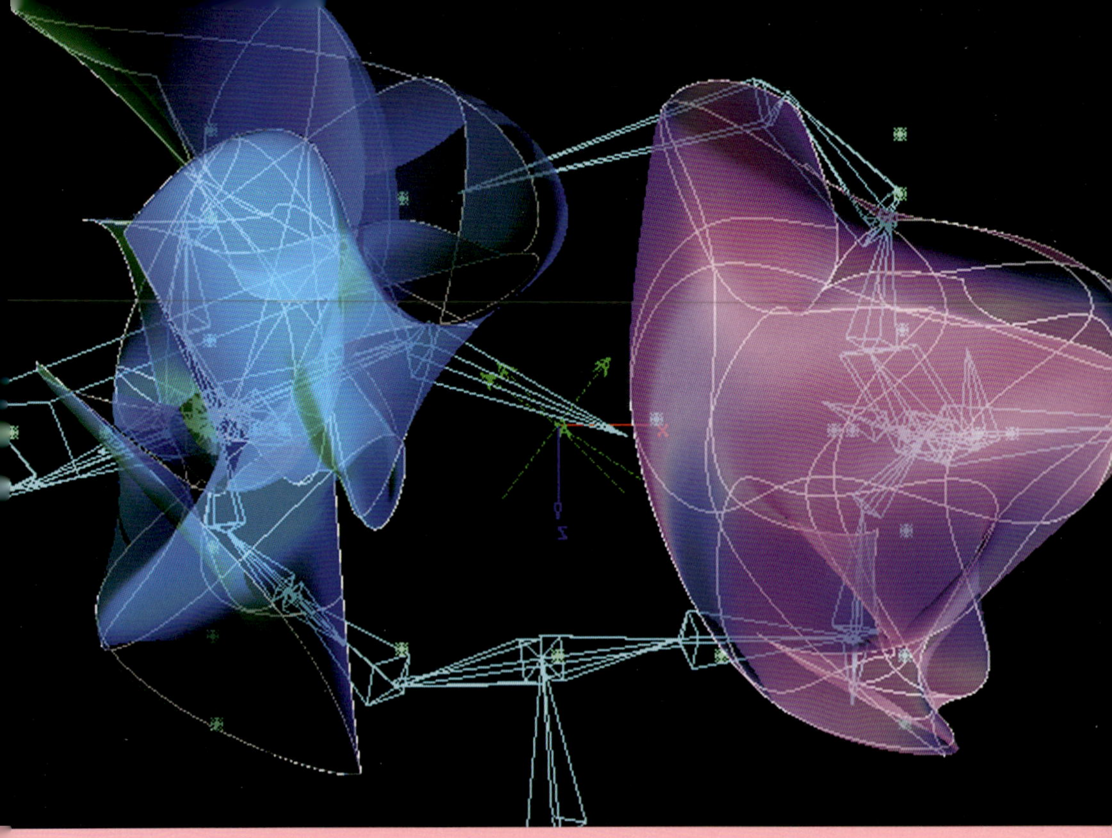

"While motion implies movement and action, animation implies the evolution of a form and its shaping forces. In its manifold implications, animation touches on many of architecture's most deeply embedded assumptions about its structure." Free-flowing forms with unstable areas of variable, fluctuating movements are a departure from conventional architecture. The architects of virtual reality speak of new spaces with new terms, for example, **Marcos Novak**, who describes his architecture with the following words: " 'Transarchitectures' or 'liquid architectures'. ... 'Transarchitectures' is a concept that places its emphasis on a perpetual becoming." **Stephen Perella** also blurs the boundary between the real and the virtual world. His hypersurfaces intermingle surface and structure, image and object, in order to create new areas

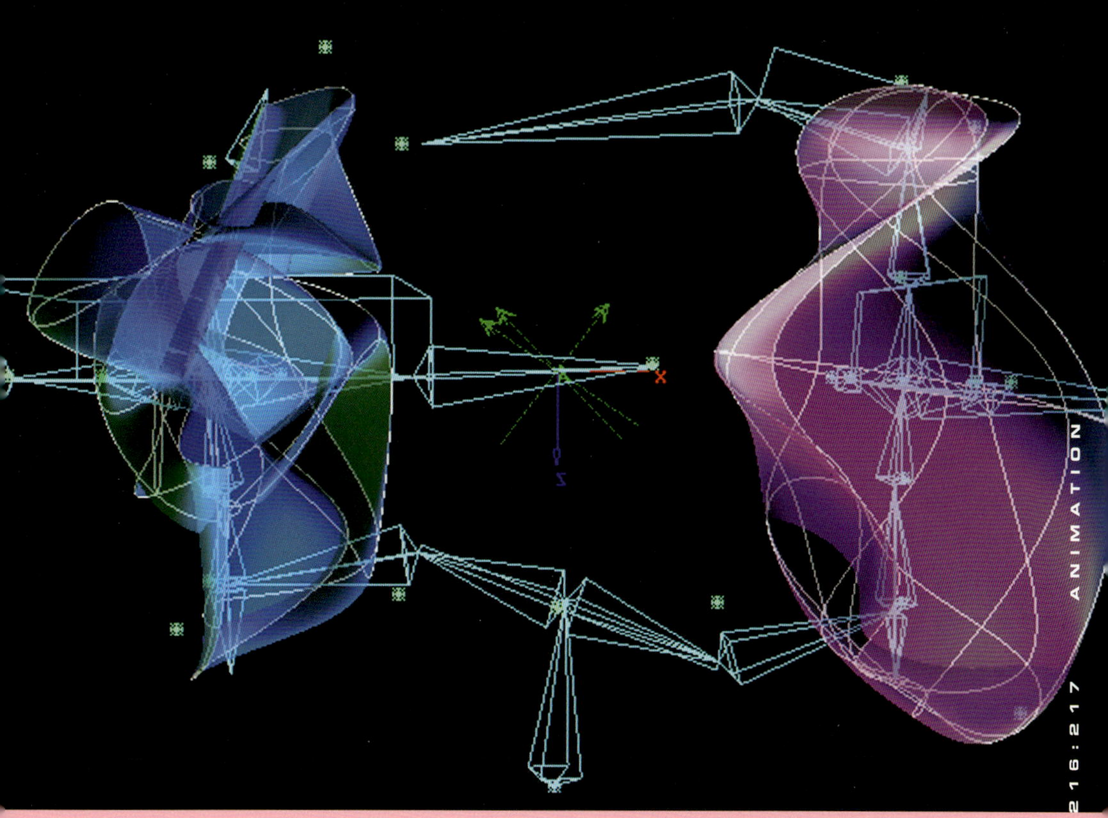

with the goal of establishing a relationship between time and space. 👁 The "Dancer in Space" project by Decoi, 1999, demonstrates how the boundaries between body and space seem to dissolve. New forms of digital architecture are constantly being created. 👁 The quality of architecture that is animated in this manner will be measured in terms of the degree to which it fulfils not only functional and rational, but also emotional requirements, to which degree the modified sense of space and time, for example, is reflected in the content, optics and texture of the architecture and how capable the latter is to inspire one's own imagination without resulting in visual overkill.

156-159

This kind of architecture can create sites of communication that correspond to the expanded experiential horizon and the fluid experience of humanity at the beginning of the twenty-first century, where entertainment finds its specific place as a component of social developments. The recognition of this task on the part of architects, and their ability to open new horizons through a differentiated awareness of quality, is not just fun and games: it is a necessity for the future. 👁 **Ocean North** speaks of a synergetic rapprochement with architecture from many disciplines. This group of architects also regard digital technologies above all as a basis for a new interpretation of how architecture has been defined thus far. In their project from 1999, Time capsule, the firm developed new configurations and new forms. 👁 Active Innerskin by **Oosterhuis Associates**, Rotterdam, is a project where the envelope is designed like an active inner skin, utilized in space travel as a working and living environment. A pneumatic grid and a flexible membrane that acts as a skin together form a data-transmitting structure that functions like a bundle of muscles.

"Transarchitectures" is a concept that places emphasis on a perpetual becoming.

MARCOS NOVAK

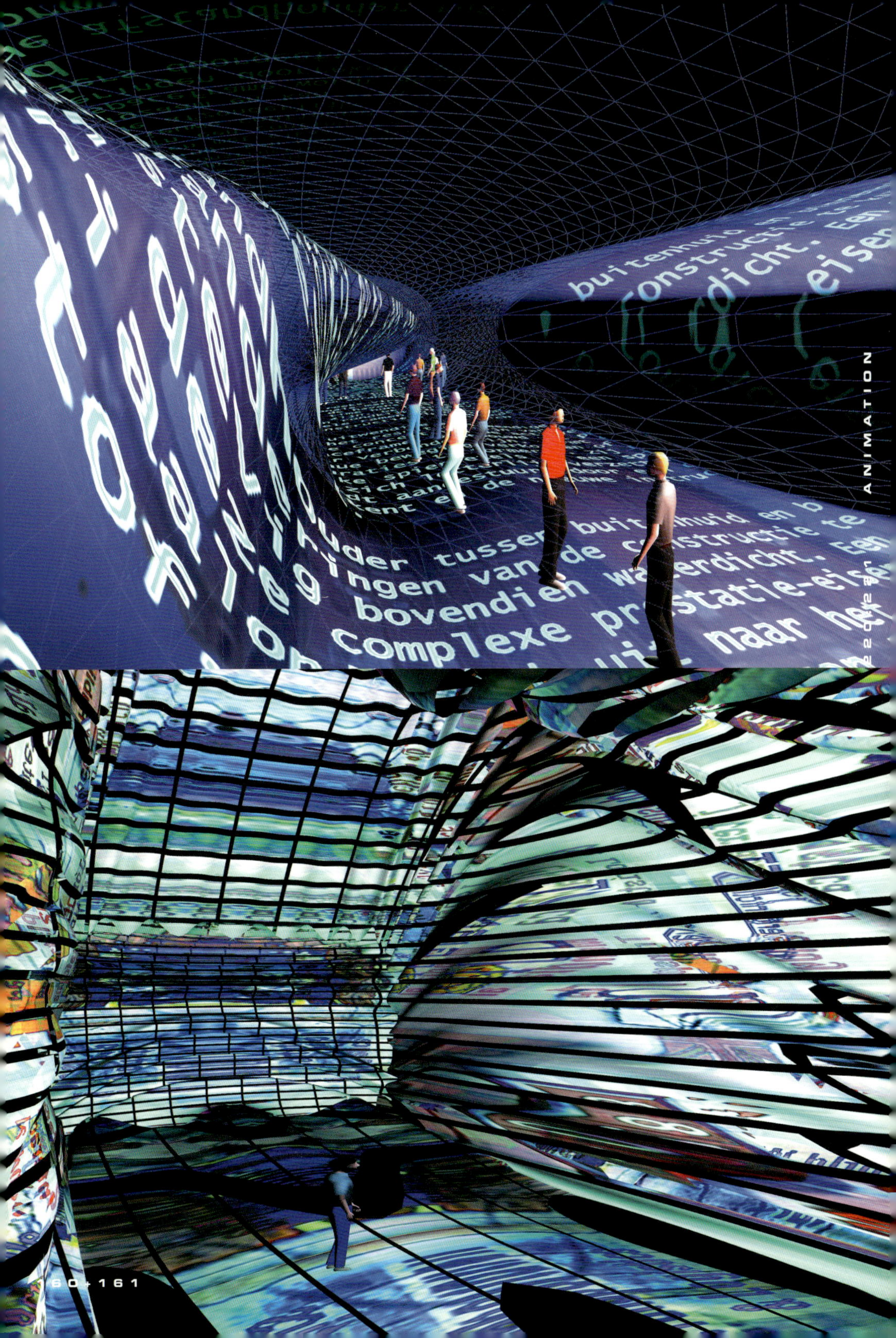

buitenhuid en
constructie te
dicht. Een
tussen buitenhuid en b
van de constructie te
bovendien waterdicht. Een
complexe prestatie-eis
naar het

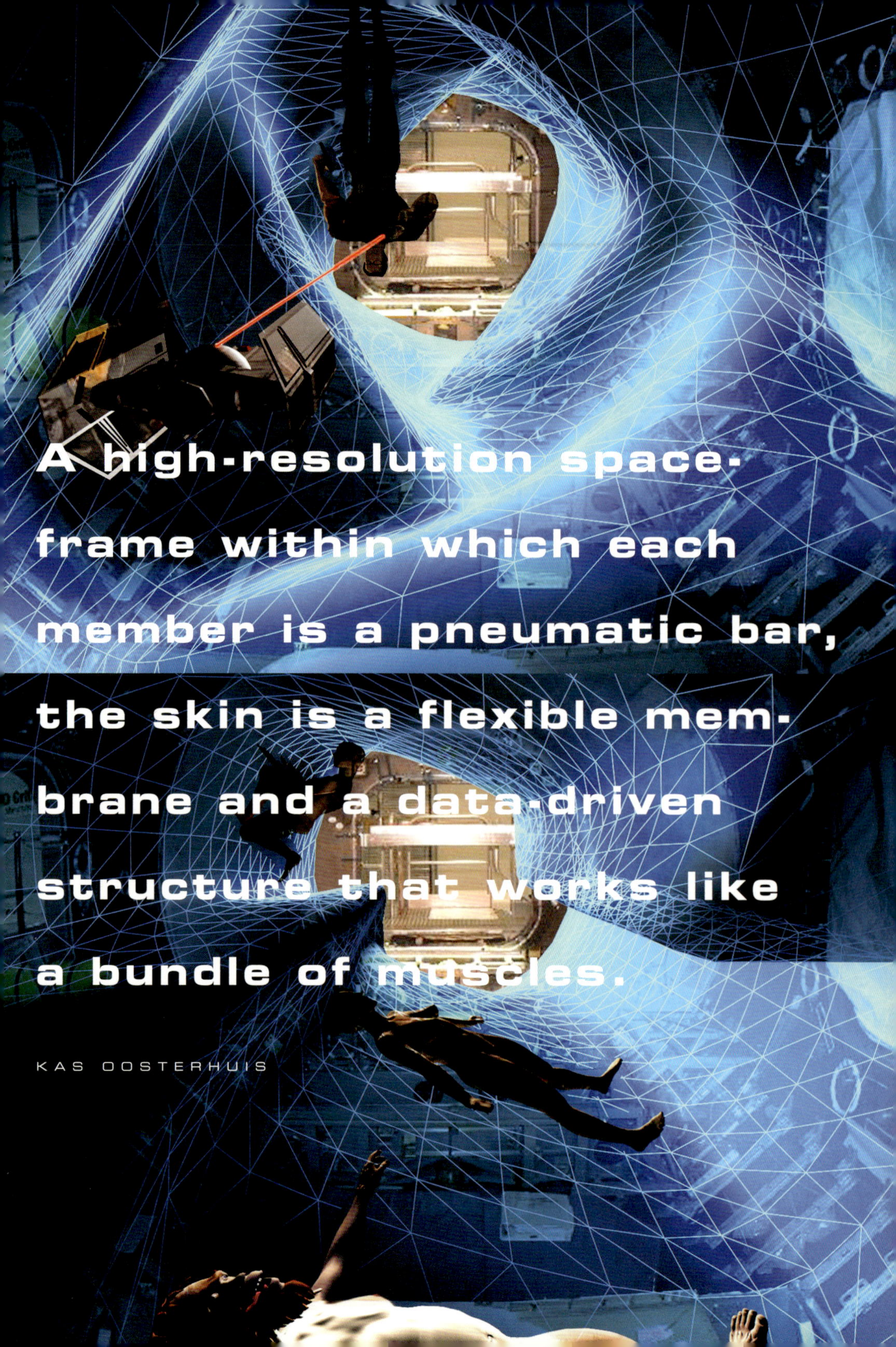
A high-resolution space-frame within which each member is a pneumatic bar, the skin is a flexible membrane and a data-driven structure that works like a bundle of muscles.
KAS OOSTERHUIS

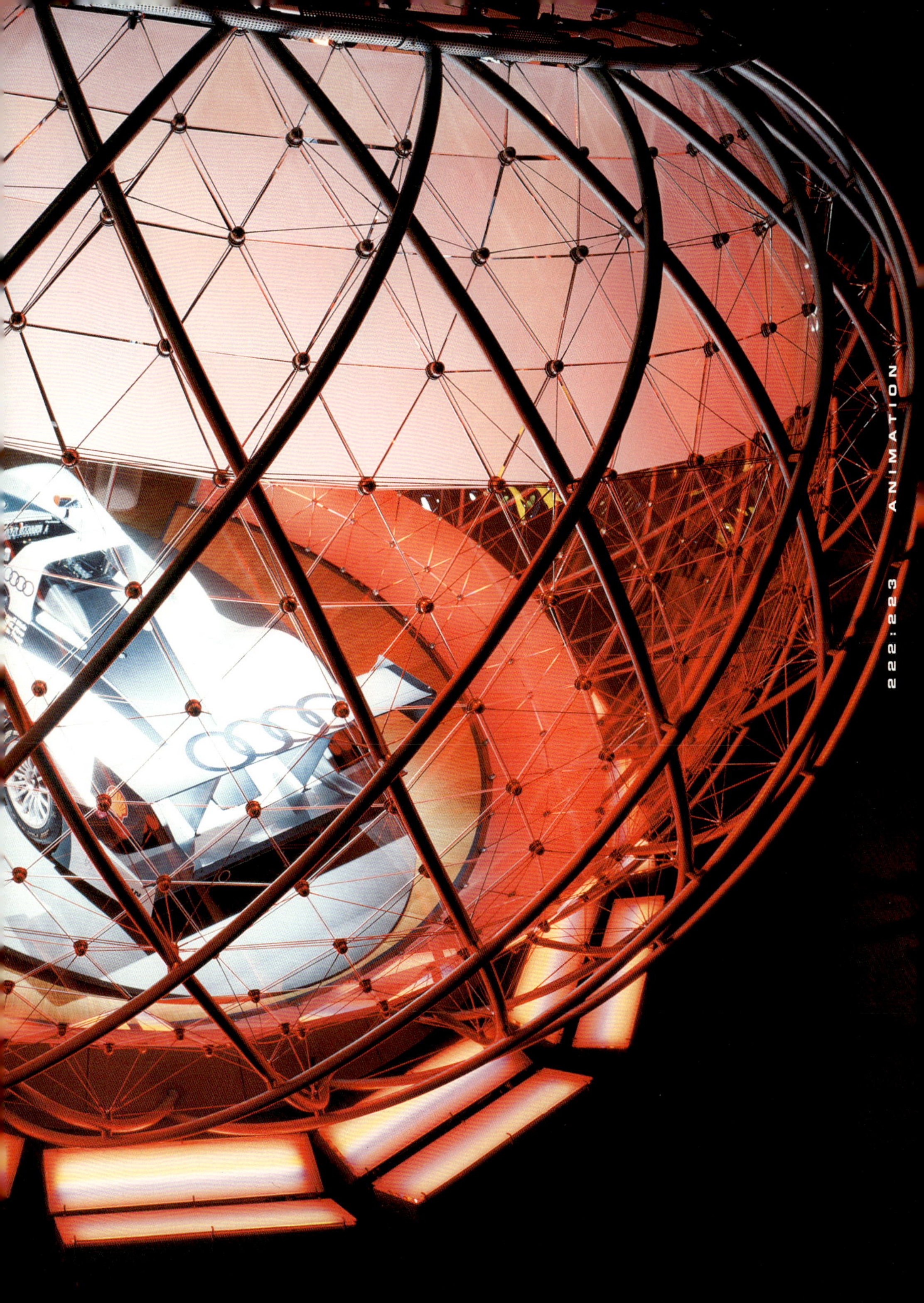

162+163+164

The architect Greg Lynn and the painter Fabian Marcaccio combine two techniques in an installation exhibition at the Wexner Center for the Arts. Digital paintings are printed on large-scale clear plastic sheets. These sheets are moulded with heat on over 100 CNC shaped foam panels to give them curvature and surface detail. The printed computer-moulded panels are then assembled to form a three dimensional environment. This collaborative installation of translucent, digitally painted and digitally moulded skins can be moved ...

EXHIBITION CATALOGUE "PREDATOR"

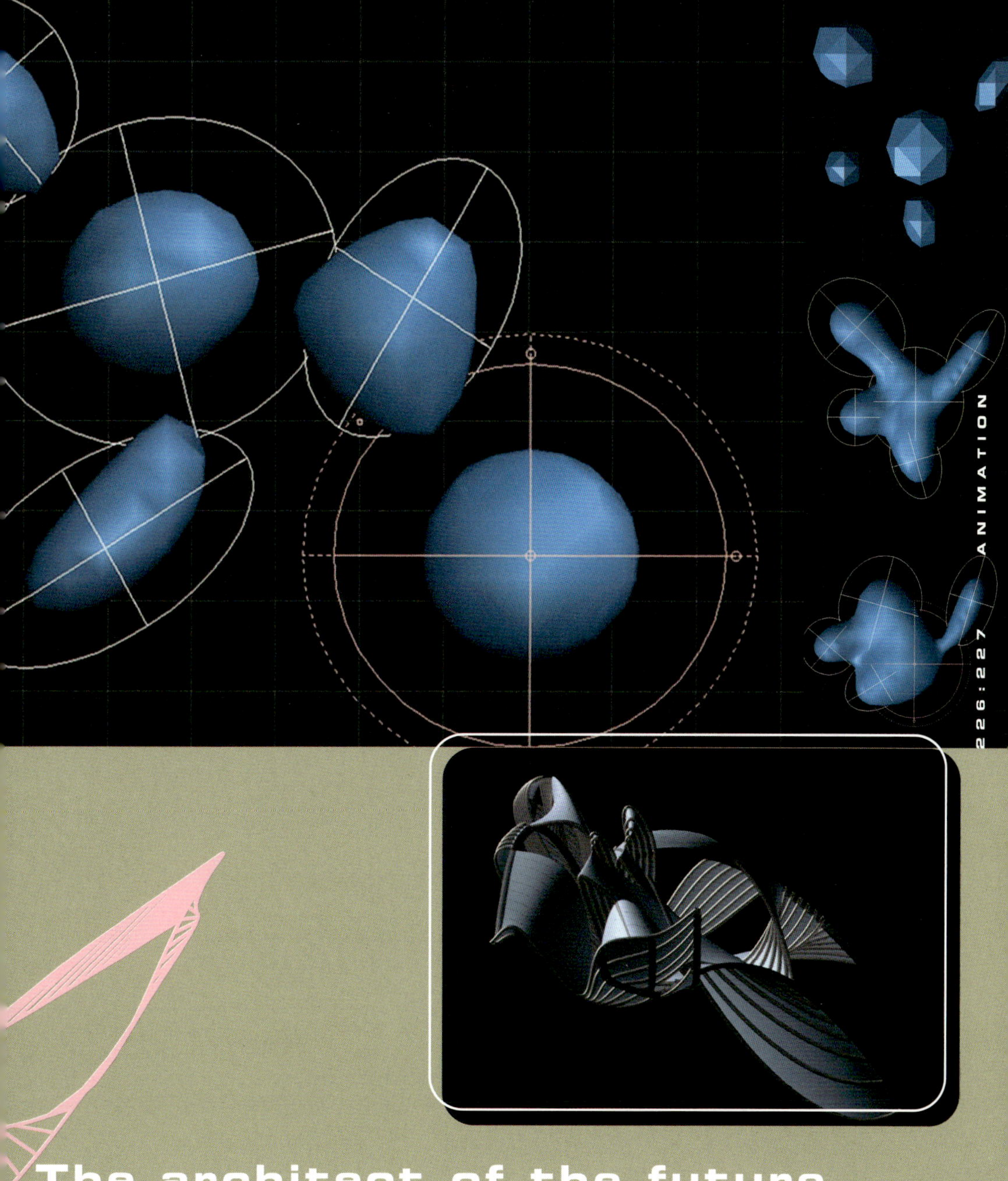

The architect of the future is an animation designer.

167+168+169+170

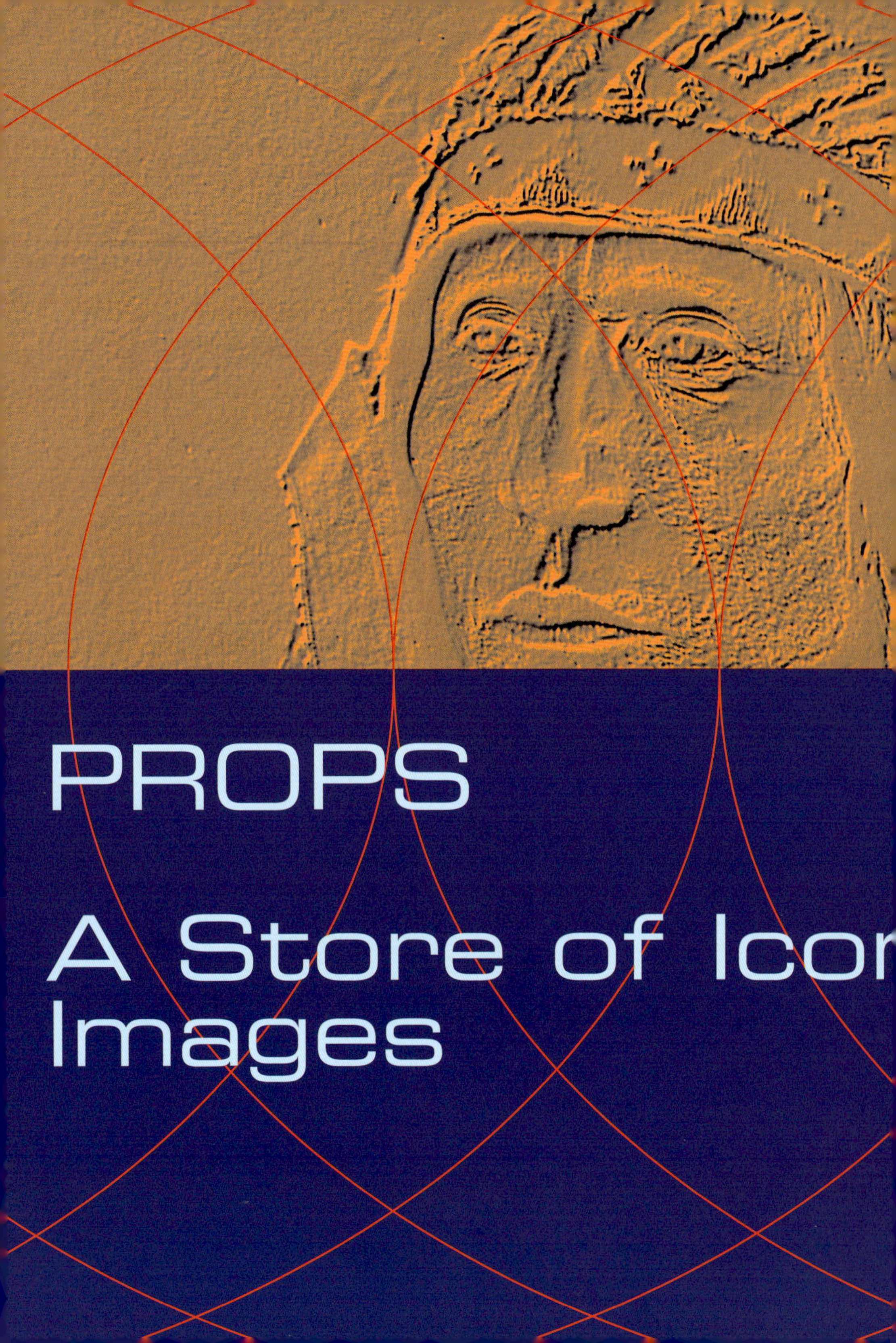
PROPS
A Store of Icon
Images

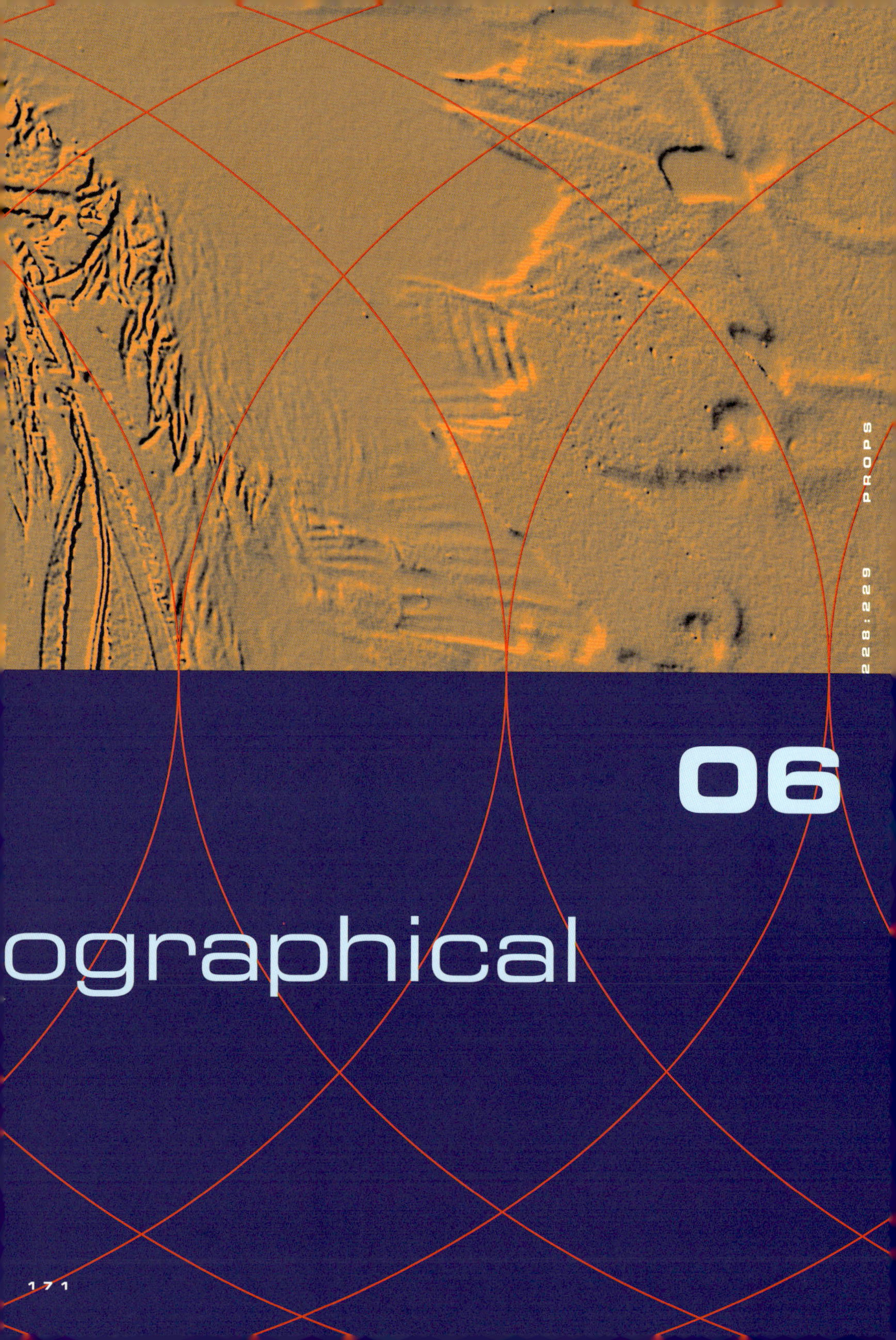
PROPS
228:229
06
ographical

Columbus

Candish

Gomez

Diaz

Franklin

Cook

Livingston

Pizarro

MODELS

The store of original images and free fantasies seems inexhaustible. No theme reaches too far into the past or the future, no trend is too current, to be incorporated into animated worlds. What do the parallel worlds look like and how are the adventure seekers transported out of reality? Which store of images are designers dipping into? What props are used to create a sense of freedom and adventure, suspense and activity, familiarity and recognition? What are the means of animation? 👁 Travel diaries by Columbus, Candish, Gomez, Diaz, Franklin, Cook, Livingston, Pizarro and many others are a store of ideas for the entertainment industry, as the accounts of seafarers and conquerors who explode the boundaries of the known world. Adventurers, pirates, heroes of the Wild West and prospectors are the protagonists of countless tales of danger and heroism. These stories provide the material from which the dream images are woven in the contemporary animated worlds of amusement parks, shopping malls and hotels, serving as a hybrid somewhere between model and copy. These environments offer a spatial experience of the journey into the past, set against a nostalgic backdrop.

THE IDYLL OF THE WILD WEST

Anyone who deals in dreams understands the power of the idyll of the Wild West. Tales of the Wild West and movies of the genre are a popular source for animated worlds. Clearly children aren't the only ones who enjoy playing cowboys, sheriffs or Indians. Outlaw heroes like Billy the Kid and Jesse James embody the dream of freedom and adventure and are brought back to life in the parks. Leisure parks resurrect many heroic figures from the store of classic westerns, embodied in Hollywood by actors such as Gary Cooper and John Wayne. 👁 The stories vary. The operators decide whether they are going to re-enact the conquest of the Wild West or the struggle of cattle farmers against the wilderness, Indians or bandits. Ballads of folk heroes are also very popular and bandits are often presented in a heroic manner. The western town is replete with recognizable symbols: the sheriff's badge, the barbershop sign, the names above the saloon. Banks, hotels and telegraph offices are also among the indispensable props. ◉ Disneyland Resort, for example, recreates the set of *High Noon* in the Cheyenne Hotel. The rooms feature over a thousand Wild West themes.

RIDES

The so-called rides are another element of amusement environments. All types of transportation means are employed to furnish the association with travelling: from monorail to "milk train," from old-timer cars, early double-decker buses, horse-drawn carriages and carousels to futuristic vehicles and breathtaking underwater rides, cozy steamboats or roller coasters. The journeys go into the past and into the future. The traveller encounters twinkling stars, meteors, the moon and extraterrestrials in the galaxy, while other journeys take him down to the mysterious depths of the ocean. ◉ Reconstructions of famous original versions of ships and spaceships as classic symbols of a mythical expansion of the horizon are especially popular. In Discoveryland at the Disneyland Resort, modelled on **Jules Verne**'s *20,000 Leagues Under the Sea*, visitors can see Captain Nemo's submarine breaking the surface and diving again. And the café "Hyperion," of the same name as the airship from the film The Island at the Top of the World (1974), at the entrance of Videopolis in Discoveryland, is a reminder of daring journeys of discovery. The renowned British firm Happold developed the engineering concept. ◉ In 1973 the astronaut

174+175+176

HYPERION
Not everyone can be an astronaut, but we can all experience the illusion of a journey into the universe.
FANTASYLAND SLOGAN

Norman Cousins wrote: "To be able to lift off from the earth, to be able to see the relationship of the planet Earth to other planets from a space station, to be able to imagine the billions of factors in precise and grandiose combination, which make human existence possible; to be able to ponder a meeting between the mind and spirit of man and space ... all these things expand the human horizon." The intergalactic adventure beckons. Not everyone can be an astronaut, but we can all experience the illusion of a journey into the universe: space and space travel are part of the thematic repertoire of every major leisure park. Clever video, sound and transportation systems transport us into unknown spheres. Futuristic buildings, spectacular and replete with allusions to outer space, create the illusion of time travel: "Experience the future now!" A space travel exhibit in Disneyland, Orlando, complements informative material on the theme of journeys into space with a simulated flight to the moon. Wonderworld in Corby also advertises a range of attractive rides, for example, a journey into the interior of the human body. The architect **Derek Walker** has designed a giant human, with the ride passing through the mouth, past lungs, heart and veins into the interior of the body. The American architecture firm Wimberly, Allison, Tong & Goo is currently planning two attractions: the World City Ship and the Airship Hotel. The ship will accommodate six thousand passengers; the Airship Hotel is a luxurious hotel suspended in the air, called Airient Express.

177+178+179

FAIRY TALES AND ADVENTURE NOVELS

The world of fairy tales and adventure novels also furnishes fantastic themes and fanciful images. Some of the literary models for idea and design consultants are, among others, Joseph Conrad's *Island of the Damned*, Robert Louis Stevenson's *Treasure Island*, Samuel Taylor's *Old Sailor*, Herman Melville's *Moby Dick*, *Sinbad the Seafarer* from the tales of *A Thousand and One Arabian Nights*, *The Secret Island* and other Jules Verne novels, *Münchhausen's Adventures* of Gottfried Bürger, and Jack London's *Call of the Wild*. The boundaries between reality and fantasy are blurred in these novels. 👁 The images conjured up by childhood are different: discovering the world, building forts, smoking in secret, staying away from home for days on end, surviving in the dark forest – these are the experiences Mark Twain imagines for his protagonist Tom Sawyer. They serve as an inspiration for Disney's theme park Tom's Island. 👁 Whether the fairytales of the Brothers Grimm, von Hauff, Andersen or Perrault serve as a design model depends entirely on the preferences of the park operator. Grimm's fairytales are among the most popular models in Europe. Originally handed down as oral tales, the stories were compiled by the Brothers Grimm and published in book form for the first time in 1812. Ever since, the texts have been enriched through the artistic interpretations of painters and illustrators. These illustrations conjure up a wide variety of moods and reflect the various eras as well as the personal traits of the artists. 👁 Disney, who also takes the fairytales as the basis for many animated films, transforms them, changing some parts entirely or adding new passages. Later, he creates a physical environment in the amusement parks for his characters based on these fairytales, usually village-like in character or, as in Toon Town, merrily colourful and cheerful. 👁 **Derek Walker** invents a fantasy village with motifs from the "land of milk and honey" for Wonderworld in Corby, Great

180+181+182

Britain. There is a tower made of cheese, houses that are oversized confectionary pastries and roofs made of liquorice. A huge coffee pot beckons visitors to take a ride on the carousel. 👁 The fairytale town Village Rhyme in Wonderworld even features its own fantasy inhabitants created by British designers Jain Quicke and Gerry Baptist. 👁 A medieval village opens its doors to visitors in the Heidepark in Soltau. Here, Hans really is "in luck" and **Tatjana Hauptmann**'s magical drawings leap off the page of the fairytale book into the reality of the amusement park. 👁 As in the fairytale, the real world is complemented by a world beyond, inhabited by fabulous creatures such as dragons, demons, giants, dwarfs, sirens, good and evil magicians and fairies of all kinds. In a mix of horror, fantasy and science fiction, countless hybrid forms are created. 👁 One successful example of an imaginary dragon has been realized by the architect and designer **Matteo Thun** for Philips in the Bavaria Filmpark in Kirchhellen. The management of Philips asked Thun to create a spectacular action-style architecture, which was realized in 1993.

FUTURE AND SPACE

The visions, discoveries and inventions of humankind are also given credit, thematically and architecturally, in the world of entertainment. As early as the fifteenth century, Leonardo da Vinci believed that humans could fly. Scientists and poets anticipated the day when we would overcome the restraints of gravity; Jules Verne dreamt of journeys into the unknown.

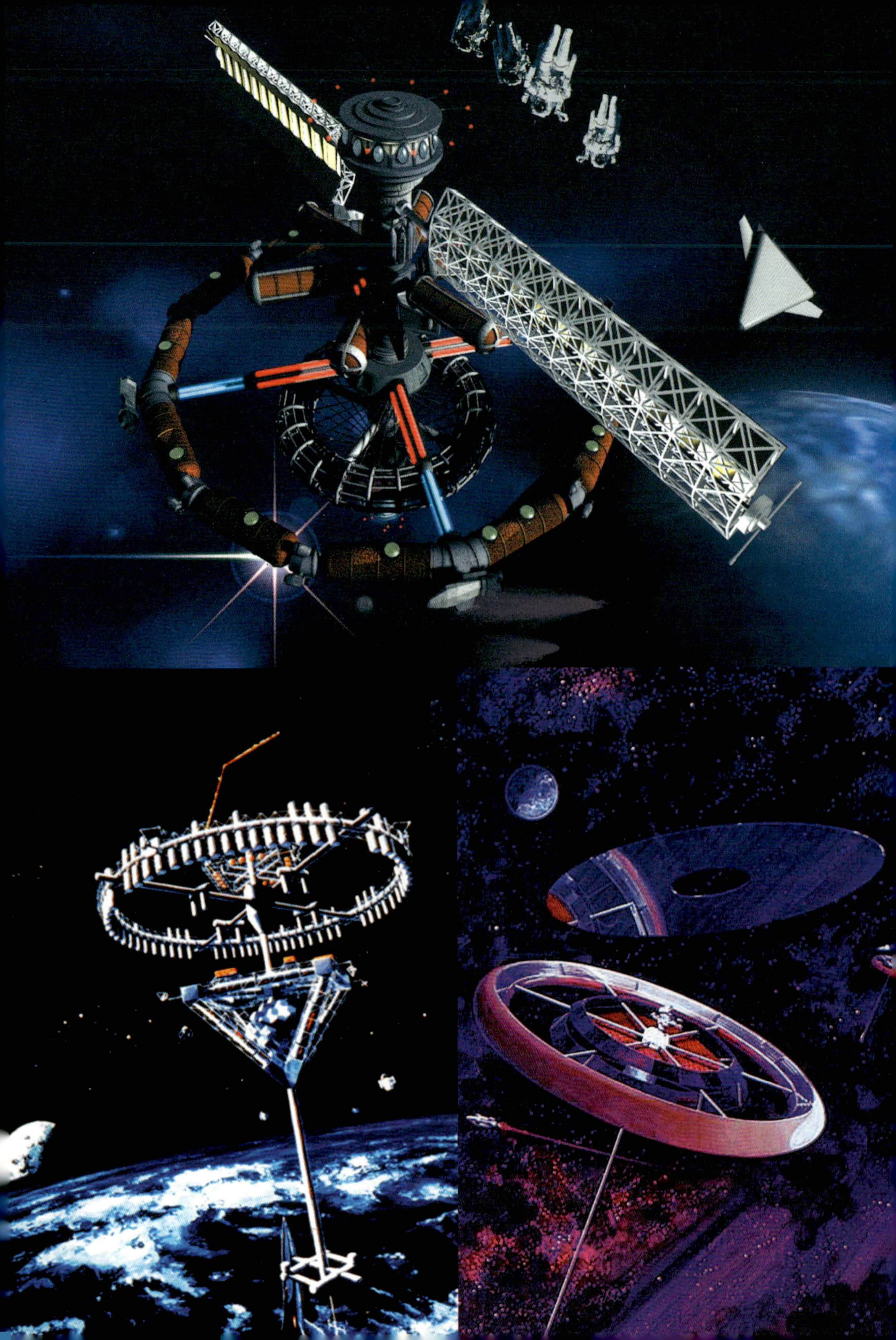

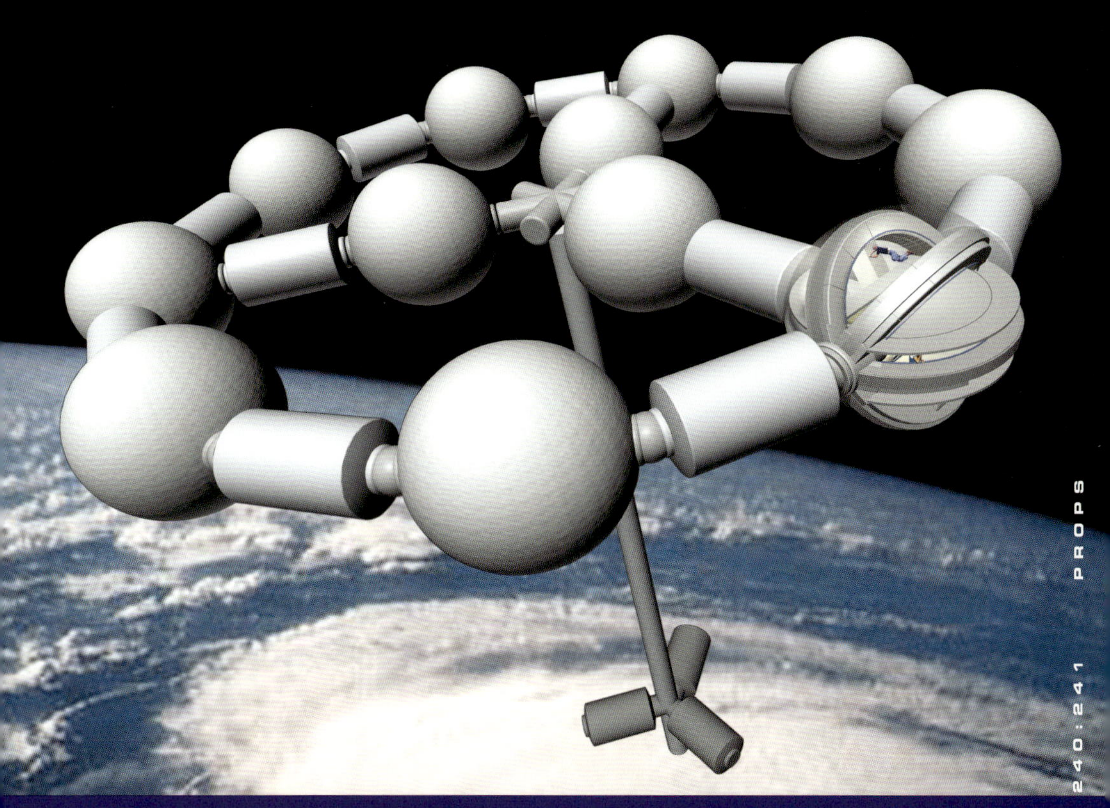

Have you any idea how big the world is?

Do you know where the light comes from

or what the source of the darkness is ...?

JOB

186+187+188+189

Tomorrowland in Anaheim, USA, is the prototype of this kind of futuristic theme world. But the task proved to be a challenge for Walt Disney and his team. What they imagined as Tomorrowland some forty years ago, leaves every visitor unmoved today. Disney comments: "The only problem with anything of tomorrow is that at the pace we are going right now tomorrow would catch up with us before we got it built." 👁 The world of the future, constructed in high-tech architecture foreseen by great visionaries, is the attraction today in Tomorrowland. Space Mountain, Star Tour, Videopolis, and Café Hyperion are some of the names for the theme area dedicated to the future and outer space. 👁 In Walt Disney World in Florida, Spaceship Earth in the EPCOT Center stands as a symbol of the future and technology. But the true landmark of the EPCOT Center is the soaring silver sphere that symbolizes the Earth. Replicated in many European amusement parks, the sphere serves as a logo for nearly every park. 👁 The artist **Robert T. McCall** also designs fantastic space architectures. 👁 The Space Park in Bremen (2001), designed by architects **Rhode, Kellermann, Wawrowsky** from Düsseldorf, is Germany's first entertainment centre with a futuristic theme. Visitors are treated to an experience of space exploration. The restaurants are called Milky Way or UFO Bar, the lobby is referred to as the command bridge, conference rooms are galaxies and the wellness club is called Fit for the Future. Shopping isn't just shopping: it's Starwalk Shopping. Everyone has to play a game of cosmic bowling; planets and commanders, extraterrestrials, starwalkers, space capsules, space station Moon Base One – they all cross paths in the Space Park in Bremen. 👁 The effect on the human body is perhaps the most interesting aspect of space exploration. Anyone with a dream to actually live in space one day is wholly dependent on technology and architecture.

190+191

W-882
W-882

375-S
75-S
10375-S

The architects of this new living environment have to take the survival, health and comfort of the users into account. Pondering the idea of living in space has inspired some architects to imagine the unimaginable and to realize these ideas in new projects. The **Shimizu Corporation** for Space Tourism, for example, presented new designs for 2002. 👁 Space tourism is the latest idea in the quest for the extraordinary experience. The moon is the travel destination of the future. The lobbyists who support the idea of making space accessible to tourists have become so powerful that space agencies around the world are beginning to face up to this new demand. Hilton is planning to build a hotel on the moon: the Lunar Hilton is to stand 325 m tall; it will have a private beach on its own lake and accommodate 5,000 guests. This is not science fiction, but a press release issued by the Hilton Corporation. Engineers and architects of the German-American space travel corporation Daimler-Chrysler Aerospace are also planning a space hotel. NASA designed fictitious space stations as early as 1970, to provide a living environment for as many as 10,000 people: a giant wheel turning in space acts as an artificial source of gravity. 👁 The Shimitzu Space Hotel provides space for 100 guests. A waiting list of interested parties has already been drawn up. A former astronaut and several space travel agencies advertise short trips and excursions into space. Designers are in the process of creating space-appropriate furniture. The very first space design products have been created under the aegis of British architect Richard Horden: a table-chair combination, a space shower, a bed and a rubbish bin. Aleksandra Konopek's dissertation also bears witness to the current interest in space tourism: Pneo is a foldable living module designed for use in space. Pneumatics and a flexible, space-compatible skin are employed to transport the folded module into orbit in a conventional space shuttle and to inflate it into a sphere, the "Konopek Sphere."

EXOTIC ENVIRONMENTS – DISTANT LANDS AND FOREIGN CULTURES

The more one has a sense of knowing the world through the media, the greater the yearning to immerse oneself bodily in an exotic environment, be it only a make-believe world. Every leisure park has a transcultural potential in and with the global culture industry. The architecture of all nations is part of the animated worlds. Fascinated by the foreign, architectural ensembles from around the world are mixed and matched. The architecture of cultural variety that is found there conveys a clear, three-dimensional message: it's a small world. Travel seems superfluous where exoticism can be found around the next corner: let's take the streetcar to the South Seas. Extras costumed in national dress, cultural customs as well as typical national culinary fare create the perfect illusion of being able to experience foreign cultures first hand. The visitor returns home with the feeling of having learned something about life in Polynesia, China or Hawaii and of having looked into the eyes of the true descendants of the native inhabitants. Original or fake? Authenticity is unimportant: "Original – We don't use that word!" comments Kisho Kurokawa. An authentic experience of the foreign place has little in common with the yearnings that are being awoken and satisfied in these environments. Import transforms the palaces, temples, pilgrimage sites and shrines into snack bars and souvenir shops. Reconstructions in amusement parks offer the opportunity to share in the experience, for example, of Captain Cook's discovery of the island of Hawaii on his third journey to the South Seas in 1778. Impressed by the dances performed by Hawaiian men, he spends a night on the foreign island and is subjected to numerous adventures and surprises, which the awed public can experience with him. The times of the Maya have long since passed. A journey to the original sites,

Original – We don´t use that word!

KISHO KUROKAWA

300 years after the end of the civilization, is no longer necessary. Visitors to Disneyland, Anaheim, California are treated to a daring mix of Maya temple with Cambodian details as they embark on their journey of discovery: the secret temple of Indiana Jones. The past is the present. Architecture reconstructs forgotten or lost worlds: Atlantis, ancient Rome, Maya temples and other sites of civilizations that have disappeared long ago. In 1998, an article in *Bauwelt* reported on Japan's old and new theme parks under the heading "The World as Copy". The Japanese have a special preference for these sites, where they glory in the idyll of the past of their own country and of Europe. Japan, perhaps more than any other country, has numerous theme- and museum-villages. Little World, for example, is a two-and-a-half-kilometre-long architectural promenade of homes from many different countries, some of which are originals, while others are reconstructed as true copies down to the last detail. This exhibition of architecture from around the world includes Thailand, Korea, Burkina Faso, Peru and Sweden. It displays aboriginal abodes from Africa, tepees, Peruvian haciendas, Indonesian and Micronesian huts and Nepalese monastery, as well as a typical Alsatian village. To a Japanese, a dirndl is as exotic as African headdress is to a European. The highlight of the Japanese leisure park Little World in Inuyama is a Bavarian village complete with garden gnomes, church, the "Bavaria" inn and the "Fairytale Forest" gift shop. The Gasthof offers beer, pork knuckles and sauerkraut on its menu. Visitors can borrow a traditional costume for a small fee and take a photograph home as a memento. What is true for Little World in Japan is equally true for Las Vegas in the United States. A Las Vegas tourist hit the nail on the head: "We live in the best country in the world, and if we have Venice right here we don't have to go to Europe." **Julian Barnes** takes it even further. He prefers the replica to the original. In 1999, Barnes wrote: "It is well established ...

that nowadays we prefer the replica to the original. We prefer the reproduction of the work to the work of art itself, the perfect sound and solitude of the compact disc to the symphony concert in the company of a thousand victims of throat complaints, the book on tape to the book on the lap. ... Now, the question to be asked is, why is it that we prefer the replica to the original? ... Once there was only the world, directly lived. Now there is the representation – let me fracture that word, re-presentation – of the world. It is not a substitute for that plain and primitive world, but an enhancement and enrichment, an ironisation and summation of that world. This is where we live today. A monochrome world has become Technicolor, a single croaking speaker has become wraparound sound. Is this our loss? No, it is our conquest, our victory. In conclusion, let me state that the world of the third millennium is inevitably, is ineradicably modern, and that it is our intellectual duty to submit to that modernity, and to dismiss as sentimental and inherently fraudulent all yearnings for what is dubiously termed the 'original'. We must demand the replica, since the reality, the truth, the authenticity of the replica is the one we can possess, colonise, reorder, find jouissance in ..."

NATURE – BEAUTY AND HORROR

Those who are unable to see the Matterhorn in Switzerland can climb the mountain in the leisure park: here, the reproduction replaces the original. Many famous unique beauties of nature are reproduced in animated environments. For the manufacturers of the illusions this is no problem. Even the Grand Canyon – in miniature reconstruction and animated with 3-D films – has its double in Florida. The grandiose is diminished, the natural wonder is made available as a tamed version of the original for a carefully controlled pseudo-dangerous experience. Interaction is the second component of artificial nature and fast rides, especially, are part of the standard repertoire of the reconstructed experience of nature. The first classic horror ride in a bobsled was created for the Matterhorn complex at Disney. Artificially staged avalanche disasters, volcano eruptions, waterfalls, earthquakes or tsunami waves, all recreated at close quarters, offer horrifically beautiful, but always safe, experiences of horror and fright.

SHOW BUSINESS

Animation sites can no longer survive without show business. The first theme parks tap into successful entertainment productions, mostly from Las Vegas, the Mecca of show business. But legendary shows are also imitated, like those staged at the Lido de Paris, which market above all the glamour of the "showgirls, at least six feet tall, with a frozen, fat, red smile, thirty pounds of feathers on their heads and the longest artificial lashes you have ever seen" are the standard and are employed to ornament every performance. 👁 Pop stars are the true kings and queens of show business today. There is a constant stream of superstars – real ones or stand-ins – who achieve cult status and exert an incomparable magnetism on the public. Whereas real stars perform in Las Vegas and entertainers such as Dean Martin, Frank Sinatra, Bill Cosby or Tom Jones have their "debuts" there, most leisure parks have long ago adopted a policy of hiring their less expensive imitators who are available year round. 👁 Live entertainment with special effects is the most recent evolution: musical events and video culture deliver the new images. Cinematic legends, for example Star Wars, are also brought to the stage combined with 3-D projections and in collaboration with Hollywood's right hand, George Lucas. Star Tours premiered in Disneyland in 1986: an intergalactic excursion into the universe that dazzles visitors with a technical extra-

vaganza of 150 special effects: all of it presented on a fibre-optics stage that simulates a galaxy. These are developments which re-position live entertainment in a new fashion after Disney's death. In true Hollywood style, the Disney Company inaugurates every newly developed attraction with a 60-hour-long party show. 👁 In the meantime, no shopping centre or mall is operated without some show or entertainment elements thrown into the mix, as the numerous urban entertainment centres already proclaim in their name. Elaborate opening shows are celebrated and tendered as complex management contracts. Often arenas or large stadiums are created especially for the show component and subsequently utilized for a variety of other attractions. They are frequently spatially linked to the shopping centre, although sometimes they are set up temporarily for a specific performance.

There is

a constant stream

of superstars –

real ones

or stand-ins.

FORM FOLLOW

Entertainment Architecture

VS FUN
07
FORM FOLLOWS FUN
254:255

AMUSEMENT PARKS

It is all about things that wobble in the night and surprise you in the morning.

PETER COOK

Following on the success of the major American amusement parks, Disneyland and Disneyworld, leisure parks began to spread across the globe. Ever since Disneyland opened its gates in July of 1955, it has been viewed as a symbol of contemporary American culture, as a synonym for American hegemony in entertainment, but also for the blurring of the difference between reality and fiction. Once Disney's architecture of illusion was exported to Florida, Japan and Paris, it became unstoppable, in the form of amusement parks, shopping centres and vacation villages. This development went hand in hand with a shift in public expectations with regard to urban design, entertainment settings, and architecture in general. 👁 The classic type is explored in a never-ending stream of new variations. Even the most recent leisure parks, especially those found in Japan, which also offer animated environments with virtual worlds, are no exception. In the meantime, there are as many variations as there are names: amusement park, theme park, adventure park, movie park, fairytale park, computer park, aquapark, holiday park, fun park, Seaworld park, safari park, animal park, water park, play park, entertainment park, family fun park, Happyland park and dreamland park, or simply The Big One. 👁 The Association of German Leisure Park Operators has defined the terms leisure park and adventure park in its charter. According to this definition, these parks are operations with the following characteristics:

VARIETE SHOW
LASER SHOW
ARENA
PLAZA DEL MAR
Neu
TOWER OF TERROR
PONY POST
METRO TINERO
Alter Jahrmarkt
Kiddie Camp
HEIDE-PARK
野外民族博物館
リトルワールド案内図
メルヘン バルト
ガストホフ バイエルン
「アルザス」
「エル・パティオ」
「ロスアンデス」
197+198 99+200 201+202

"A leisure park is an enterprise operating fixed installations on an enclosed or fenced-in site, where game and sports facilities, large models, animals, green space, and technical and cultural facilities are presented either together or in part and made available for public use ... An entry fee is usually charged for access to a leisure park or parts thereof. The use of the facilities and installations in the park can be made available on a flat-fee basis charged at the gate or on an individual ticket basis." ◉ There are approximately fifty large leisure parks and three hundred smaller operations in Germany. The density is quite high in Holland, where fifteen large and thirty smaller operations are distributed across an area one-sixth the size of the Federal Republic. Roughly 3.3 million visitors flock to the five large Belgian theme parks annually. Great Britain has almost as many large and medium-sized leisure parks as Germany, while France is notable for a much smaller number of similar facilities. ◉ The holiday resort introduced yet another type of theme park designed with the potential of reaching a large public. Of forty major theme parks in the United States, twelve are located in California and eight in Florida.

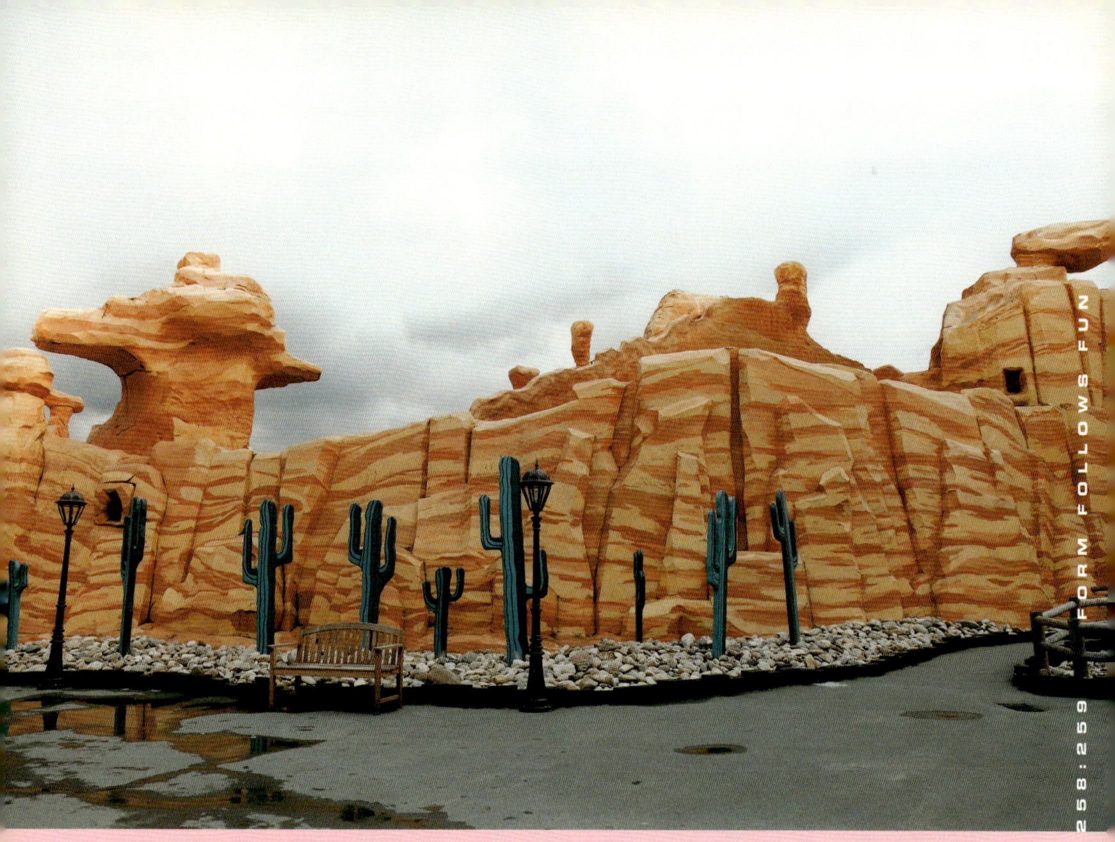

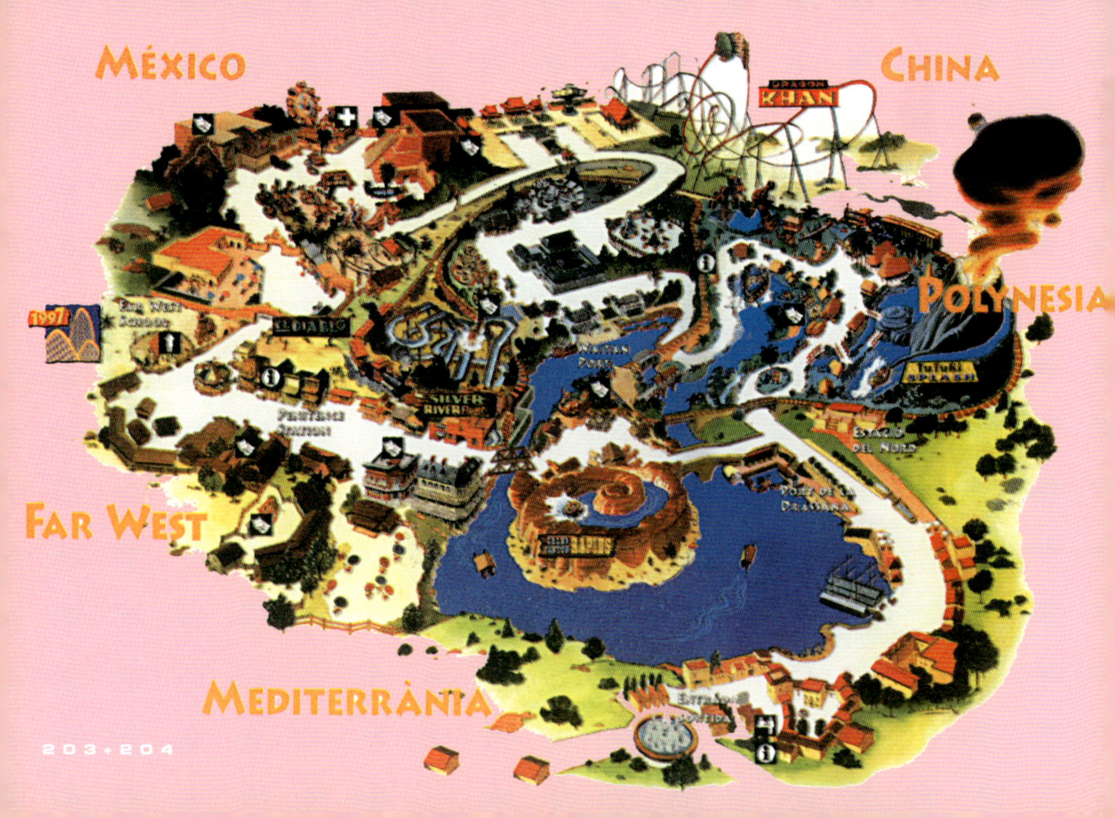

México
China
Polynesia
Far West
Mediterrània

203+204

Il Giardino dei Tarocchi In contrast to the aforementioned examples, there are parks whose appeal is not founded in elaborate technology but first and foremost in the individual artistic design. The Giardino dei Tarocchi is an especially imaginative example: inspired by Antonio Gaudí's Parque Güell in Barcelona, it was created from 1979 to 1996 on the basis of designs by the artist **Niki de Saint Phalle** in Capalbio in the Italian province of Grossetto. The unique amusement garden features twenty-two monumental sculptures, some large enough to walk through or designed as habitable spaces. The cement-encased iron structures, based on the Arcana Maiora of the Tarot, are covered in mosaics composed of mirrors, glass and colourful ceramics. The empress as goddess and high priestess even served for a while as an apartment for Niki de Saint Phalle (1930–2002), one of the most important artists of the twentieth century. In addition to the Tarot Garden, she designed several large projects in collaboration with the sculptor Jean Tinguely.

Legoland Günzburg The Danish toy manufacturer Lego constructed the fourth Legoland for €150 million in 2002. The 60-hectare site in Günzburg, halfway between Munich and Stuttgart, is easy to reach. Tokyo had been discussed as an alternative site, but Germany, the second-largest Lego market in the world, was the ultimate choice. 👁 The centre of the new complex in Günzburg is Miniland, which features miniature reconstructions of Hamburg, Berlin and Frankfurt and their landmarks on a scale of 1:20. In addition to Miniland, the park features the building and test centre, an adventureland with rocks, meat-eating Lego plants, a railway that speeds through a waterfall, the Land of Knights and the Lego Racer-Drome. 👁 Visitors can expect to see fifty million Lego blocks, over forty attractions and many shows. 👁 The first Legoland opened its gates in 1968 in the Danish town of Billund, right next to the head office of Lego.

A second park followed in 1996 in London near Buckingham Palace and in 1999, to the joy of Americans, the third Legoland was inaugurated in California.

Wonderworld Wonderworld, an unrealized project from 1982 that was planned for the town of Corby, Great Britain, would have been an alternative to amusement park design in the style of Disney. British architect Derek Walker was in charge of the overall planning and artistic direction. Different theme areas were assigned to architects such as Eva Jiricna and Ron Herron from London. Major international engineering firms such as Ove Arup and Partners were in charge of engineering, while the firm Happold was commissioned to design the lightweight load-bearing structure. Wonderworld was conceived as an edutainment centre for the whole family. Although Walt Disney's concepts were taken into the consideration, the innovative architecture conveyed an entirely different image. The British tradition of crystal palaces – exemplified by the Crystal Palace in Paxton, which has been a major attraction since 1851 – served as an additional source of inspiration. 👁 Wonderworld was intended as a site where shows and exhibitions, music festivals and many other uses were to be assembled in a flexible manner for the first time: a new leisure city. The Wonderworld themes are: Land, Safety, Rhyme, Communication, The Body, Concerthall, Disco, Rollerway, The World, Resort Area, Stadium, Energy, Sea, and Hospitality Zone. 👁 The project is currently being revised and it seems it may be realized after all within the foreseeable future.

Wonder

World

FORM FOLLOWS FUN

264-265

208-212

MACHINES FOR MASS CONSUMPTION

Retail arcades or shopping centres, mega-malls, super-malls and mega-stores: they all evolved in the postmodern consumer society and have become the very centre of major cities around the world. They demonstrate the linkages between amusement, pleasure and experience and economic aspects on the one hand, and the emergence of new spatial structures on the other. All of these "machines" are semi-public spaces embellished with symbols and images aimed at representing or, at the very least conveying, a new style of mass consumption and living. Inner cities are overtaken by shopping malls and retail arcades. In her book *The City as Event*, **Regine Bittner** paints a vivid image of the mechanisms of such urban experiential spaces: "In the age of economic globalisation and multi-media communication, cities have become theatres for stage productions of urbanity. While lavish presentations of history and culture on the one hand emphasise the uniqueness of each place in order to attract investors, tourists and residents with spending power, on the other hand the inner cities of this world are decked out with shopping malls and arcades that are the same everywhere. Modern inner city space is essentially established by practices of consumption and enjoyment, giving the impression that cities are growing more and more alike."

Shopping Centre Over the course of the past fifty years, the boundaries between shopping, leisure and entertainment have become blurred. The singular function of the distribution of goods seems to be superannuated. As a precursor to malls, shopping centres have gradually evolved in the direction of shopping as experience, an impression that is emphasized by the installation of food courts. Snack bars on wheels have been replaced with permanently installed restaurants. The result is a blend of eating and shopping. This creates an opportunity to encourage the consumer to spend as much time as possible in the centre. Early on in their development, shopping centres begin to offer additional services, such as cinemas, restaurants, fast-food services, gambling casinos and skating rinks – an indicator of the growing importance of the shopping centre with regard to leisure behaviour. The competition for the customer's attention with the help of a variety of media such as sound, information boards, video arcades and, last but not least, experiential architecture, is growing more and more fierce. In the footsteps of the historic department store, the retail arcade and the galleria, the new type of shopping centre has firmly established its own place: a large, climate-controlled complex with multifunctional facilities, all under one roof.

Bercy Shopping Centre The Bercy shopping centre is located on the eastern outskirts of Paris. Its architect, **Renzo Piano**, has deliberately chosen a form reminiscent of an airship that has just landed: a readily recognizable large shape that is memorable even to passing motorists. The structure was erected from 1987 to 1990. The geometry of the complex consists of three segments with different radii and varying lengths in profile, which combine into an unusual form. This 100,000 m² centre accommodates retail stores, boutiques, and a food court. The complex is subdivided into three atria. The middle atrium contains a garden with a small forest. Visitors, who arrive predominantly by car, enter from the underground garage into the centre with direct access to the stores. Each of the atria contains escalators leading to the upper levels. In contrast to malls, which feature entire theme parks, shopping centres beckon with more understated attractions.

Mega-Mall The mall evolved out of the shopping centre over the last three decades. The mega-mall is an expansion of the conventional mall through the addition of a theme park.

BERCY 2
CENTRE COMMERCIAL
P
NIV. 8.74
NIV. 3.70
NIV. 0.17
NIV. -3.02
NIV. -5.87
cacharel
GUCCI
PAROLE

1

We want to dislodge gravity. We want to create a lighter, more playful, new architecture that expresses the spirit of the present day. The building itself conveys only one principal message: "the immaterial."

RENZO PIANO

213+214+215

Entertainment is another new component, as is a style of architecture that harks back to Disney's philosophy. Theme parks have become fixtures in the functional repertoire of every mega-mall the synthesis of theme park and shopping centre. This type, which is much more than a monumental terminal for the movement of goods, first developed in the United States. The mega-mall is usually one to three storeys high, with two to five axes and the aforementioned attractions. In *Blueprint*, no. 127, 1996, the journalist **Frances Anderton** asks: "What is better than a theme park or a mall?" Answering his own question, his immediate reply is: "A theme mall." The architect **Fritz Eller** also explores the building type of the mega-mall: "A dream house or ... a world that has been turned upside down? An ambiguous world? The attempt to create a new counter world, free of work, free of constraint, of monotony, of being alone, of duty and

performance? A world of stimulation, excitement, adventure, and informality? It seems to me that everyone is aware how much their behaviour falls victim to a forced artificiality. One experiences, one feels the ambiguity; the overpowering seduction of everyone to behave as they were intended to behave from the very beginning ultimately produces a kind of disillusionment. The illusory world is but a diversion from the world in which we live, or is it an alternative world? Everything we see, the entire architecture, is but an illusion."

City Walk Mall The City Walk Complex in the United States, realized by **Jon Jerde** in 1996, is an example of a mall focussed on shopping for fantasy. City Walk employs extreme colours, building forms and symbols that represent familiar buildings in Los Angeles that have taken on a landmark character. 👁 The City Walk mall is integrated into MCA Universal Studios. Once again,

216+217+218

Number Eleven

the surprise effect is the key to success: "... it's gotta be entertaining." Retail stores, multiplex cinemas, high-tech games, theme shops and theme cafés represent an artificial sampling of what a big city has to offer, albeit without the dark sides of the "real" metropolis. Here, and this is the wish of the creators, one can enjoy the glittering ambience untroubled by the danger of being mugged or the grunge of rear courtyards.

West Edmonton Mall The first mega-mall of the world, the West Edmonton Mall, was inaugurated in Canada in 1985. All the functions are arranged along a central axis: 830 individual retailers and eleven department stores are integrated into the complex. The mall also features a water park with twenty-nine submarines, a wave pool and a skating rink, as well as the leisure park Fantasyland, the Europe Boulevard and a large golf hotel. The name mega-mall is a reference to the size of the complex: roughly 500,000 m². In 1987, **Dietmar Steiner** wrote in the *Stadtbauwelt*: "The mall looms over Edmonton's suburban homes like cathedrals did in earlier times, with the difference that it does not offer architecture that engages the mind or the spirit. Rather, it gives the impression of having been placed there without an architectural concept. The mall makes no contribution to the debate on architecture. It is an unimaginative box in a horrible sea of parking lots." 👁 **Margaret Crawford**'s views on this new building type are far more differentiated. In issues 114, 115 of *Arch+* from 1992, she writes: "The Edmonton Mall adopted another design principle of Disney: the spatial density of different motifs. Where the images were separated by a spatial scene change at Disney, the mall gives one the impression of seeing all the images simultaneously. In the West Edmonton Mall, on the other hand, this element of the land, the guiding principle of Disneyland, is finally eliminated. This unleashes a veritable whirlwind of detached images and ideas without context ... and the impression one could gain in the West Edmonton Mall is one of receiving all channels simultaneously."

Centro Oberhausen The first mall for the new generation in Germany – the Centro – was opened in 1996 in Oberhausen in the Ruhr region. Aside from the shopping area, the mall includes an amusement park, a multi-purpose hall, a promenade, a multiplex cinema, sports facilities, parking garages and apartments, as well as a hotel and a business park. The Centro has the appearance of an autonomous city, with streets and squares, which seem to replace the conventional urban structure and compete with it. The complex, which was planned and realized by the architects **Rhode, Kellermann and Wawrowsky** from Düsseldorf, covers an area of 830,000 m².

Lotte World Where am I? In the South Seas or in Germany, in the Middle Ages, in Italy or China – or only in the supermarket, after all? Lotte World, which was created in Seoul in 1989, is another example of the total synthesis of theme park and commerce. The operator, the Lotte-Group, engaged the architectural firm **Battaglia Associates** to realize a large complex with a shopping mall, a hotel, and a sports and recreation centre, as well as an indoor and an outdoor theme park. In contrast to the West Edmonton Mall, this complex has a differentiated formal language, which ensures that the internal functions are legible on the facade. While Canada's West Edmonton Mall is a faceless box on the exterior, columns, arches, numerous mirrors and clever lighting are employed in this instance to signal a certain value status.

Sony Center The European Sony headquarters on Potsdamer Platz in Berlin has occupied its site like a large circus tent since 1999. The attractions are grouped around the tent: a Sony Style store, a 3-D Imax and a multiplex-cinema, the Arsenal theatre with the film museum and the German Kinemathek Foundation, exotic restaurants and the torso of the old Esplanade Hotel, displayed like a museum exhibit. ◉ Once upon a time, this was the centre of Berlin and if it were up to the wishes of the Sony empire, it would be again. The Sony Center utilizes typologies that have been employed in a series of Sony construction projects in Japan and in the United States and which are part of the corporation's worldwide marketing strategy: elements of an office building, an urban entertainment centre and a showroom are combined into a kind of instant city. The uses of the building components grouped around a central courtyard also correspond to the marketing strategy of the enterprise. Architecture that is as spectacular and eye-catching as possible is needed to arouse curiosity, and it has been delivered in this case by the architect **Helmut Jahn** with his transparent, asymmetrical tent roof. ◉ Frank Roost comments: "... never before has urban entertainment been as much a part of a multi-media consumer chain as is the case today with the entertainment centres of the global media corporations. ... a commercialisation that threatens to dominate the cities of tomorrow, in view of the growing importance of the culture of fun, leisure and events, of urban tourism and multimedia communication." (*Bauwelt* 48/2000)

Urban Entertainment Centre Like cinema operators and theme park organizers, entertainment impresarios recognize the potential of mass retailing in combination with cinemas and theme parks. The result is an urban entertainment centre. Cinemas, theme parks, video arcades and slot machines are complemented by alternative forms of dissemination such as the Internet,

222+223+224

direct mail, and outlets. One example is Universal City, located on a 160-hectare hill in the Verdugo mountains a few miles northwest of downtown Los Angeles. In the 1990s, the former studio city with sound stages and film sets was transformed into an urban entertainment centre that attracts eight million visitors a year. The goal is to combine the disparate individual buildings of Universal City into a new urban centre. The existing activities are complemented by additional services such as restaurants, retail stores, entertainment venues, offices and classrooms. The sports package and other attractions generate the highest profit, according to operator estimates. The idea of total entertainment, where shopping, sports, play and leisure are combined into a single experiential world, is clearly recognizable. ◉ At the full-service agencies in Santa Monica, which manage these types of sites, the architects work in direct consultation with show designers, set designers and graphic designers. These teams employ film jargon in describing the developmental process of their projects: the first phase is referred to as brainstorming a project, while the second phase is dedicated to storyboarding or scripting the theme of the building. And finally, there is the Wow factor – the key to success. ◉ The stimulation of all senses is characteristic of UECs – urban entertainment centres, which are sprouting like mushrooms from the ground in the United States, Asia, and most recently also in Germany, where fifty new centres are planned for the future.

Horton Plaza Another project by the architect **Jon A. Jerde**, who has been nicknamed the King of Theme Malls, is the Horton Plaza in San Diego: a project conceived to rejuvenate San Diego's downtown with a variety of uses such as retail, hotel, entertainment, residential, cinema, gallery and theatre. Jon A. Jerde describes his concept as follows: "We composed the project out of fragments of buildings already existing in San Diego: it was composed of the language of the city that was pre-existent: the arcades of Santa Fe railroad station, the heights and towers of buildings, tile domes. The initial challenge was to decode the language of the city ... to discover its fantasy."

Canal City Hakata Given the average age of its 1.3 million inhabitants – thirty-five years – Fukuoka is the second youngest city in Japan and, after Kyoto, the city with the highest student population. The demand for the latest trends in shopping and entertainment is correspondingly high. Here as elsewhere the most sought after expert is the architect as imagineer. Developers are competing worldwide for experts who know how to satisfy both the requirements of global investors and local yearnings. Fulfilling these requirements is the goal of **Jerde Partnership**, which has grown into a worldwide operation and which designed the five experiential areas grouped along a canal at Canal City Hakata.

JVC Guadalajara Urban entertainment centres invariably offer the same programs: cinemas, restaurants, bars, clubs, shops, fitness and wellness facilities and offices. The new entertainment centre at Guadalajara in Mexico charges international architects, for example **Coop Himmelb(l)au, Daniel Libeskind, Enrice Norton and Morphosis**, with the task of creating an animated environment for multiple functions. ◉ The concept of the JVC entertainment and business centre, which includes a research and development department for technology, is intended to lead the way in the evolution of the entertainment and consumer industry toward new possibilities of information exchange and knowledge enrichment. ◉ The lot covers an area of 295,730 m² with 96,000 m² of useable area. Building costs run to $ 136 million, an indication of the massive scale of the new centre, which is to be realized in the coming years.

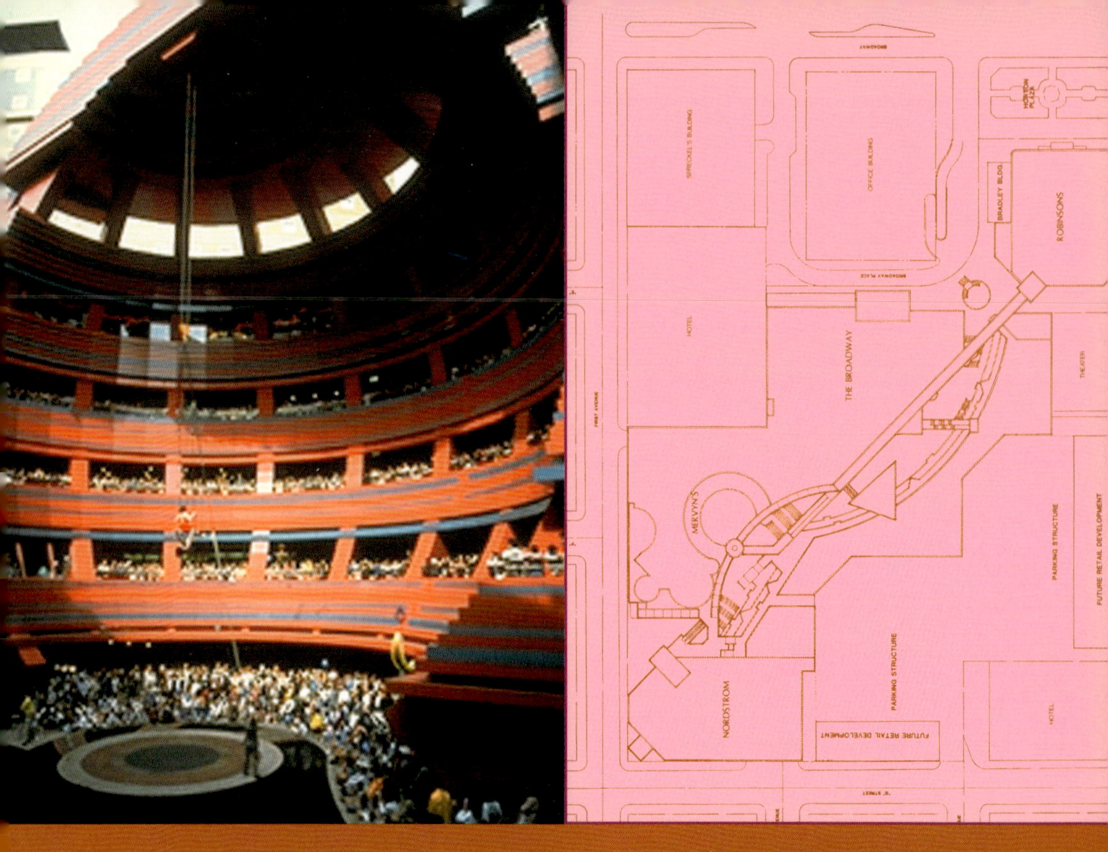

The initial challenge was to decode the language of the city ... to discover its fantasy.

JON A. JERDE

JON A. JERDE

225+226+227+228

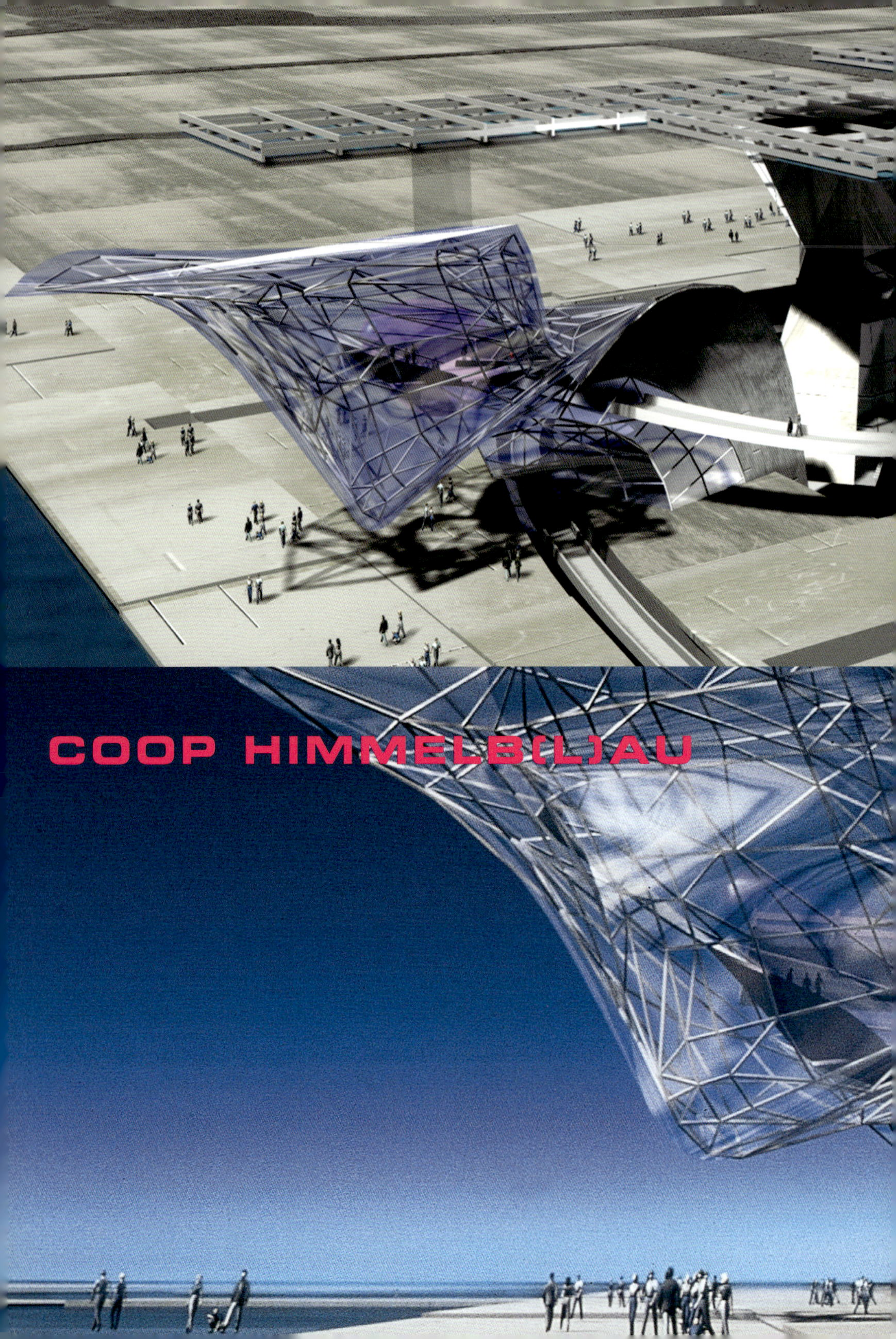
COOP HIMMELB(L)AU

FORM FOLLOWS FUN
282:283
229:230

DANIEL LIBESKIND

231+232

WILLIAM ALSOP

TRAVEL AS EXPERIENCE – NEW RAILWAY STATIONS

Railway stations have long since ceased to be sites for facilitating smooth transit; mere now they are designed to include many other uses and experiences. The railway stations of the new type are enriched with additional functions such as restaurants, cafés, conference rooms, retail areas and, recently, also theatres, museums or recreation centres.

Central Station Rotterdam The British architect **William Alsop** emerged as the winner of the first competition for a $ 2.3 million project in the centre of Rotterdam. The 20-hectare complex is composed of 310,000 m^2 of office space, 185,000 m^2 of residential space and 110,000 m^2 of retail and entertainment space. According to Alsop's spectacular design, Rotterdam's new railway stations will be transformed into a transportation terminal on three levels, integrating not only subway, regional and intercity trains, buses and streetcars, but also offering all kinds of experiences and entertainment. 👁 The railway station sits atop a sculpture reminiscent of wine goblets, with which Alsop does justice to his reputation for extravagance. Nine crystal goblets raised on pilotis accommodate a municipal museum, bookstores, cafés and theatres, thus linking the transportation terminal and the city centre.

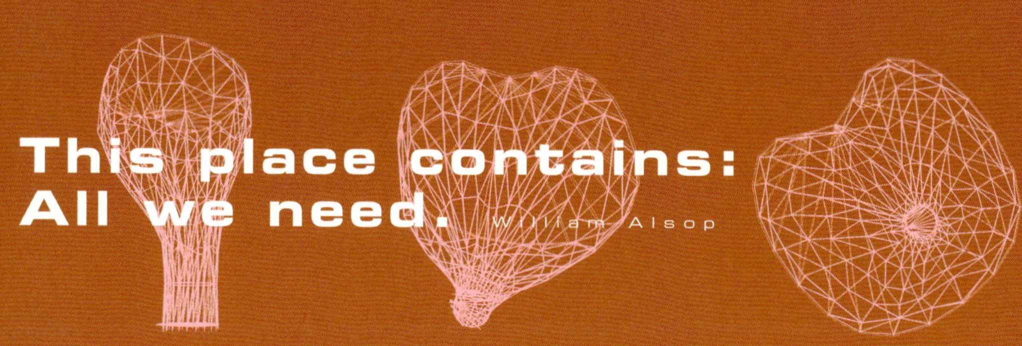

This place contains:
All we need. William Alsop

233+234+235

WILLIAM ALSOP

bioskoop

UN STUDIO

Central Station Arnheim The Dutch city of Arnheim has engaged the architectural firm **UN Studio, Ben van Berkel and Caroline Bos** from Amsterdam to realize its new main railway station. The "One Terminal" concept for all types of transportation that has been developed for the railway station is more than just an answer to the actual streams of traffic. The organization of the railway site has created an urban landscape that provides space for leisure programs such as entertainment, shopping, restaurants, and recreation. This railway station, too, is an example of the new generation of multifunctional railway terminals. Instead of the classic railway terminal with tower and clock, what is being created here is a different type of terminal and a different kind of parking garage. UN Studio is building a railway station with the goal of actually making it disappear.

UN STUDIO

CHRISTOPH INGENHOVEN

Stuttgart Railway Terminal In 1997 the architectural firm of **Ingenhoven und Partner** won the international competition for the Stuttgart railway terminal, setting new standards with their design for the station buildings of the twenty-first century. A self-supporting shell structure stretches across the subterranean tracks and platforms and is illuminated by light falling through large circular "light eyes." The load-bearing structure – flowing forms inside and out – which was developed in collaboration with **Frei Otto**, creates a continuous spatial sequence. The construction depth of the efficient load-bearing shell structure could be reduced down to one hundredth of the span width, which has drastically diminished the material use. The "zero-energy-station" designed by Christoph Ingenhoven requires no heating, cooling or mechanical ventilation. The new construction of the subterranean railway station and the fact that the platforms run underground offers the opportunity to link the city above across the castle park with the inner city project called Stuttgart 21. The transition from the designed exterior space to the underground interior space is a special experience. Four large filigree shells in glass and steel stretch across the main entrances to the station. Set back from the surrounding streets, they mark the location of the new station terminal. The access levels connect all station functions with the many service installations, which are integrated into the new structure and the heritage-protected historic building. On the surface a clearly structured station square provides access to the new urban district, with cultural facilities such as a cinema, a theatre and a museum of mobility along the edges. The project is currently in the planning stages and is to be realized by the year 2013.

241+242

CHRISTOPH INGENHOVEN

243+244

HOLIDAY FICTION

The architecture in holiday destinations has been satisfying emotional requirements for some time: a fairytale-like fantasy architecture fulfils this task by creating illusory worlds with the help of staged productions and backdrops for the purpose of recreation. As architecture critic **Ingeborg Flagge** describes in her book *Freizeitarchitektur* (*Leisure Architecture*), it is precisely not the everyday, which the holidaymakers enjoy. In architectural criticism, the debate returns again and again to the legitimacy of illusory worlds in leisure and tourism. The following examples illustrate the range of animated holiday environments.

Port Grimaud The architecture firm **Spoerry** realized a complete reconstruction of a Côte-d'Azur locale by creating an artificial lagoon city in southern France. In contrast to many other examples, the project is rigorously faithful to the original model of a lagoon city. There are no shifts in scale, nor is the result an entirely new architecture. The strategic placement of post office, church, shops and mooring docks, groups of houses, squares and bridges forms a tourist attraction that has been successfully used for decades. Historicizing facades hide the standard row housing in concrete panel construction.

Club Méditerranée Since 1950 Club Méditeranée, known simply as Club Med, has established itself as a professional holiday operator in all corners of the globe through animation with specially designed holiday architecture. All Club Med bungalow villages are based on the proto-

type of a Polynesian village. The facilities, such as restaurants, bars, supermarkets, and sports and medical facilities, as well as the bungalows themselves, are grouped around a centre consisting of a pool and a theatre. ◉ A feeling of belonging is deliberately encouraged through a casual tone in interaction. A radio program from 1991 captures the tone perfectly: "Hi, I'm Ricky. That's my artist's name. My real name is Manfred. I'm an animator at the club. I provide real entertainment. Some people also call me the Sammy Davis of the village. On Tuesdays, there's a Jeep safari. That's always exciting. Looking at lions and real aboriginals. It's great fun. Yeah, and on Wednesday we go on a pirate excursion on a real ship with headscarf and eye patch. At night, we'll have a Spanish Evening with barbecue and then we'll choose Mr. Tarzan. That's life here at the Club."

Center Parcs The Club's successful recipe of providing a trouble-free and almost clinically pure tourist experience led in 1970 to the idea of the Center Parcs, most of which are located in the Netherlands and in Belgium. Whereas the Club still seeks out original holiday destinations, installing its own world on site, Center Parcs manage without this step and utilize the latest technology to create the conditions for climate control under large domes in order to offer Balinese, Congolese, Algerian or Thai enclaves in the home country. ◉ In the Center Parc world, temperatures are always maintained at a paradisiacal 29 degrees Celsius. The ensembles consist of 400 to 600 bungalows and a wide range of restaurants and leisure programs. Each Parc has a

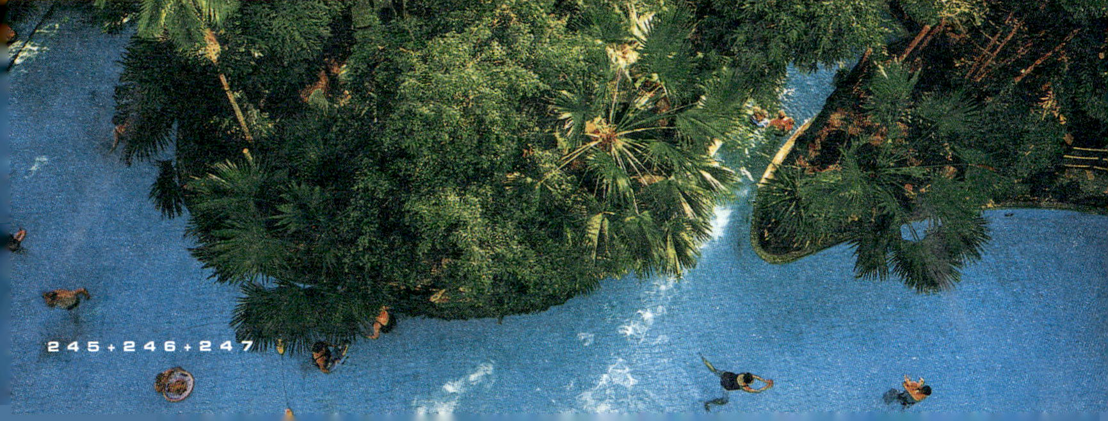

245+246+247

Parc Plaza at the centre. In addition to restaurant, bar, disco and supermarket, it also features a sports hall, several bowling alleys and a subtropical bathing paradise.

FUN POOLS AND ALLROUNDER LEISURE CENTRES

The classic pool has long since become outdated. Since 1971 facilities are built around the world with names such as leisure pool and fun pool or name creations that suggest vacation associations, such as Alpamare, Tropamare, Aquarena or Solemar, thereby indicating a change in the indoor pool type. Extended opening hours, adapted to the increase in leisure time, and bathing fun in all imaginable variations are the characteristics of this change. Since these facilities tend to target a wider market, they also require a new planning strategy. More parking spaces, larger entrance areas, and expanded and multifunctional pool areas, as well as lounge areas near the pools, are all essential components of the concept. ◉ The conventional rectangular pool is often transformed into an imaginatively designed bathing landscape, and the building becomes an experiential place for a new cult of the body, defined first and foremost by the need for fun and diversion. But the atmosphere of fun and adventure is also promoted by a plethora of additional attractions in these sites. A wide variety of water plays are constantly in operation: jet streams, water throwers, spray nozzles, water slides, wild water streams, gurgling springs and artificial waves. Saunas with matching sauna landscapes, as well as solariums complete with meadows for sunbathing are also part of the inventory. People tend to spend more time here, which increases the need for communication that is served by the provision of bistros, restaurants and poolside bars. A multi-functional screen is frequently incorporated into the plan for additional entertainment programs. ◉ The key difference from the user's experience in a classic indoor pool lies in the feeling of spending a true vacation day. The transparent and filigree construction of vast roofs with unobstructed light falling into the space from the outside creates a completely new ambience in this pool type. Visitors often have the illusion of being under the open sky.

Itäkeskuksen Uimahalli The pool in Itäkeskuksen, a neighbourhood in Helsinki, was realized by the architect **Hyvämüki-Karthunen-Parkkinen** from 1991–1993. It features numerous pools of differing sizes and shapes, saunas and solariums, a shop and a cafeteria which is reminiscent of a ship's bridge. The architecture cites marine props at every turn: landing stages, lookouts, and raised flags. The design of the vault creates the illusion of a natural rock formation; at the same time, it also resembles an animated cloud formation, suggesting the open sky.

Ocean Dome With an artificial beach beneath the largest glass dome in the world, designed by the architect **Yoshinobu Ashiwara**, Japan launched the holiday vision of the next millennium on Kyushu, the country's third largest island, in 1999. With day pass in hand, visitors ride through the portal on an escalator. Inside the dome, they are transported into a Caribbean summer with a temperature of precisely 30 degrees Celsius, where tropical birdsong is broadcast from loudspeakers. During the night shows, Seagaia's engineers transform the miniature sea into a stage for film projections, preceded by an atmospherically staged sunset. The name Seagaia is a combination of "sea" and "gaia" (from the Greek for earth). A similar project in Germany may soon offer visitors an opportunity to go island-hopping within a contained area: In Grevenbroich, near Düsseldorf, the most beautiful lagoons of the world are to be reconstructed next to a hotel complex and a large shopping centre: sections of the Copacabana, the Great Barrier Reef, Honolulu beaches and much more. The plans, by the architects **Rhode, Kellermann, Wawrowsky**, have already been completed. Now it is a matter of finding investors.

YOSHINOBU ASHIWARA

248+249

8,000 Cubic Metres

La Laport Ski Dome SSAWS The counterpart of the artificial summer paradise, the Ski Dome of the Kajima Corporation offers Japanese the opportunity to enjoy winter sports year round in Chiba, a district in the urban conglomeration of Tokyo. The roofed, 80-m-long and 70-m-wide ski slope provides an environment that is completely independent of the real temperatures outside. The indoor temperature in the Ski Dome is kept at a constant 5 degrees Celsius. The acronym SSAWS is comprised of the initials of the four seasons – spring, summer, autumn, and winter – and snow!

# of White Splendour

Allrounder Winterworld Neuss The Tokyo site was followed by others in the Netherlands, in The Hague (1996) and Amsterdam (1999): all are profitable operations. And in what German locations is snow guaranteed? Neuss and Bottrop! What these sites have in common is a frost-inspired structural transformation, where former garbage heaps and slag heaps are developed for alpine fun. Snow machines generate 8,000 cubic metres of the glorious white stuff in no time at all, creating a 40-cm layer of snow on the artificial moguls, which are steep enough to challenge even an expert skier. The new site designed by the architect **Burkhard Schramm** in Neuss is especially notable. With a length of 800 m, a width of 60 m, a maximum incline of 28 percent, an elevation of 50 m, two tow lifts and four chair lifts, the silver colossus looms over the flat landscape on the Lower Rhine.

250+251+252+253

RICHARD ROGERS RENZO PIANO

EDUTAINMENT

There is hardly a museum or a cultural centre that does not take the aspect of entertainment into account. The latest generation of museums offer novel experiential spaces and contemporary forms. The museum, which is also understood as an instrument of communication and entertainment, is no longer simply a place for contemplating art, but a setting for a multitude of additional, even interactive uses, in keeping with its new functions and the political and cultural demands for communicating knowledge in an entertaining fashion.

Centre Pompidou The transformation of the classic museum into a public meeting place also dedicated to spectacular events began with the Centre Pompidou in Paris in 1977. Conceived

by the architects **Richard Rogers and Renzo Piano**, it is less a cultural centre than an experiential centre with information and entertainment. The flexible container of the dynamic communication machine accommodates exhibition spaces for modern art, a library, a design centre, a roof terrace restaurant and a cinema. The square surrounding the museum replaces the agora of antiquity: fire-eaters and street musicians enliven the area with spectacular performances. Movement and fun play an essential role.

Parc de la Villette Where former French president de Gaulle once planned to erect the world's largest and most modern abattoir in Paris, the Parc de la Villette today overwhelms hordes of visitors with a vast program of art and technology, science and music, architecture

and horticulture. The decision to transform La Villette into a cultural complex was taken in 1982. An architecture competition was launched for a national museum of science, technology and industry, as well as an adjacent park. The architect **Bernhard Tschumi** emerged as the winner of the competition and realized the futuristic cultural complex in 1998. An extensive network of gardens, axially arranged galleries and winding paths was created on a 500,000 m² site. The conspicuous red cubes, pre-fabricated pavilions, housing cinemas, restaurants, an information centre, a playhouse, studios and much more, serve as orientation markers. They are called follies, in the manner of the eighteenth-century pleasure pavilions. The architect **Adrien Fainsilber** is to develop the concept for the museum and the cinema. He will not build a museum in the classic sense, but a Cité Technique, a forum with open and transparent halls. Visitors are encouraged to participate interactively at various computer terminals and projection walls. They are also given opportunities to experiment, to ask questions and to use programs. The central atrium of the Cité is surrounded by six exhibition levels. The exhibition themes range from submarine to space shuttle. The adjacent structure is the unmistakable Géode, a futuristic metal sphere with a reflective external skin, which houses an Omnimax theatre. The buildings of the Cité de la Musique, conceived by Christian de Portzamparc as a small music city, complete the Villette complex. The ensemble on the southwestern edge of the park, opened for occupancy in

1990, is home to the National Conservatory of Music and Dance, accommodating classrooms and practice rooms, concert halls, and a media and music library, as well as apartments for guests and teachers. ◉ La Villette has become an important public park in Paris. In the daytime, school classes pass through the park, while evening events contribute to the cultural life of the city.

Guggenheim Museum Bilbao The Guggenheim Museum by **Frank O. Gehry** in Bilbao, Spain, illustrates how museum architecture functions as a tourist attraction: visitors to the building inaugurated in 1997 are drawn to it first and foremost because of the spectacular architecture, with the exhibits playing only a secondary role. Modern architecture gained a popular image through this project: the more outrageous and dramatic its presence, the more successful is the reception on the part of the public. ◉ The Guggenheim Museum in Bilbao is located on a site at the mouth of the Nervión River. The museum building is one of several major projects undertaken by the government of the Basque region, which suffered greatly as a result of the crisis in the shipping industry. Industrial sites lie fallow, districts fall into disrepair, and old warehouses stand vacant. The goal of the museum, and a series of other buildings, is to breathe new life into this urban enclave. ◉ The design concept consists of a series of connected building sections arranged around a large atrium. A cantilevered external stairway leads directly to the main entrance. The exhibition areas are accessed via a variety of bridges, several panorama lifts

256-259

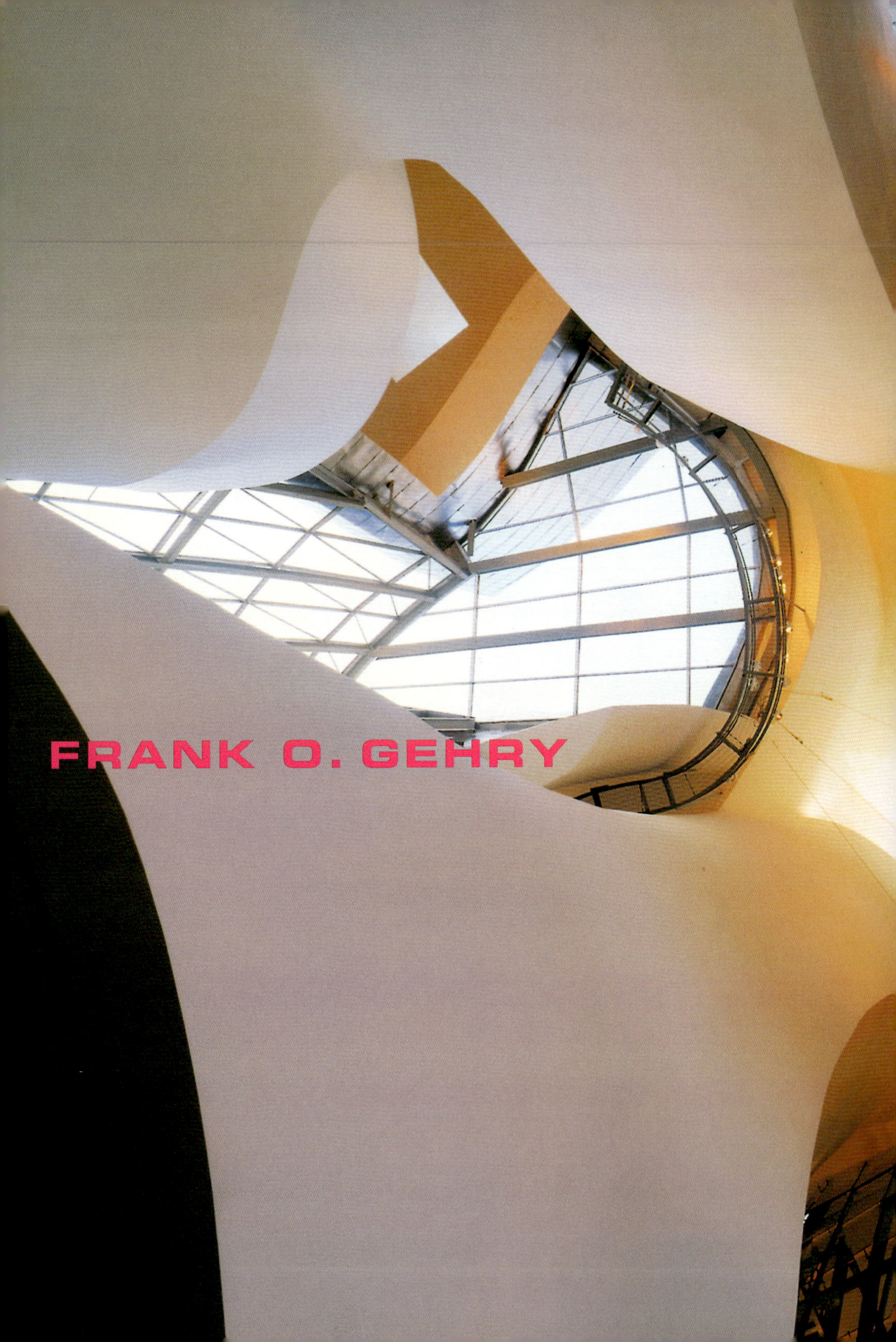
FRANK O. GEHRY

and staircase towers. Different materials, such as stone, steel, glass and titanium, which define the building, communicate a sense of variety and vitality. There is no doubt that Gehry's museum in Bilbao generates powerful aesthetic and spatial impressions in the opinion of **Javier Mozas**. In *Bauwelt* issue 13/1997, he writes: "The form of the museum creates the impression of something never seen before, of a dream world made concrete, of an encounter with a living organism."

Futuroscope and Cinemax Futuristic buildings and monuments are popular attractions for thousands of visitors. In 1990, rural France joined in by creating a futuristic project for the twenty-first century in Poitiers. This blend of science-fiction park, engineering academy and technology centre symbolizes the linkages between leisure, education, research, training and further education, as well as production and services. In accordance with the principle of division by theme, the Cinemax and the various pavilions constitute the leisure area of the park. The themes are communication, earth, water, health and time. The competition brief stipulates that the architecture should depict the world of tomorrow: spectacular, highly informative, and rigorously futuristic. **Denis Laming** is the architect, who realized the Futuroscope and the Cinemax. His temple of the future constitutes the centre of the ensemble in an architecture that combines two simple shapes: prism and sphere. Next to the Futuroscope, the complex is defined by the silhouette of an oversized mountain crystal.

DENIS LAMING

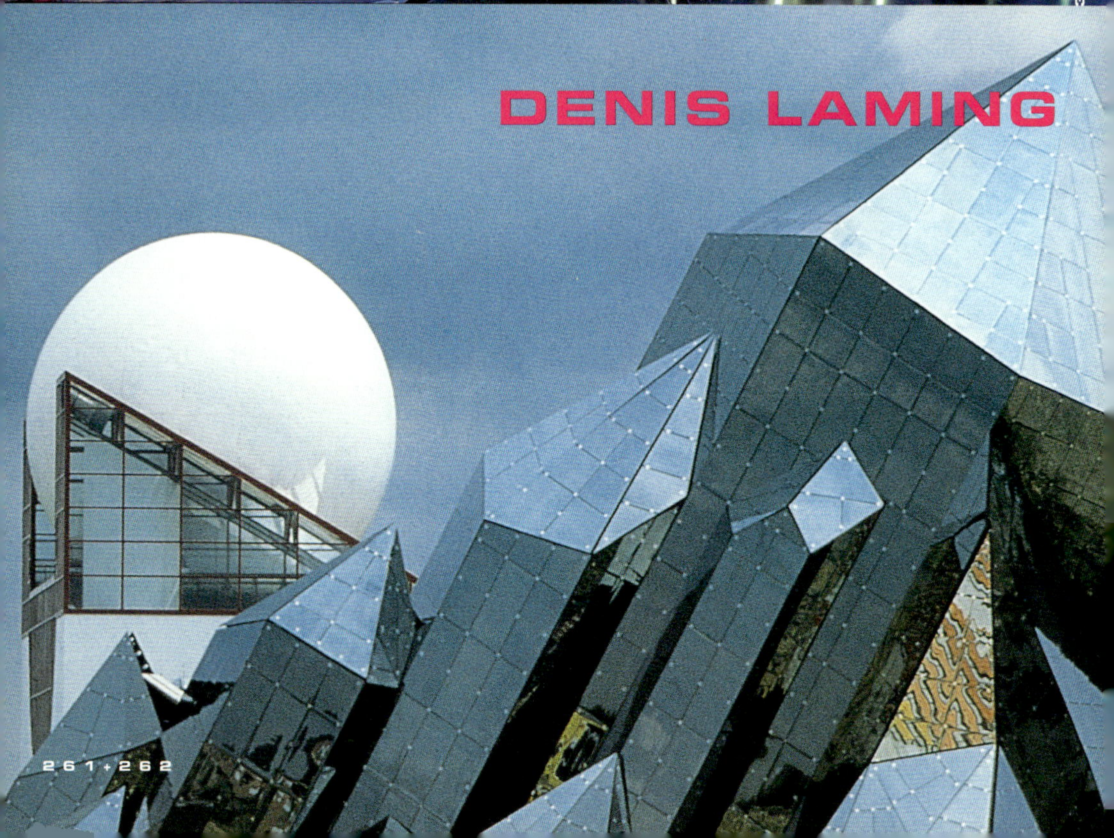

261+262

ITSUKO HASEGAWA

Cultural Centre Shonandai The Shonandai Cultural Centre in Tokyo, Fujisawa Kanagawa Prefecture, was inaugurated in 1991. The area surrounding two spherical buildings is structured with aluminium roofs staggered according to size and tree-like sculptures. The spheres accommodate a children's museum, workshops, galleries and several theatres. These facilities are grouped around a central park like a small urban community. The aim of the architecture, designed by Japanese architect **Itsuko Hasegawa**, is to evoke a kind of second nature and draws upon narrative architectonic elements to do so. The architect animates the complex with a wide range of themes in the hope of creating a futuristic cosmic environment. An earth sphere, a geodesic dome, a moon sphere, and a model of the universe serve as her sources of inspiration. In Hasegawa's own words, one of the principal themes of this project is to create a world of emotions and a landscape filled with new natural forms.

I would like to create a world of emotions and a landscape filled with new natural forms.

ITSUKO HASEGAWA

263+264

National Centre for Popular Music **Doug Branson and Nigel Coates** conceived an unconventional museum for the city of Sheffield. The National Centre for Popular Music, opened in 1999, offers the first interactive attraction in the world dedicated to music, according to the city's official publicity. In addition to the Meadowhall shopping complex at the edge of Sheffield, an artificial ski slope and a new cultural industry district in the city's core, the National Centre for Popular Music offers yet another site for fun, entertainment and information. The architects designed four bulbous pavilions, deviating slightly from the horizontal plane, reminiscent of drums, tank lids or the so-called bumpers of pinball machines. In the interior, the history of popular music is visually and acoustically communicated through videos and songs.

Automobile City Wolfsburg In 2000, Munich-based **Henn Architects and Engineers** realized the master plan of an urban concept centred on the theme of the automobile on a 250,000 m² site immediately adjacent to the Volkswagen headquarters in Wolfsburg. The goal was to achieve a link between this area and downtown Wolfsburg through a fluid transition between the various public areas of commerce, culture and communication. An automobile museum has been designed as a two-part experiential building; pavilions exhibit products manufactured by VW and its partners. The pavilions were designed and realized by different architects. Alfredo Arribas from Barcelona designed the Seat pavilion, Bellprat Associates from Winterthur the Lamborghini pavilion, and Furneaux Stewart from London together with Berlin-based Grüntuch Ernst the VW pavilion. The firm Confino from Lussan designed the Audi pavilion, while KSS Architects and Furneaux Stewart, both from London, realized the Bentley pavilion. Jack Rouse Associates, Cincinnati, designed the automobile museum Zeithaus. Tong Chi Associates developed the plans for the KonzernForum (corporate forum) and the piazza, and the Prague

DOUG BRANSON NIGEL COATES

HENN ARCHITECTS AND ENGINEERS

firm Sipek was commissioned to design and build the Škoda pavilion. The comprehensive plan offers a wide-ranging program: a client centre, a corporate forum, a conference centre, glazed stacking towers to showcase VW models, a luxury hotel – all of this set into the organic environment of a Japanese garden landscape. A cableway, a so-called people mover, connects the complex with downtown in one direction, and with Castle Wolfsburg, an art museum and a cultural centre in the other direction. Mobility and its significance for the future of humankind is the theme of the infotainment area. The theme is presented, among other things, by means of 3-D animation projected onto textile facades. The car city is open to the public 24/7: show towers, exhibitions, restaurant, café and cinema invite visitors to enjoy a well-rounded experience.

267+268+269+270+271

COOP HIMMELB(L)AU

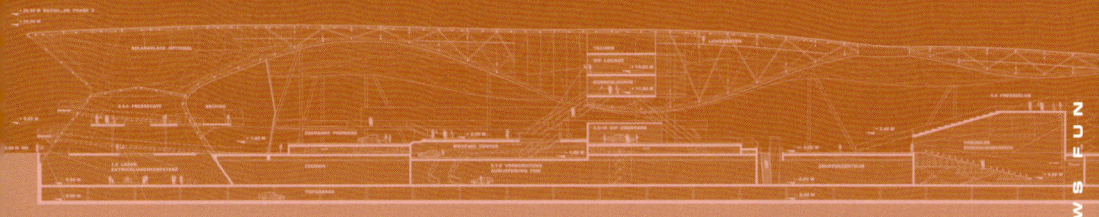

BMW Experience and Delivery Centre The BMW Delivery Centre in Munich seems to be the car manufacturer's response to Volkswagen's car city. The Viennese architecture firm **Coop Himmelb(l)au** won the design competition in July 2001. The new centre is being constructed in the immediate vicinity of the Olympic park, the BMW Group corporate headquarters and the BMW plant in Munich. Conceived as a central place of communication and interaction for clients and the general public, the BMW board explains: "The experience and delivery centre on a roughly 25,000 m² site is intended to not only reflect BMW's identity but to promote a lasting impression. At the same time, it will embody the lifestyle and leisure world of the Bavarian metropolis." The BMW Group will invest more than €100 million in the new centre. 👁 There are two underground levels and three above-ground storeys. The building length is roughly 180 m, the maximum width 125 m. The centre is scheduled to open at the end of 2004. 👁 The entire complex is arranged according to the principle of theme worlds. The program ranges from service to interactive technology, entertainment and lifestyle, and also includes dining and wining in a sophisticated ambience. A forum for a wide variety of events will be another highlight of the experience and delivery centre. Up to 600 spectators can gather to take in artistic as well as technological presentations.

COOP HIMMELB(L)AU

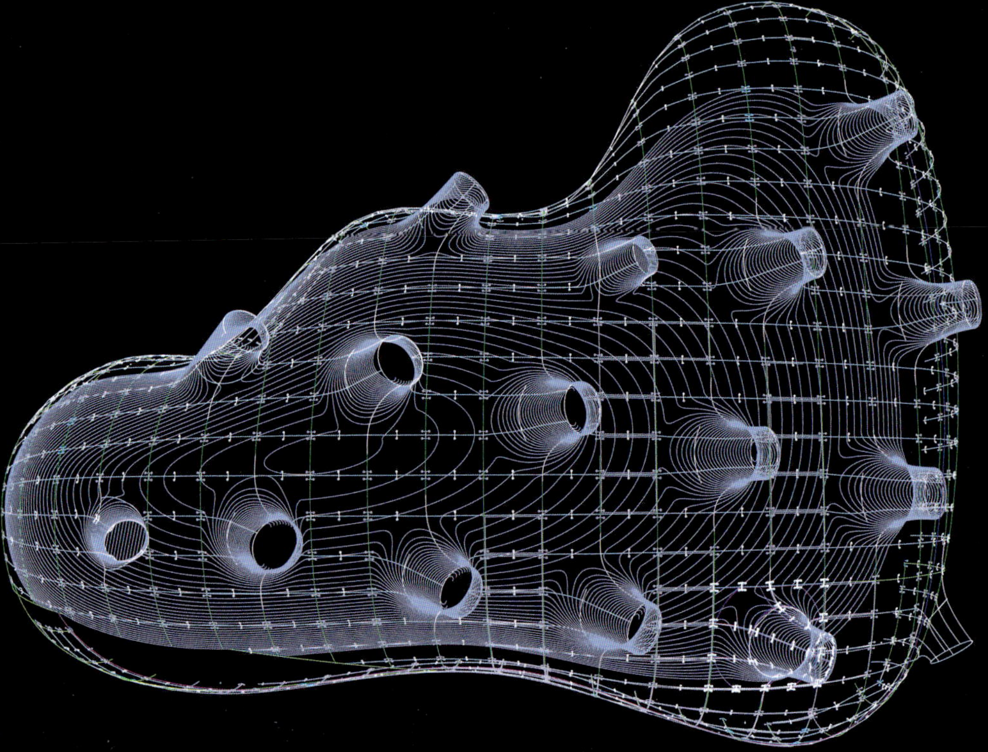

PETER COOK
COLIN FOURNIER

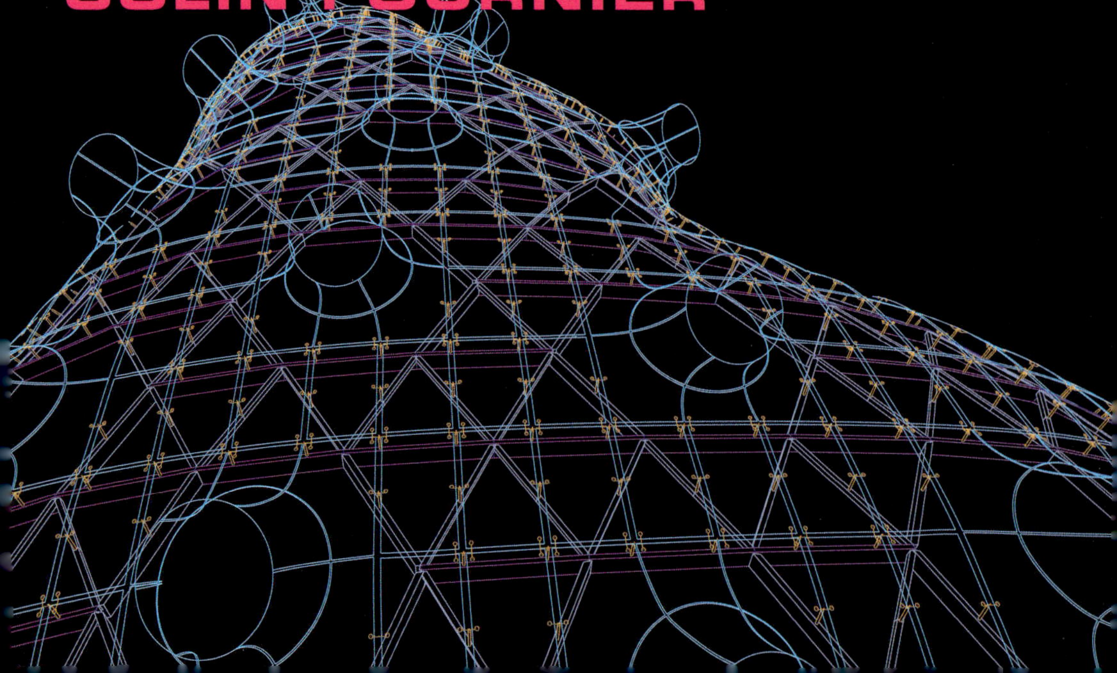

Kunsthaus Graz **Peter Cook and Partners** won the international competition for the Kunsthaus Graz, Austria, in April 2000. The project is conceived as an organically shaped structure with two exhibition levels. The entire structure is raised on a few columns. Visitors to the museum glide through the glazed ground floor on an inclined electronic travelling ramp (PIN) to the exhibition areas on the upper levels, which are enveloped in the biomorphic, double-curved outer skin. Here too the architecture, which has long since outshone the exhibits, is exotic, unusual and playful. Like a journey of discovery, the architecture has much to offer. Visitors to the museum can expect to be surprised, promises architect Peter Cook. "Strange things appear and disappear within this skin ... At night, these apparitions – or perhaps they are bait? – will be even more exotic in appearance."

A friendly alien

276+277+278

ZAHA HADID

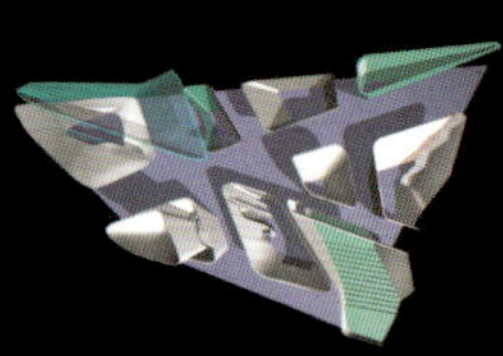

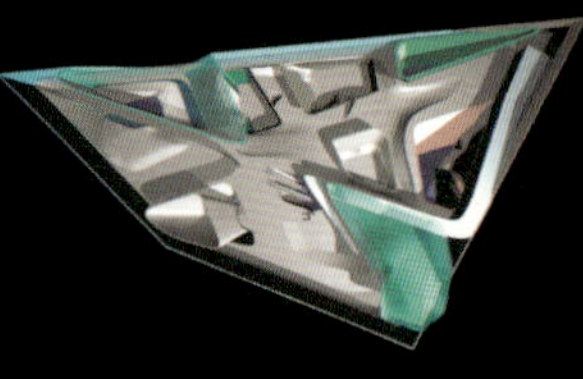

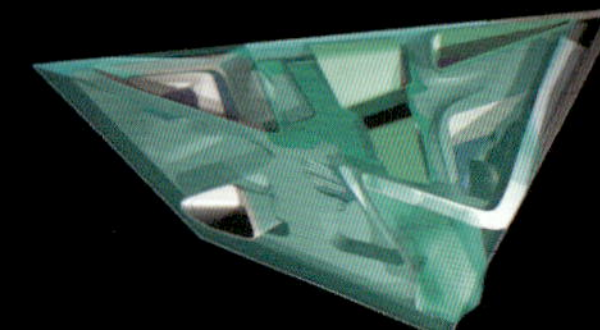

Science Centre Wolfsburg Wolfsburg is the recipient of another highly unusual building, designed by the architect **Zaha Hadid**. A floating disk – an avant-garde structure – an extraterrestrial spaceship. Journals and the daily press enter into a race of superlatives in describing this building project, which is conceived to communicate new ways of understanding the natural sciences and technology. The architecture of the science centre will be a key element in awakening visitors' curiosity and extending an invitation to embark on a journey of discovery. The structure operates without conventional access systems and offers new spatial experiences, similar to those created by Frank O. Gehry. With a clear height of 6.5 m, Zaha Hadid creates an unfettered space and utilizes open structures to provide many diverse sightlines. With 250 experimentation and interactive stations, the centre has little in common with conventional museums of technology displaying the items in the collections.

279+280+281

SUCCESS OF EXCESS – LAS VEGAS

Las Vegas is the world's capital of animation. Las Vegas is everything at once: a city, an amusement park, a vacation paradise, and a gigantic urban entertainment centre. ◉ It all began with the first casinos established on Fremont Street toward the end of the nineteenth century, followed in subsequent years by the gradual development of the Las Vegas Boulevard – better known as "The Strip." While El Rancho and The Last Frontier are still simple gaming saloons with a matching rusticated architecture in the western style, the Casino Flamingo marked the dawn of a new era. Bugsy Siegel, the owner of the Flamingo, quickly realized that lasting success required more than decks of cards and a few tables for the players. Architecture and design imitate the elegant hotels in Miami, like the Desert Inn. ◉ Las Vegas is an entirely artificial city, tailored to entertain the masses. The gambler's paradise of yesteryear has evolved into a vacation paradise. Today, the Strip is a city and the masses are now also drawn there because of the architecture. Las Vegas is booming. Aside from the theme architecture, lighting takes centre stage: as dusk falls, the city is transformed through gaudy bright colours. Hundreds of neon and lighting designers, show designers and engineers toil to invent new and ever more elaborate light shows. ◉ As in an amusement park, the architecture is defined by themes. Scaled-down versions of New York's famous landmarks – the skyline of Manhattan, Brooklyn Bridge, the Statue of Liberty and Central Park – create a miniature metropolis. The Casino Treasure Island dazzles with spectacular theatrical presentations: guests are treated to the awe-inspiring spectacle of the sinking of a frigate. The Hotel Luxor conjures up an image of Egypt in the days of Tutankhamen. Excalibur adopts freely interpreted elements of the Middle Ages. The Venetian, finally, offers a replica of Venice complete with Grand Canal and Italian singers. The Strip is a bewildering mix of different

5:10
BOARDWALK
PLAY
COOL

The illusory world is but a diversion from the world in which we live, or is it an alternative world? Everything we see, the entire architecture, is but an illusion.

FRITZ ELLER

283+284

themes, scales and building types, albeit without a comprehensive concept. ◎ The import of culture is by no means restricted to facades; the restaurant trade and the supporting program also convey the European way of life to the guests. Recently, the Guggenheim corporation has even erected a museum with 4,000 m^2 of exhibition space on the parking lot of the Venetian: a steel and concrete container designed by **OMA/Rem Koolhaas**. ◎ Las Vegas, hitherto the Mecca of forgeries, aspires to a new level of attractiveness by presenting original masterpieces – by introducing an element that had been lacking thus far: authenticity. ◎ Many writers and philosophers are predominantly critical in their commentaries on animation phenomena like Disneyland or Las Vegas. They reject the artificiality, the imitation. In *Travels in Hyperreality* (1987), the Italian prominent author **Umberto Eco** writes under the heading "The City of Robots": "In the United States, on the contrary, as everyone knows, there exist amusement cities. Las Vegas is one example; it is focused on gambling and entertainment, its architecture is totally artificial, and it has been studied by Robert Venturi as a completely new phenomenon in city planning, a 'message' city, entirely made up of signs, not a city like the others, which communicate in order to function, but rather a city that functions in order to communicate." ◎ The dissemination of entertainment and amusement in the American style coincided with the development of so-called adventure or fantasy hotels, which attract their clientele with a multitude of entertainment programs that go far beyond the purely visual impression. These hotels, developed with high capital investment, are often indiscriminate in the opulence of the historic or folkloristic architectural styles they cite. Dolphins standing on their heads as fountain décor, Indian tombs, fire-spewing volcanoes in the forecourt – they are all part of the encyclopaedia of carefree taste. ◎ Kitsch architecture, writes the architectural historian

Heinrich Klotz, "is the clinical symptom of architecture that ignores the requirements for an environment rich in experiences and exposes the signal effect of subjective self-representation as pointless, superfluous, a poor compromise and morally suspect. A city cleansed of all antics, where the advertising sign dominates as the only symbol that is tolerated, pushes its inhabitants into the suburban paradises, where the well-heeled build homes for garden gnomes, for princes and princesses, for hunters in green tunics, for James Bond, for Bavarian, Old English and Asturian landed gentry, for Hansel and Gretel, for Bonnie and Clyde, for streamline minds and wrought-iron antiquarians. And when even this sphere fails to satisfy the expressive urge, vacation villages take in the sick, who refresh themselves in smart paradises and homeland idylls. An entire iconography of ersatz architecture has evolved, whose wealth of formulae, metaphors and citations is justified in the guise of taking revenge against the dogma of the modern architectonic hygiene."

"May I be your slave?"

Entertainment hotels came into fashion in the early 1950s. Pop stars like Frank Sinatra, Sammy Davis jr., Harry Belafonte and many others were booked for permanent engagements. Casinos and hotels like The Sands, The Dunes, and The Stardust became magnets for the masses. The Stardust tried to outdo all others with the Lido de Paris show imported from Paris. Recreating a Parisian street scene, the show featured fireworks under the Eiffel Tower and loads of show-girls. **Jay Sarno** had the Caesar's Palace built in the Roman style in 1966. Every costume, every detail and the hotel logo are „done up" in the Roman style. At Circus Circus, conversely, wild animals, fire-eaters, acrobats and clowns take centre stage. 👁 The small downtown hotels of the 1950s have given way to the large theme hotels; only mega-enterprises can keep up with the pace. The thematic variety expands into the outdoor space and turns three-dimensional. Venturi refers to Las Vegas as a disneyfied boulevard. 👁 The most recent generation of theme hotels such as Treasure Island, Manhattan, Luxor, Paris, Bellagio, Tropicana and the Venetian enable the visitor to stroll from one world into another. Each hotel offers a unique spectacle. A giant sphinx stands guard in front of the Luxor complex. The Tropicana attracts visitors with free interpretations of the massive, stone-carved statues of heads on the Easter Islands. Guests in the Bellagio enjoy a view of Lake Como, although it is only 50 cm deep here. The most recent and most spectacular example is the Venetian with reconstructions of St. Mark's Square, the Campanile and the Doge's Palace on a scale of 1:1.

HAPPY ENDIN

Make the Peop
Feel Good

G
08
le

Today, especially, the architect has three tasks: I, to build ...; II, to create the new cultural image ...; and III, to stimulate a desire for building ... This implies that totally new modes of presenting projects have to be devised, not only the ground plans which make architecture seem a purely technical matter ...

BRUNO TAUT

... but we also want *magic*.
We want our visitors to feel
that they have passed through
a mirror, that they have left
their own worlds and
Heaven's

Gate

entered a new one, different yet strangely familiar, where things are not done as in other parts of the inhabited planet, but as if in a rare dream.

JULIAN BARNES

... I have in mind the tomorrow and the after-tomorrow when happy people will live with "other cathedrals" and "churches," with "other schools" and "new sources of energy" ...

WENZEL A. HABLIK

For one had never stopped hoping that one day the heavenly Baroque portal really would open. HEINRICH KLOTZ

Imagination

What in all the world does a child have to be scared of? The old Persians, your people, called their walls *daeza*. *Pairi* meant anything that surrounds.
See? *Pairi daeza*. You have a wall running all the way around you. That, my little Tai-Jan, is the source of Paradise. RICHARD POWERS

L O

O

K

A new world with new symbol

and formulae

FRITZ ELLER

SOURCES

001 Mickey Mouse. ©The Walt Disney CompanyPhoto 002+003 View of the Earth from the moon. Photo: NASA 004 Union Rave. Photo: Andreas Gursky 005 Axial view of the Lion's Court in the Alhambra at Granada. Spain, 14th century. Photo: Henri Stierlin 006 Transformation from: Union Rave and Vivian, 1977. Photo: Joel Meyerowitz 007 Rush Hour in Wall Street. Photo: R. Stack 008 Francisco Asensio Cerver, Theme and Amusement Paks 009 Tokyo 98. Photo: Beat Streuli 010 Sydney 98. Photo: Beat Streuli 011 Labourer. Photo: August Sander, The Photographic Collection/SK Cultural Foundation – August Sander Archives, Cologne 012 Mass motorization. Photo courtesy of: IFA-Bilderteam 013 Joyopolis. Las Vegas. Street facade. Photo: Prof. Volker Martin 014 42nd Street 1964. Richard Lindner. ©VG Bild-Kunst, Bonn 2001 015 Project. Architects Wimberly, Allison, Tong & Goo 016 Underwater-Sea-Hotel. Architects Wimberly, Allison, Tong & Goo 017 Digital composition by John Lund. Photo: Tony Stone Images 018 British self portrait. Millennium Dome, 1999. Architect: Richard Rogers. Photo: Lorenzo Apicella 019 Body Zone. Millennium Dome. London 2000. Architects: Doug Branson and Nigel Coates. Photo: Ralph Richter 020 Millennium Dome. London 2000. Architects: Doug Branson and Nigel Coates. Photo: Christian Richters 021 Roll. Photo: Frei Otto 022 Bone interior. Photo: Frei Otto 023 Bone structure of the beak of a black stork. Photo: Frei Otto 024 Sea urchin shell. Photo: Frei Otto 025 Transformation from: Barbie dolls. ©2001 Mattel, Inc. All rights reserved + Meteorite Essen. Kaleidoscope sphere. Photo: Ralph Richter 026 Entrance to Millennium Dome. London. Architect: Richard Rogers. Photo: Ralph Richter 027 Meteorite Essen. Kaleidoscope sphere. Photo: Ralph Richter 028 Model seen from above. Architects: Foster and Partners. Photo: Foster and Partners 029 Master plan. Architects: Foster and Partners. Photo: Foster and Partners 030 Universum-Science Centre Bremen. Architect: Thomas Klumpp. Photo: Samuel Zuder 031+033+034 Guggenheim Virtual Museum. Architects: Asymptote: Lise Anne Couture, Hani Rashid. Photo: Asymptote 032 Transformation from: Manimal 1998. Daniel Lee + exhibition catalogue *Europäische Phantasien*. Montage after Henri Rousseau. Design: Prof. Günther Kieser 035 Cybercouture 2000. ©Pia Myrvold and cybercouture.com 036 Exhibition catalogue *Europäische Phantasien*. Montage after Henri Rousseau. Design: Günther Kieser 037 Manimal 1998. Daniel Lee 038 Parascape. Architects: Oosterhuis Associates. Rotterdam 039 The Legible City. Jeffrey Shaw 040 Transformation from: Michelangelo. *The Creation of Adam*. Detail of ceiling fresco in the Sistine Chapel. Rome 1508–1512 + Space Glove reproduced from: Bernd Willim, Designer im Bereich Animation und Cyberspace. Berlin 1992. Bernd Willim (ed.) 041 Transformation from: Taj Mahal. Detail. Photo: Ralph Richter + golden statue of Buddha. Photo courtesy of: Tony Stone Images 042 Transformation from: *The new city, the New Jerusalem*. Woodcut, 16th century, reproduced from: Badde, Paul: *Die himmlische Stadt*. Munich 1999 + golden statue of Buddha. Photo: Tony Stone 043 Adam and Eve. Jasmin Joseph. Haiti 1967. ©Davenport Museum of Art 044 *The Expulsion of Adam and Eve from Paradise*. Tommaso Masaccio (1401–28). Brancacci Chapel of the Carmelite Church in Florence (Sta Maria del Carmine). Italy ©The Bridgeman Art Library 045 Golden statue of Buddha. Photo courtesy of: Tony Stone Images 046 *The new city, the New Jerusalem*. Woodcut, 16th century, reproduced from: Badde, Paul: *Die himmlische Stadt*. Munich 1999 047 Wells Cathedral. View of ceiling vault. Photo: Florian Monheim 048 *Two Angels Building the Heavenly Jerusalem*. Schwarzrheindorf circa 1170. Photo: Prof. Rolf Sachsse 049 Sah mosque. Isfahan. Iran 1612– 1630. Photo: Kurt-Michael Westermann 050 Veiled Islamic woman. Photo courtesy of: Tony Stone Images 051 General view of the Lion's Court in the Alhambra at Granada. Spain, 14th century. Photo: Henri Stierlin 052 Taj Mahal at dawn. Agra. India 1631–1653. Photo: Ralph Richter 053 Hindu deity. Photo courtesy of: Tony Stone Images 054 Kate Moss in: *Sacred Figures*. Olga Tobreluts. Photo: Olga Tobreluts 055 Praying child. Postcard 056 Bettina Rheims/Serge Bramly *"Crucifixion I"* reproduced from: *I.N.R.I.* ©Bettina Rheims/Serge Bramly, Kehayoff Verlag, Munich 1998 057 Michael Schirner, *Salvation*, 1999, sound installation, exhibition "Heaven," Düsseldorfer Kunsthalle 058 Walt Disney Studios Park. ©The Walt Disney Company 059 Transformation from: Walt Disney Studio Park Paris + Mickey Mouse. ©The Walt Disney Company 060 Mickey Mouse as the sorcerer's apprentice in the animated feature film "Fantasia." ©The Walt Disney Company 061 Cinderella Castle. Disneyland Resort. Paris. ©The Walt Disney Company 062 Neuschwanstein Castle. Summer residence of Ludwig II of Bavaria 063 Entrance to Videopolis. Disneyland Resort. Paris. ©The Walt Disney Company 064 Space Mountain. Disneyland Resort. Paris ©The Walt Disney Company 065 Mark-Twain steamboat. Disneyland Resort. Paris. ©The Walt Disney Company 066 Railroad. Disneyland Resort. Paris. ©The Walt Disney Company 067 „It's a small world." Facade detail. Disneyland Resort. Paris. ©The Walt Disney Company 068 Disneyland Hotel. Architects: Wimberly, Allison, Tong & Goo. ©The Walt Disney Company 069 Hotel Magic Kingdom. Architects: Wimberly, Allison, Tong & Goo. ©The Walt Disney Company 070 Disney Village. Disneyland Resort. Paris. Architect: Frank O. Gehry. ©The Walt Disney Company 071 Disney Village. Disneyland Resort. Paris. Architect: Frank O.Gehry. ©The Walt Disney Company 072 Disney Village. Disneyland Resort. Paris. Architect: Frank O. Gehry. ©The Walt Disney Company 073 Catastrophe scenarios in production courtyard. Walt Disney Studio Parks. Paris. ©The Walt Disney Company 074 *Pollice verso* ("Thumbs down"). Jean-Léon Gérôme 1872. Phoenix Art Museum 075 Japanese glass industry pavilion. World's fair Osaka 1970. Architect: Ohbayashi-Gumi Ltd. 076 *Pollice verso* ("Thumbs down"). Jean-Léon Gérôme 1872. Phoenix Art Museum 077 Colosseum. Rome. Ground plan and section. 078 Colosseum. Rome. Italy. 1st century AD. 079 Circus Maximus. Rome. 2nd century AD. Photo: Eberhard Thiem, LOTOS-FILM, Kaufbeuren 080 Chariot race. Ullstein Bild 081 Baths of Caracalla. View of interior. Ullstein Bild 082 Reconstruction of the Baths of Caracalla from a bird's eye perspective, by Rauscher, 1894 083 Baths of Caracalla. Ground plan 084 Quacks at Medieval fair. Ullstein-Bild 085 Tournament. Medieval amusements. Courtesy of: AKG Images 086 View of the Grotto of Venus at Castle Linderhof in green light. Photo: Bavarian Administration of State Castles, Parks and Lakes 087 Versailles. Master plan by André Le Nôtre, 1710. Photo: Jeannie Baubion-Mackler 088 Highly aesthetic domestication of the wilderness. Photo: Jeannie Baubion-Mackler 089 Pergola-like bridge with "bull's eyes.". Villa Garzoni. Photo: Martin Claßen 090 Villa d'Este. Tivoli near Rome. Photo: Martin Claßen 091 Fountain of Rome. Villa d'Este. Photo: May Woods 092 Elephant, throwing a legionary. Park Bomarzo. Middle of 16th century. Photo: Martin Claßen 093 Statue of elephant next to the Café Moulin Rouge in the gardens of the Moulin Rouge. Photo: Uwe Fichtner and Rudolf Michna 094 Fountain in the park of Castle Herrenhausen. Photo: Martin Claßen 095 Gothic-Chinese arcade in Vauxhall circa 1750. Photo: Prof. Stefan Koppelkamm 096 Itinerant entertainers, harpists and barrel organ players in the Brigittenau park of Vienna. Prater. Photo: Uwe Fichtner and Rudolf Michna 097 Ferris wheel. Prater, Vienna. Austria circa 1938. Photo: Uwe Fichtner and Rudolf Michna 098 Concert hall in the Tivoli, 1902. Architect: Arne Petersen.

Photo: Prof. Stefan Koppelkamm 099 Panorama rotunda. Architect: Jacob Ignaz Hittorff. Photo: Rheinisches Bildarchiv, Cologne 100 Panorama rotunda. Section. Architect: Jacob Ignaz Hittorff. Photo: Rheinisches Bildarchiv, Cologne 101 Hippodrome, 1855. Architect: Jacob Ignaz Hittorff. Photo: Rheinisches Bildarchiv, Cologne 102 Main entrance to the Luna Park. Coney Island. New York. Vintage postcard 103 Loop. Coney Island. New York. Vintage postcard 104 Central Tower. Coney Island. New York. Vintage postcard 105 Waterslide "Shooting the Chutes." Luna Park. Coney Island. New York. Vintage postcard 106 View down Surf Avenue. Luna Park. Coney Island. New York. Vintage postcard 107 Roller-coaster on Coney Island, 1920. Photo: Uwe Fichtner and Rudolf Michna 108 Waterslide. Luna Park. Berlin. Photo: Uwe Fichtner and Rudolf Michna 109 Palace Pier. Brighton. Photo: Ursula Schulz-Dornburg 110 Palace Pier. Brighton. Elevation. Photo: Ursula Schulz-Dornburg 111 "Pavilion" theatre. Palace Pier. Brighton. Photo: Ursula Schulz-Dornburg 112 Crystal Palace. Great Exhibition. London, 1851. Architect: Joseph Paxton. Photo courtesy of: Deutsches Museum, picture and film library 113 Tower by Gustave Eiffel. Exposition universelle. Paris 1889. Photo courtesy of: Klartext Verlag 114 Ferris wheel by George W. Ferris. Columbian World's Fair. Chicago 1893. Photo: Jeffrey Howe 115 Plan of New York World's Fair 1964 116 Globe on the central plaza. New York World's Fair 1964 117 German pavilion. Montréal EXPO, 1967. Architects: Frei Otto and Rudolf Gutbrod. Photo: Frei Otto 118 planet m. Bertelsmann. EXPO 2000. Hanover. Triad Berlin. Architects: Karl Karau in collaboration with Axel Büther and Becker, Gewers, Kühn & Kühn Architects. Photo: Michael Lange 119 Universe Corporate Headquaters. Los Angeles. Architect: Greg Lynn 120 Wooden doll ©The Walt Disney Company 121 Pinocchio. ©The Walt Disney Company 122 Long house on Borneo. Julian Davison, in Singapur & Malaysia, Guides Gallimard. ©Editions Nouveaux Loisirs 123 Iban long houses on Borneo. Photo: Gerhard Rauchwetter 124 Common room in long house. Photo: Gerhard Rauchwetter 125+127 Squash and stretch. ©The Walt Disney Company 126 Wooden doll. ©The Walt Disney Company 128 "Ginger & Fred" National building of the Netherlands in Prague. Czech Republic, 1992-96. Architect: Frank O. Gehry. Photo: Ralph Richter 129 Arcs. The human figure in motion. ©The Walt Disney Company 130 Dumbo. ©The Walt Disney Company 131 The wicked witch as embodiment of evil. ©The Walt Disney Company 132 Asahi Beer: "Super Dry" hall. Tokyo. Japan 1989. Architect: Philippe Starck 133 Roof installation object. Asahi Beer: "Super Dry" hall. Tokyo. Japan 1989. Architect: Philippe Starck 134 Egg yolk. Photo: Holger Knauf. Düsseldorf 135 Der Whopper. ©Burger King 136 Netherlands pavilion. EXPO 2000. Hanover. Germany. Architects: MVRDV ©MVRDV. Computeranimation: GroupA 137 Attic storey of Netherlands pavilion with pool, island and wind mills, EXPO 2000. Hanover. Germany. Architects: MVRDV. ©MVRDV. Computeranimation: GroupA 138 Staatsgalerie Stuttgart. Germany, 1984. Architect: James Stirling 139 Piazza d'Italia. New Orleans. USA 1986. Architect: Charles Moore 140 "Tuned Suburb". 1968. Ron Herron. Archigram 141 A Space-Comic serves as a welcome source of inspiration: Archigram 1969 142 Cloud. Germany, 1968-72. Coop Himmelb(l)au. Wolf D. Prix, Helmut Swiczinsky. ©Coop Himmelb(l)au 143 EXPO-Dome. Montréal. Canada, 1967. Architect: Richard Buckminster Fuller 144 Bees in honeycomb. Photo: Frei Otto 145 Eden Project. Cornwall. GB 2001. Architects: Nicholas Grimshaw and Partners. Photo: Ralph Richter 146 Eden Project. Cornwall. GB 2001. Architects: Nicholas Grimshaw and Partners. Photo: Ralph Richter 147 Gossamer web in grass wet with dew. Photo: Frei Otto 148 Aviary at Hellabrunn Zoo. Munich. Germany, 1970. Architect: Jörg Gribl. Engineer: Büro Happold. Consultant: Frei Otto 149+150 Bionic pavilon. Case study. Architects: 3deluxe 151+152 Youth media world "Scape". EXPO 2000. Hanover. Germany. Arch: 3deluxe 153 New York Tunes. Time capsule. Competition. Helsinki. ©OCEAN north 154 Tschekpo Dan Agbetou. Dance company. Bielefeld. Photo: Ursula Kaufmann 155 Newtimes two dance. ©OCEAN north 156-159 Saltwater pavilon. Oosterhuis Associates. NL 1997 Photo: Oosterhuis 160+161 TransPORTs 2001. Oosterhuis Associates. Photo: Oosterhuis 162+163 Active innerskin. Rotterdam 1999. Oosterhuis Associates. Photo: Oosterhuis 164 Audi pavilion. IAA Frankfurt 1999. Architect: Christoph Ingenhoven. Photo: Jan Esche 165+166 Predator – Wexner Center for the Arts. Columbus. Ohio. Architect: Greg Lynn in collaboration with painter Fabian Marcaccio. New York. Photo: Greg Lynn FORM 167+168 Greg Lynn FORM. Meta Blob. Photo: Greg Lynn FORM 169 Study for a pavilion. Oosterhuis Associates. Photo: Oosterhuis 170 *Animate Forms*. Greg Lynn FORM Photo: Greg Lynn FORM 171+175 Jack Red Cloud. Photo: National Anthropological Archives, Washington 172 Pyramid of Kukulcán. Chichén Itzá. Yucatan. Mexico. 1982. Photo: Marilyn Bridges 173 Submerged city. Phantasialand Brühl 174 Hotel Cheyenne. Disneyland Resort Paris. Architect: Robert Stern. ©The Walt Disney Company 176 The Body (a ride through the human body). Architect: Derek Walker. Photo: Derek Walker 177 Hyperion. Photo: Büro Happold 178 Flume Ride. Wonderworld Corby. Derek Walker. Photo: Derek Walker 179 *Hans in luck*. Water-colour. Reproduced from: Tatjana Hauptmann: *Das große Märchenbuch*. ©1987 Diogenes Verlag AG, Zurich 180 Medieval village in Heidepark Soltau. Photo: Heidepark Soltau 181+182 Philips Fantasy Worlds. Architect: Matteo Thun. Photo: Matteo Thun 183 *The Prologue and the Promise*. Space Architecture by Robert T. McCall 184 Space Tourism. Shimizu Corporation 185 *Argosy*. Robert T. McCall 186 Space Resort. Wimberly, Allison, Tong & Goo. Photo: Wimberly, Allison, Tong & Goo 187 Leisure parks in Space. Fictitious space station. Design: NASA 1979. Photo: NASA 188 Space hotel Shimitzu. Photo: NASA 189 Pneo – a foldable living mobile: Hotel configuration in the Earth's orbit. Concept: Aleksandra Konopek. ©VG Bild-Kunst. Bonn 190 Columbia, the first space transporter prior to the first flight in space. Photo: NASA 191 Space Park Bremen. Model. RKW Architects. Photo: Holger Knauf 192 Space Park Bremen. Model. RKW Architects. Photo: Drees & Sommer. Project office Spacepark 193 The Matterhorn. Zermatt Switzerland 194 Nuba woman with headdress. Photo: Leni Riefenstahl. ©1972 Leni Riefenstahl-Produktion and AVA GmbH, Munich-Breitbrunn 195 Jerry Hall in a robe of Thierry Mugler. Photo: Patrice Stable 196 Guggenheim-Museum. Bilbao. Spain, 1998. Architect: Frank O. Gehry. Photo: Ralph Richter 197 Hansapark Sierksdorf. Germany, 1970 198 Heidepark Soltau. Germany, 1970. Photo: Heidepark Soltau 199 Little World. Inuyama. Japan, 1985. Reproduced from: *Bauwelt* 35/1998. Photo: Jörg Gleiter 200 Nasu Highland Park. Nasu. Japan, 1996 201 Holiday-Park. Hassloch, 1971 202 Europa Park Rust. Germany, 1975. Photo: Europa Park Rust 203 Magic Worlds, North American mountainous landscape, Bottrop-Kirchhellen, 1998. Photo: Thomas Wrede 204 Port Aventura. Salou. Spain, 1995 205 The sun as bird. Il Giardino dei Tarocchi. Capalbio. Italy, 1979. Architect: Niki de Saint Phalle. Photo: VG Bild-Kunst, Bonn 206+207 Miniland Frankfurt. Legoland Günzburg 2000. Photo: Legoland 208 Wonderworld Corby. Project, Great Britain, 1982. Plan for various theme areas. Architect: Derek Walker 209 Wonderworld Corby. Master plan. Project, Great Britain, 1982. Architect: Derek Walker 210 Wonderworld Corby. Concert hall. Section. Project, Great Britain, 1982. Architect: Derek Walker 211 Wonderworld Corby.

Illustration for "The Land" theme area. Project, Great Britain, 1982. Architect: Derek Walker **212** Wonderworld Corby. Body Area Zone. Project Great Britain, 1982. Architect: Derek Walker **213+214** Bercy shopping centre. Paris, 1990. Architect: Renzo Piano. ©RPBWPM: Michel Denancé **215** Bercy shopping centre. Cross section. Paris, 1990. Architect: Renzo Piano **216** City Walk complex. Universal City. Los Angeles. USA 1993. The Jerde Partnership International Inc. Architect: Jon A. Jerde. Photo: The Jerde Partnership **217** City Walk complex. Ground plan. Universal City. Los Angeles. USA 1993. The Jerde Partnership International Inc. Architect: Jon A. Jerde. Photo: The Jerde Partnership **218** Horton Plaza. San Diego. USA 1984. The Jerde Partnership International Inc. Architect: Jon A. Jerde. Photo: The Jerde Parnership **219** Wave pool. West Edmonton Mall. Alberta. Canada, 1981. Photo: Fuhrmann Consulting **220** Europa Boulevard. West Edmonton Mall. Alberta. Canada, 1981. Photo: Fuhrmann Consulting **221** The Centro-Promenade. Architects: Rhode, Kellermann, Wawrowsky and Partners. Photo: Michael Neuhaus **222** Opening ceremony of Lotte World shopping mall. Seoul. Korea 1989. Architects: Battaglia Associates **223+224** Sony Center. Berlin. Architect: Helmut Jahn. 1999. Photo: Ralph Richter **225** Canal City Hakata. Fukuoka. Japan 1996. Architects: The Jerde Parnership. Photo: Hiroyuki Kawano **226** Horton Plaza. San Diego. USA 1984. Ground plan. Architects: The Jerde Partnership **227** Canal City Hakata. Fukuoka. Japan 1996. Ground plan. Architects: The Jerde Partnership **228** Canal City Hakata. Fukuoka. Japan 1996. Architects: The Jerde Parnership. Photo: Benny Chan **229+230** JVC The New Urban Entertainment Center. Guadalajara. Mexico 1998–2001. Architects: Coop Himmelb(l)au. Animation: Armin Hess **231+232** JVC The New Urban Entertainment Center. Guadalajara. Mexico 1998–2001. Architect: Daniel Libeskind. Photo: Torsten Seidel **233** Rotterdam railway station, 2000. General view. Architect: William Alsop. Animation: Alsop Architects **234** Rotterdam railway station, 2000. Partial view. Architect: William Alsop. Animation: Alsop Architects **235** Rotterdam railway station, 2000. Design study. Architect: William Alsop. Animation: Alsop Architects **236** Rotterdam railway station, 2000. Interior perspective. Architect: William Alsop. Animation: Alsop Architects **237** Arnheim railway station. Computer animation. Architects: Ben van Berkel und Caroline Bos. UN Studio. Amsterdam **238** Arnheim railway station. Sectional drawing. Architects: Ben van Berkel und Caroline Bos. UN Studio. Amsterdam **239** Arnheim railway station. Interior. Architects: Ben van Berkel und Caroline Bos. UN-Studio. Amsterdam **240** Arnheim railway station. Model. Architects: Ben van Berkel und Caroline Bos. UN Studio. Amsterdam **241-244** Stuttgart railway terminal, 1997–2013. Architects: Ingenhoven und Partner, Düsseldorf. Photos: Holger Knauf, Düsseldorf **245** Port Grimaud. France, 1982. Photo: Daniel Philippe **246** Club Mediterranée. Polynesian village in Cefalù, Sicily. Photo: DERTOUR GmbH **247** Center Parc. De Vossemeren. Belgium **248** Ocean Dome. Seagaia. Kyushu. Japan 1994 **249** Empty Dream. New York 1995. Photo: Mariko Mori and Deitch Projects **250+251** La Laport Skidome. "SSAWS." Chiba. Japan 1993. Architects: Kajima Corporation **252+253** Allrounder Winter World Neuss. Germany, 2000. Architect: Christian Schramm. Photo: Holger Knauf, Düsseldorf **254+255** Centre Pompidou. Paris. France, 1977. Architects: Richard Rogers and Renzo Piano. Photo: Renzo Piano **256-259** Modern follies. Parc de la Villette. Paris. France 1998. Architects: Bernhard Tschumi and Adrien Fainsilber. Photos: Bernhard Tschumi **260** Guggenheim Museum. Bilbao. Spain, 1998. Architect: Frank O. Gehry. Photo: Ralph Richter **261+262** Futuroscope and Cinemax Park. Architect: Denis Laming. Photo: Denis Laming **263+264** Shonandai Cultural Centre. From: Tokyo. World Cities. Architect: Itsuko Hasegawa **265** National Centre for Popular Music. Sheffield. Great Britain, 1999. Architects: Doug Branson and Nigel Coates **266** National Centre for Popular Music. Sheffield. Great Britain, 1999. Ground plans. Architects: Doug Branson and Nigel Coates **267** BMW Experience and Delivery Centre. Section. Animation: Armin Hess. Photo: Coop Himmelb(l)au **268** VW Automobile City Wolfsburg. Car stacking towers. Architect: Günter Henn. Photo: Henn Architects & Engineers **269** VW Automobile City Wolfsburg. Entrance to pavilion with telescoping lift gate. Architect: Günter Henn. Photo: Henn Architects & Engineers **270** VW Automobile City Wolfsburg. Footpath across water to client service center and to car stacking towers. Architect: Günter Henn. Photo: Henn Architects & Engineers **271** Lamborghini pavilon. VW Automobile City Wolfsburg. Architect: Henn Architects & Engineers **272** BMW Experience and Delivery Centre. Munich. Interior. Architects: Coop Himmelb(l)au **273** BMW Experience and Delivery Centre. Munich. Section. Architects: Coop Himmelb(l)au **274** BMW Experience and Delivery Centre. Munich. General view. Architects: Coop Himmelb(l)au **275** BMW Experience and Delivery Centre. Munich. Panorama. Architects: Coop Himmelb(l)au **276+277** Kunsthaus and Stadthalle Graz. Acrylic glass panels. Architects: Peter Cook, Colin Fournier and Klaus Kada **278** Kunsthaus and Stadthalle Graz. Light funnels. Architects: Peter Cook, Colin Fournier and Klaus Kada **279-281** Science Centre Wolfsburg. Elevations. Architect: Zaha Hadid **282** Holiday Inn Boardwalk Casino. Las Vegas. ©AKG Berlin **283** Luxor Hotel & Casino. Architect: Veldon Simpson. Photo courtesy of: Tony Stone Images **284** The Tropicana. Las Vegas. ©Transglobe Agency **285** Caesar's Palace. Las Vegas. 1966–2000. Architects: Melvin Grossmann/Marnell Corrao Associates Inc. Photo: Marnell Corrao **286** Neon signs. Las Vegas. Photo: Keith Collie. ©AKG Berlin **287** Heaven's Gate. Detail. Jeffrey Shaw **288** Domed structure. Günther Günschel. 1957 **289** Video installation: Heaven's Gate. Jeffrey Shaw **290** *Domstern.* Bruno Taut 1919. Photo: Foundation archives of the Academy of Fine Arts, Berlin BTS–24–104/33 **291** National Library. Singapore, 1998. Imagination. Architects: UN-Studio. Ben van Berkel, Caroline Bos. Rotterdam **292** William Blake. *The Ancient of Days*, 1794. From *Europe: A Prophecy.* Photo courtesy of: Fitzwilliam Museum **293+294** Compound eyes of an insect. Photo: Claude Nuridsany/ Agentur/Focus **295** Photo: Holger Knauf, 2004

p.12 "There all is order and beauty ...," Charles Baudelaire, *The Flowers of Evil*, trans. Francis Duke (University of Virginia Press, 1961) p. 99. Gerhard Schulze, *Die Erlebnisgesellschaft* (Frankfurt/New York, 1993). **p.16** "... some are characterized by a hurry ...," after Djuna Barnes, *New York, Geschichten und Reportagen aus einer Metropole* (Berlin, 1987). **p.21** "The environmental planning of an age ...," *Jeffrey Shaw – a user's manual* Edition ZKM, (Ostfildern: Edition ZKM, Cantz, 1997), p. 148. **p.22** "Today, work is only half of life ...," after Horst W. Opaschowski: "Freizeit – Wann, Wieviel, Wozu?" in: *Animation* no. 7/8, 1983. **p.23** "The respect we have for mobility ...," after Rainer Hank, *Arbeit – Die Religion des 20. Jahrhunderts* (Eichborn, 1995). **p.24** "A society that is continuously engaged in hard work ...," after Rainer Hank, *Arbeit – Die Religion des 20. Jahrhunderts* (Eichborn, 1995). **p.25** "More and more, *work* gets all good conscience ...," Friedrich Nietzsche, *The Gay Science*, Book Four, aphorism 329, trans. Josefine Nauckhoff, (Cambridge University Press, 2001), pp. 182, 184. **p.27** "The city is always running ...," Lars Lerup. *After the City.* 2000. **p.31** "People as toys, enslaved by the pleasures of consumerism ...," after Wieland Schmied, *Katalog zur Ausstellung Bund NW* (Kestner Gesellschaft, 1989). **p.32** "We are still processing how to handle this new condition ...," after Gerhard Schulze, *Die Erlebnisgesellschaft* (Frankfurt/New York, 1993). "... failed to take into account ...," Aldous Huxley *Brave New World Revisited* (Chatto & Windus, 1964) p. 55, cited in: Neil Postman, *Amusing Ourselves to Death* (London: Heinemann, 1986) p. viii. **p.33** "People must be entertained ...," after Charles Dickens, *Harte Zeiten* (Frankfurt am Main: Insel Verlag, 1986). "Entertainment is the supra-ideology ...," Neil Postman, *Amusing Ourselves to Death* (London: Heinemann, 1986) p. 87. **p.33+34** "Modern man no longer cares ...," Friedrich Nietzsche, *The Gay Science*, Book Four, aphorism 329, trans. Josefine Nauckhoff (Cambridge University Press, 2001) pp. 182, 184. **p.37** "Together, this ensemble of electronic techniques ...," Neil Postman, *Amusing Ourselves to Death* (London: Heinemann, 1986) p. 77. **p.37/38** "For the first time in history ...," Neil Postman, *Amusing Ourselves to Death* (London: Heinemann, 1986) p. 77. **p.38** "We dream of a fantastic extraterrestrial ...," after Claude Nuridsany and Marie Pèrennou, *Mikrokosmos.* (Bern, Munich, Vienna: Scherz Verlag, 1997). **p.42** "And we haven't even begun ...," Claude Nuridsany and Marie Pèrennou, *Mikrokosmos.* (Bern, Munich, Vienna: Scherz Verlag, 1997). **Page 48** "One of the characteristics of popular culture ...," after Umberto Eco, *Über Gott und die Welt* (Munich, Vienna, 1986). **p.50** "... a trivial culture, preoccupied with ...," Aldous Huxley, in: Neil Postman, *Amusing Ourselves to Death* (London: Heinemann, 1986) p. vii. **p.55** "Virtual: ...," (New York: Random House Unabridged Dictionary). **p.61** "*As human beings* ...," Hani Rashid, Lise Anne Couture, *Asymptote Flux* (London: Phaidon 2002). **p.62** "By representing new things in new ways ...," Aaron Betsky, *NAI Ausstellungskatalog 2000.* **p.67** "Then the Lord God planted a garden in Eden ...," *The Good News Bible*, Today's English Version, Genesis 2 (Toronto: CBS, 2nd edition, 1992) p. 3. **p.70** "... it renders heavenly order ...," after Rolf Toman (ed.), *Die Kunst der italienischen Renaissance. Architektur-Skulptur-Malerei-Zeichnung* (Cologne, 1994). "And then I saw a new heaven and a new earth ...," *The Good News Bible*, Today's English Version, Revelation 21 (Toronto: CBS, 2nd edition, 1992) p. 1803. **p.76** "There will be no more death ...," *The Good News Bible*, Today's English Version, Revelation 21 (Toronto: CBS, 2nd edition, 1992) p. 1803. **p.78** "Even the smallest rose, the most humble poppy ...," Aldous Huxley, *Amina. Okada, Taj Mahal*, 1993. **p.81** "The global religious renewal ...," Roland Robertson in: Samuel P. Huntington, *The Clash of Civilizations* (New York: Simon and Schuster, 1996). **p.86+90/91** "I'm building a dream," Walt Disney, Derek Walker *A.D.* no. 88, 1990. **p.88+110/ 111** "When we set out to plan Disneyland ...," Walt Disney in: Thomas, B., *Walt Disney, An American Original* (New York, 1976). **p.88+ 116** "Here you leave today and ...," Walt Disney in: Randy Bright, *Disneyland, Inside Story* (New York, 1987). **p.89** "Happiness is truth and truth is happiness." after *Geo-Special: Kalifornien-Las Vegas*, no. 3, June, July 2000. "I never meant ...," Walt Disney, Derek Walker *A.D.* no. 88, 1990. "When we consider a new ...," Christopher Finch, *The Art of Walt Disney, from Mickey Mouse to the Magic Kingdom* (New York, 1973). **p.90** "Disneyland is a work of love." (...) "All I want is that ...," (...) "All of us who use ...," (...) "We seem to know when ...," Walt Disney in: Frank Thomas, Ollie Johnston, *Disney Animation* (New York: Abbeville Press, 1981). "You know, the only way ...," Walt Disney in: Frank Thomas, Ollie Johnston, *Disney Animation* (New York: Abbeville Press, 1981), p. 119. **p.90+92/93** "I think I am an innovator ...," Walt Disney in: Randy Bright, *Disneyland Inside Story* (New York, 1987). **p.92** „Ich will nicht, dass die Besucher die Welt ...", Walt Disney. In: Randy Bright: Disneyland Inside Story. New York, 1987, p. 61. **Page 97** "The only problem of anything of tomorrow is ...", Derek Walker, *Architecture and Themeing, A.D.* no. 88, 1990. **p.98/99** "It's show business and I am a showman." Walt Disney, Derek Walker *A.D.* no. 88, 1990. **p.101** "In truth, happiness can only mean: to escape." After Theodor W. Adorno, *Minima Moralia.* **p.104** "The facades of Main Street USA are presented as ...," after Umberto Eco, *Über Gott und die Welt* (Munich, Vienna, 1986). **p.104/105** "All I want is that people ...," Walt Disney, Derek Walker *A.D.* no. 88, 1990. **p.105** "Disney World – an absolutely staggering New Town ...," Peter Blake in: Peter Cook, *Archigram* (Basel: Birkhäuser, 1991). "Building the World of Tomorrow, for Peace and Freedom." Erik Mattie, *Weltausstellungen* (Stuttgart, 1998). **p.106/107** "We seem to know when...," Walt Disney in: Frank Thomas, Ollie Johnston, *Disney Animation* (New York: Abbeville Press, 1981). **Page 114** "You know, the only way I've found ...," Walt Disney in: Frank Thomas, Ollie Johnston, *Disney Animation* (New York: Abbeville Press, 1981) p. 159. **p.118** "The Roman people, who once ...," after Juvenal in: H. Bender, *Rom und Römisches Leben im Altertum* (Tübingen). "I came upon a spectacle by chance ...," after Seneca in: H. Bender, *Rom und Römisches Leben im Altertum* (Tübingen). **p.124** "... where persons of leisure and pleasure seekers ...," after Dieter Hennebo, *Entwicklung des Stadtgrüns von der Antike bis in die Zeit des Absolutismus* (2nd edition, Berlin, Hannover, 1979). **p.127** "Arcadia is the land where everyday life is golden ...," Torsten Olaf Enge, Carl Friedrich Schröer, *Garden Architecture in Europe, 1450–1800* (Cologne: Benedikt Taschen, 1990) p. 12. **p.129/130** "You, who roam the world You, who roam the world ...," after Bosco Sacro, Bomarzo in: Torsten Olaf Enge, Carl Friedrich Schröer, *Garden Architecture in Europe, 1450–1800* (Cologne, Benedikt Taschen, 1990) p. 76. **p.131** "The Baroque was an epoch of fast living ...," Torsten Olaf Enge, Carl Friedrich Schröer, *Garden Architecture in Europe, 1450–1800*, (Cologne: Benedikt Taschen, 1990) p. 108. **p.138** " Already I hear the uproar of the village ...," Johann Wolfgang von Goethe, *Faust*, Part I, trans. Randall Jarrell, Farrar (New York: Straus & Girous, 1976) pp. 50, **p.139** "Persons of high stature ...," after Johann Peter Willebrand in: Uwe Fichtner, Rudolf Michna, *Freizeitparks* (Freiburg, 1987). "... commoners at pain of corporal punishment ...," after Dieter Hennebo, *Entwicklung des Stadtgrüns von der Antike bis in die Zeit des Absolutismus* (2nd edition, Berlin, Hannover, 1979). **p.140** "Anything is possible in Paris now ...," *Jakob Ignaz Hittorf*, exhibition catalogue Wallraf Richartz-Museum (Cologne, 1987) p. 212. **p.143** "... henceforth and from now on ...," after H. Pemmer, N. Lackner, *Der Prater, Von den Anfängen bis zur Gegenwart* (Vienna, Munich, 1974). **p.145** "Is it a park? No. ..." after Adalbert Stifter in: E. Lorbek: "Wo Wien sich selber spielte, Zwischen Raimundbühne und Riesenrad, die Leopoldstadt," in: *Westermann Monatsmagazin* no. 7 (Brunswick, 1971). "The dull, muffled sound of music ...," after Stefan Zweig in: Hofmann, J. und W.: *Wien* (Munich, 1956). **p.148** "Buildings are by no means conceived for eternity ...," after Thomas von Joest, *Jakob Ignaz Hittorf*, exhibition catalogue Wallraf Richartz-Museum (Cologne, 1987). **p.150** "... be renewed like ...," Thomas von Joest, *Jakob Ignaz Hittorf*, exhibition catalogue Wallraf Richartz-Museum (Cologne, 1987). **p.152** "This was no longer a fairground,...," after R. G. Blomeyer, B. Tietze in *Bauwelt* 12/1996 "Kleine Sozialgeschichte des großen Vergnügens, Lunaparkkultur." **p.153** "... It was in the snack bars on Coney Island ...," after R.G. Blomeyer/B. Tietze, "Musik und Bewegung: 25 Jahre Scharouns Philharmonie," in *db*, 3/1989, pp. 88–96. **p.154** "Slides polished to a high shine ...," after Djuna Barnes, *New York – Geschichten und Reportagen aus einer Metropole* (1915). **p.165** "World's fairs become a public place ...," after Kretschmer, Winfried, *Geschichte der Weltausstellungen* (Frankfurt, 1999). p.172 Animation, *n.* 1) *general*: the process of making inanimate objects appear to move, after Brockhaus Encyclopaedia, 1996. p.174 "The Dasun in Borneo ...," after Edward O. Wilson, *Die Einheit des Wissens* (Berlin: Siedler, 1998) pp. 205ff. p.183 "The villain must be ...," Walt Disney in: Thomas, Frank and Johnston, Ollie, *Disney Animation* (New York, 1981). p.194 "Disney deserves credit ...," Paul Goldberger in: *The New York Times*, 1991. p.199 "Archigram tuned into the broad innovative impulses ...," Herbert Lachmayer in: Peter Cook, *A Guide to Archigram 1961–1974* (London: Academy Group, 1994) p. 421. "Coop Himmelb(l)au is not a colour ...," Wolfgang Prix, *Coop Himmelb(l)au, Architektur ist jetzt* (Stuttgart: Verlag Gerd Hatje, 1983). "We are tired of ...," Wolfgang Prix, *Coop Himmelb(l)au, Architektur ist jetzt* (Stuttgart: Verlag Gerd Hatje, 1983). "Our architecture is based ...," Wolfgang Prix, *Coop Himmelb(l)au, Architektur ist jetzt* (Stuttgart: Verlag Gerd Hatje, 1983) pp. 5-7. p.202 "A new science, bionics, tries to ... In addition to the pure adaptation of the forms ...," Frei Otto in a letter to the author. p.203 "Buildings should therefore not imitate nature ...," after Arthur Schopenhauer (1851), in: Rudolf Bannasch, "Vorbild Natur" in *Design Report* 09/2002. p.205 "What really interests me ...," Richard Buckminster Fuller, *Your Private Sky* (Zurich: Lars Müller, 1999) p. 444. "Through a kind of digital ...," Peter Zellner, *Hybrid Space* (London: Thames & Hudson Ltd., 1999) p. 111. p.206 "Soon buildings will be able to change ...," Nicholas Grimshaw cited in: Hugh Pearman, "Equilibrium" in *Nicholas Grimshaw & Partners, Buildings and Projects* (Berlin: Ernst & Sohn, 2000) p. 242. p.209+211 "We can discover sensuality in the computer ...," brochure, 3deluxe. p.213+216 "... animation implies the evolution ...," (...) "While motion implies movement ...," Greg Lynn in: Peter Zellner, *Hybrid Space* (London: Thames & Hudson Ltd., 1999) p. 38. p.216+220 "'Transarchitectures' is a concept," Marcos Novak in: Peter Cachola Schmal (ed.), *digitalreal. blobmeister – first built projects* (Basel: Birkhäuser – Publishers for Architecture, 2001), pp. 238/239ff. p.222 "A high-resolution spaceframe ...," Kas Oosterhuis in: Peter Zellner, *Hybrid Space* (London: Thames & Hudson Ltd., 1999) p. 81. p.225 "The architect Greg Lynn and the painter Fabian Marcaccio ...," exhibition catalogue "Predator", 1999. p.227 "The architect of the future is an animation designer." Regina Dahmen-Ingenhoven. p.234 "Not everyone can be an astronaut." Fantasyland Slogan. p.235 "To be able to lift off from the earth ...," Norman Cousins cited in: Joseph P. Allen, *Entering Space* (New York: Stewart, Tabori & Chang, 1984). p.241 "Have you any idea how big the world is?" Job 38:18, 19, *The Good News Bible*, Today's English Version (2nd edition, 1992) p. 633. p.242 "The only problem ...," Walt Disney in: Derek Walker, *Achitecture and Themeing, A.D.* no. 88, 1990. p.247+248 "Original – We don't use this word!," Kisho Kurokawa in: *Bauwelt* 35/1998. p.247 "... let's take the streetcar to the South Seas!" Traders Vic – advertising slogan for a restaurant in Düsseldorf. p.249 "We live in the best country ...," after *Geo-Special: Kalifornien–Las Vegas*, no. 3, June/ July, 2000. p.249+ 250 "It is well established ...," Julian Barnes, *England, England* (London: Jonathan Cape, 1998), pp. 53–55. p.251 "showgirls, at least six feet tall ...," J. Graham, *Vegas, live and in Person* (New York, 1989). p.253 "There is a constant stream of superstars – real ones or stand-ins ...," Regina Dahmen-Ingenhoven. p.256 "It is all about things that wobble ...," Peter Cook in: *Blueprint* no. 127, April 1996. p.258 "A leisure park is an enterprise ...," after *AIEST*, "Tagesausflugsverkehr und seine Auswirkungen" (St. Gallen, 1988). p.266 "In the age of economic globalisation ..." after Regine Bittner, *The City as Event* (Frankfurt, New York: Campus, Edition Bauhaus, 2001), preface, p. 7. p.270 "What is better ...," Frances Anderton after *Blueprint*, no. 127, April 1996. "A dream house ...," after Fritz Eller, *Architektur Canada* (Stuttgart/Zurich, 1988). p.273 "The mall looms over ...," after Dietmar Steiner, "Überall ist Mega Mall," in *Stadtbauwelt* 48/1987. "The Edmonton Mall adopted ...," after Margaret Crawford, "Warenwelten" in: *Arch+* 114/115, 1992. p.277 "... never before has urban entertainment ...," after Frank Roost in: *Bauwelt* 48/2000. p.278+279 "We composed the project out of fragments ...," after Jon A. Jerde in: *Blueprint*, No. 127, April 1996. p.280 "The initial challenge was to decode ...," Jon A. Jerde in: *Blueprint*, no. 127, April 1996. p.287 "This place contains: All we need." William Alsop, postcard. p.299 "Hi, I'm Ricky." *SWF 3*, radio broadcast, June 15th, 1991. p.312 "The form of the museum ...," after Javier Mozas in: *Bauwelt* 13/1997. p.315 "I would like to create ...," Itsuko Hasegawa, *Crossover Architecture* (Rotterdam: Nai Publishers, 2000). p.329 "The experience and delivery centre ...," BMW-board, competition report, pp. 328-333. p.331 "The illusory world is but a diversion ...," Fritz Eller: *Architektur Canada* (Stuttgart/Zurich, 1988). p.332 "In the United States, on the contrary,...," Umberto Eco, *Travels in Hyperreality*, trans. William Weaver (Orlando: Harcourt, Brace, Jovanovich, 1986) p. 40. p.333 " ... is the clinical symptom of architecture ...," after Heinrich Klotz, "Die röhrenden Hirsche der Architektur," in: *Bücherreport* (Luzern, Frankfurt am Main, 1977). p.335 "May I be your slave?", Regina Dahmen-Ingenhoven. p.340 "... the architect has three tasks ...," Bruno Taut cited in: Ulrich Conrads and Hans G. Sperlich, *Fantastic Architecture*, trans. Christiane Crasemann Collins and George R. Collins (London: The Architectural Press, 1963) p. 148. p.342 "... but we also want *magic*." Julian Barnes, *England, England* (London: Jonathan Cape, 1998) p. 120. p.344 "... I have in mind the tomorrow ...," Wenzel A. Hablik, letter reproduced in: Ulrich Conrads and Hans G. Sperlich, *Fantastic Architecture*, trans. Christiane Crasemann Collins and George R. Collins (London: The Architectural Press, 1963) p. 148. p.346 "For one had never stopped hoping ...," after Heinrich Klotz, *Jeffrey Shaw – a user's manual* (Ostfildern: Edition ZKM, Cantz, 1997) p. 7. p.348 "What in all the world does a child have to be scared of?" Richard Powers, *Plowing the Dark* (New York: Farrar, Straus and Giroux, 2000) p. 235. p.352+353 "A new world with new symbols and formulae." After Fritz Eller, *Architektur Canada* (Stuttgart, Zürich, 1988).

Translation Elizabeth Schwaiger **Editorial Services** Ute Einhoff, Claudia Grothus, Birgit Laskowski **Digital Illustrations** Gudrun Olthoff (pp. 17, 46, 55, 63, 84/85, 87) **Typesetting** Marly Riemer **Graphic Design** Sophie Bleifuß

P.O. Box 133, CH-4010 Basel, Switzerland
Part of Springer Science+Business Media. www.birkhauser.ch
Printed on acid-free paper produced from chlorine-free pulp
ISBN 3-7643-6631-1 Printed in Germany

This book is based on my dissertation for my doctorate at the RWTH Aachen in 2000. During that time I received much support and inspiration.

Thanks to my dear parents, Liesel and Wilhelm Dahmen, who always make time for me; to professor Fritz Eller, my mentor and thesis supervisor, who is a fantastic visionary and teacher; to Dr. Karl-Joseph Bollenbeck, who provided me with the key inspiration; to my husband Christoph Ingenhoven, who generously supported my undertaking at all times and is, at any rate, an extraordinary person; to Kristin Feireiss, who transformed my idea into what I had imagined and for her wonderful proposal to engage Sophie Bleifuß for the design.
Thanks also to all those who made their images available to me; to all those, who stood by me with moral and practical support, who encouraged me again and again and inspired me: Sybille Fanelsa, Michael Reiß, Ute Einhoff, Jan Esche, Birgit and Stefan Laskowski, Claudia Grothus, Ulrike Ruh, Ulrich Schmidt, Ralph Richter, Ian Douglas, Christine Köser, Ireni Xira, and Holger Knauf, and Elizabeth Schwaiger for the translation.
Special thanks to my sister Martina Schwarzlose for tea and jelly babies and loads of animation for the soul.

The Author Dr. Regina Dahmen-Ingenhoven, born in 1961, studied architecture at the RWTH Aachen (Aachen University of Technology). Immediately after her diploma, from 1986 to 1992, she was scientific assistant to the chair of Design for Building and Industrial Building, held by professor Fritz Eller. Her dissertation *Orte der Animation, Architektur für Freizeit und Vergnügen im 20. Jahrhundert* (Sites of Animation, Architecture for Leisure and Amusement in the 20th Century), was written while at the same chair, from 1987 to 2000. Regina Dahmen-Ingenhoven has been a practicing, independent architect since 1986 with a focus on design for hospitals, clinics and wellness facilities. She is married to Christoph Ingenhoven and the mother of five children.

A CIP catalogue record for this book is available from the Library of Congress, Washington D.C., USA

Die Deutsche Bibliothek lists this publication in the Deutsche Nationalbibliografie;
Detailed bibliographic data is available in the Internet at **http://dnb.ddb.de**